Jessie Kesson

WRITING HER LIFE

Jessie Kesson

WRITING HER LIFE

A BIOGRAPHY BY

ISOBEL MURRAY

CANONGATE

First published in Great Britain in 2000
by Canongate Books Ltd, 14 High Street, Edinburgh EH1 1TE

10 9 8 7 6 5 4 3 2 1

The publishers gratefully acknowledge
subsidy from the Scottish Arts Council
towards the publication of this volume

British Library Cataloguing-in-Publication Data
A catalogue record for this book is
available on request from the British Library

ISBN 0 86241 999 9

www.canongate.net

Typeset by Hewer Text Ltd, Edinburgh
Printed and bound by
Creative Print and Design, Ebbw Vale, Wales

Contents

Preface and Acknowledgements

Jessie Kesson's handwriting was as individual as she was. Her letters were typically handwritten in tiny, neat 'printed' script. Naturally, when her books were published, they were printed in the usual way. Jessie's punctuation was increasingly eccentric, and publishers and producers were irritated by it and said so. Her work, when published, was punctuated in the usual way. When, as often here, I quote unpublished work, letters, etc, I have taken the liberty of regularising the punctuation in many places. She had an abiding affection for capital letters, when indicating particular significance. I have retained some of her most significant usages, in breach, at times, of the publisher's house style. Her maiden surname, even on official records, is variously given as Macdonald, MacDonald and McDonald. As this is of some slight historical interest, I have retained this variety in the text, but regularised it to McDonald in the Index.

I first met Jessie Kesson at the Edinburgh Book Festival in 1985. I was chairing a 'Meet the Author' session with her and Iain Crichton Smith. She had agreed, despite a very tight schedule, to be interviewed by Bob Tait and myself, as part of a series of in-depth interviews with Scottish writers. An edited version of this interview, along with a later one when she was awarded a D Litt at Aberdeen University, is featured in *Scottish Writers Talking*, 1996 (pp 55–83).

Jessie's papers have been deposited in the National Library of Scotland, where in due time they will be catalogued. I have confined notes here to published sources only.

Quotations from her work will be followed by page numbers when the source is clear, and with the following abbreviations when it is not:

The White Bird Passes: WBP
Glitter of Mica: GM
Where the Apple Ripens and other stories: WAR
Another Time, Another Place: ATAP

I am most indebted to Avril Wilbourne, Jessie Kesson's daughter, for making it possible for me to write this book and for a great deal of help and kindness; to Lisa St Aubin de Terán, Jessie's literary executor, who asked me to undertake it; and to Bob Tait, who tolerated, and welcomed, a third presence in our home for many months.

I am very grateful to Aberdeen University, who gave me a year's University Research Fellowship to complete work on the book, and to the Carnegie Trust for the Universities of Scotland, who gave me two grants to help towards travel and expenses.

I have had marvellous help from archives and archivists, and have been given access to all open files. Chatto & Windus gave me access to their archives in Reading University Library, which are rich with regard to Jessie and which contain, in particular, invaluable letters to Peter Calvocoressi. Michael Bott and Frances Miller in Reading were extremely helpful. The BBC gave me access to important material in Glasgow (Libby Stanners) and Caversham (James Codd). At Old Aberdeen House, Siobhan Convey and Mrs Angus helped with some excellent suggestions about Elgin and Moray records and, at Grampian Health Board Archives, Fiona Watson helpfully gave me access to appropriate documents. Elizabeth Watson helped with scripts from the Scottish Theatre Archive at Glasgow University Library. Alistair Campbell of the Moray District Library Service, a good friend of Jessie's, organised help from several archivists, and I am grateful to him and to all of them.

I have had help from Register House, Edinburgh, the Scottish Record Office, the Library at St Andrews House and the Crown Office, and the National Library of Scotland, and am indebted to Myrtle Anderson-Smith and her staff in Special Collections in Aberdeen University, to Aberdeen Central Library; and to Wellgate Library, Dundee. In Dundee I was also helped by Alison

Cooke at D. C. Thomson and Sinclair Mathieson, editor of *The People's Friend.*

Many people who knew Jessie have helped me, and especial gratitude is due to Dr William Donaldson, who gave me full access to his correspondence with her. Others whose help has been invaluable include Elizabeth Adair; Sir Kenneth Alexander; Mrs Isabel Baird; Jill Balcon; Peter Calvocoressi; Mrs E. Cameron; Alistair Campbell; Stewart Conn; Anne Downie; Flora Garry; Carol Galbraith; Anne and George Gray of Smeaton; Paul Harris; Andrew Hewson; Mrs Chrissie Hubbard; James Hunter; Marilyn Imrie; Dr Duncan Lamont; Grace Law; Mary and David Levie; Dr Ian Olson; Michael Radford; Trevor Royle; Alastair Scott; Mrs Cath Scott; Mina and Islay Skea; George Stevenson; Mrs Audrey Stock; Mrs Betty Wilson.

Many others have also helped: Dr Carol Anderson; Andrew Bolger; Mrs Janey Buchan; Moira Burgess; Professor Ian Campbell; Charlotte Carter of *Country Living*, Aileen Christianson; Mary Dick-Smith; Maura Dooley of the South Bank Centre; Alastair and Nancy Gammie; Professor Douglas Gifford; Brian Hall; Norman Harper; Mrs Hilda Hesling; Professor David Hewitt; Larry Hutchison; Selena Jones; Andrew Kerr; Dr Jeannette King; Christina Mackenzie; Archie MacLullich; Dr Dorothy McMillan; Dr Robert McColl Miller; Dominic Mitchell; John Murphy; Wilma Murray; Dr Richard Price; Maureen Ramsay; Dr Martin Ray; Jenny Renton; Dr J. Graeme Roberts; Julia Robertson; Ali Smith; Alan Spence; Mrs Katharine Stewart; John Stocks; Edward Thomas; Sarah Thompson, student of Librarianship at Robert Gordon University in 1994–95; Professor George Watson; Jessica Williamson; Donald Withrington.

People who read my newspaper appeals for help were also most generous: Bill Cameron; Dr Ian Davidson; Rita Davidson; May Fletcher; Colin Fraser; Hugh Fraser; Mrs C. W. French; Mrs Margaret C. Irving; M. Jamieson; Ann Jones and Patricia Roberts; Miss Jean Kesson; Mrs Lamont; Jean Lindsay; Bunny Little; Calum Macleod; Morag Macleod; Nan S Macleod; Winifred Masson; Mrs Elizabeth Matheson; Patricia B. Olday; Mrs Ann Osborne; Mrs Paton; Robert Paton; Wilma Paton; Kathleen

Perkins; Tom Pow; Leslie Robertson; Margaret Rothnie; Mrs G. M. Spray; W. H. Squires; Mrs Letta Williamson; Mr Wills; Miss Wylie; and two helpful correspondents who chose to remain anonymous.

Isobel Murray
February 2000

List of Illustrations

Jessie Kesson – Introduction

Jessie Kesson had an extraordinary life and an extraordinary writing career. She is not offered here as a 'case', but as a writer, as Moultrie Kelsall put it, with a streak of genius. Candia McWilliam has described her as 'the astounding Scot, Jessie Kesson'. Nevertheless, it is astonishing to watch her gradually triumph over experiences that make even such childhoods as Charles Dickens's look tame. Her young life, in particular, was a series of violent shifts of surroundings and circumstances, with no ongoing family support to provide stability or continuity. Before she was 18, she had lived with her mother in Elgin slums, been neglected and been legally moved to a distant orphanage, where she had two matrons in succession and a shifting population of fellow orphans. After school she went to work on a farm, was sent back to another school and worked in a department store, the last two in Aberdeen, where she lived in a hostel, and met new middle-class girls at school, and lively but alien working girls in the hostel. Small wonder that when the latest matron in the hostel was vindictively unpleasant, she ended up attacking her and then attacking herself. She spent a traumatic year in mental hospital, and when she left, aged 19, was 'boarded out' with an uncomprehending and very old woman in a high and isolated area of the Highlands.

How anyone expected her to deal with this series of disjointed experiences one cannot guess. No one mentioned 'aftercare' or enquired after her again. She was not sick any more, but would need a long process of healing. Jessie herself seemed to understand that there was only one psychotherapist available – herself. She must write herself, write her life, and give it the continuity and integrity it had so signally lacked. When, as a married woman with job and baby, she began to write, it was her own story she had to start with.

She was born illegitimate in 1916, in Inverness, and much of her childhood was spent in an Elgin slum, where food, work and money were in short supply, and her mother was a small-time prostitute, a problem drinker and a bad manager. They lived in fear of the 'Cruelty Man', and eventually the authorities caught up with mother and child, and separated them, finding Liz not a fit or proper person to have custody of her daughter, who was sent to an orphanage in Aberdeenshire, not to see her mother again for many years. The scars of her early experience stayed with her all her life: she could only rarely put her early background behind her and, for Jessie the writer, it provided her main subject matter for a long time. Her first published prose was an anonymous two-part attempt to compress her two childhoods. In 'Railway Journey', the girl is travelling back from her second 'home' to her first, to find out 'which is the real me – Ness of the Orphanage, or Ness of Kelbie's Close'. She is sure to be remembered: but the story ends abruptly with her buying another single ticket: 'I should have taken a return, you know, but I'm very stupid'.[1] Titles like 'We Can't Go Back' and 'Road of No Return' recur in her work, and as late as 1990 Colette Douglas-Home presented this account of an interview in *The Scotsman:*

> She returned to the Orphanage and day after day she climbed a local hill. 'If I looked down on one side I could see buses going to Elgin where my mother was. If I looked down on the other side I could see the orphanage and the farm. I was torn between wondering where I should go and I took a nervous breakdown.'[2]

A heroic kind of self-revelation can be found in all her books, especially of course in what was at last to become the novel, *The White Bird Passes.*[3]

Readers of this, her first and best-known novel, must think they know the early biography already. They are wrong. This impression is dangerously false. The novel does not in any way conceal the slum childhood, the poverty, the consorting with tinkers and travellers, the dirt and lousy hair. It is open about the family disgrace, when Grandfather will speak to neither his daughter (Liz) nor his granddaughter (Janie), and will not allow the child to be called by her grandmother's name. It also indicates the nature of the mother's occupation – money changes hands in advance in *The White Bird Passes* – and spells out the nature of Liz's illness as syphilis. The novel might be too painful to read altogether, were it not suffused with a child's intensity of magic-making, and response to sensation, music, smells, life. The reader is not crushed by the sordid action, because the child so evidently sees it differently. She is 'intensely glad for just being alive' (12); and glories in anticipation for its own sake: 'Janie had learned to enjoy the prospect more than the reality' (65). She revels in the excitement of the fairground, and is 'intensely happy' (47) when she sees the caravan of the Green's oldest tinker. At the Diddle Doddle (Model Lodging House), among the vagrants, 'Janie instantly and warmly felt at home' (100) and, all in all, 'the Lane was home and wonderful' (86). Douglas Dunn calls her treatment of the Lane 'an outstanding union of squalor and enchantment'.[4] The excitement and vividness of the child encourage the reader to forget the hard facts, both those apparent in the novel and those the writer omitted or later tried to soften. She spent her writing life on a fine line between autobiography, fiction and poetic vision.

FACTS, FEELINGS AND MYTH

The strict facts of her early life, such as can be recovered, are much grimmer, more complex and more confusing. Here is my best example of how far the biography can diverge from Jessie's carefully honed novel account. According to the novel, Jessie went to one primary school in Elgin, the West End School, from 1921, when she was five, until she was eight, when she was separated from her mother and sent to Aberdeenshire. But school records show she left the West End School within 15 months of enrolling: a note in the register says, 'Gone to Alves – a mystery!' Alves is a scattered hamlet some six miles from Elgin, and Jessie

was enrolled at the school there in January 1923, claiming not to
have attended school before. Suspicion begins to arise that the
pair were 'on the run'. Jessie was readmitted to West End School
in April 1923 and left on 7th September, only to be readmitted
again on 19th September. She remained at West End School until
August 1926, when she was enrolled at East End School in early
September, and stayed there until her day in court, on 19th April
1927. (By then she was 10½, not eight, as in her own versions of
the story.) A copy of a letter in Old Aberdeen House says Jessie
attended the three schools mentioned above, plus Rothes Primary,
but, to date, the Rothes Primary records have not been traced.
Even this brief account casts doubt on the accuracy of the novel,
without supplying any coherent alternative. It gets worse.

A series of official letters from J. W. Macfarlane, Inspector of
the Poor, Alves, reports to Elgin Parish Council on some of the
experiences of Liz and Jessie from 1924 to 1927. They were
registered as paupers, on public assistance. On 14th January 1924
he writes of Liz:

> Your pauper, above named, had an accident on the ice on
> Saturday evening and sustained a severe wound close to the
> knee joint. She was removed to the Hospital in order to have
> the wound stitched and has meantime been detained there.
>
> Her girl has been taken charge of by a neighbour, and I
> expect I will have to pay for her keep until her mother is
> discharged.

Three weeks later he writes:

> The above named was discharged from the Hospital yester-
> day, and I have renewed her former allowance of 10/- per
> week. While she was in Hospital I paid 7/6 per week on
> behalf of her child who was being cared for by a neighbour,
> and trust this will have your approval.

Every six months now, there are bills for Elgin Parish Council.
The accident on the ice resulted in the following:

April 1924   Elizabeth McDonald

Nov 30 Aliment	Jan 24 8 weeks @ 10/-	£4	0	0
Feb 5 do.	May 15 14 1/2	7	5	0
Hire removal to Hospital			2	6
Jan 18 Aliment (child Jessie) Feb 14 3@7/6		1	2	6
Medicines 2/2 Beef steak 7/-			9	2
Clothing 29/10 Books 1/6		1	11	4
Boots 12/9 Boot repairs 7/7		1	0	4

In February 1925 Liz applied for admission to the Poorhouse, 'stating that she cannot manage to exist on the allowance of 10/- per week': she was given a further 5/- per week. On 17th November 1926 the Inspector writes: 'I have to inform you that Jessie McDonald, child of the above named, was admitted to Morayshire Poorhouse on 15th inst'. She was discharged a week later: presumably this was in the nature of a final warning to Liz about her neglect of the child. Poorhouses were still used, on occasion, 'as a temporary shelter before a child was found a more permanent home'.[5] If this was the strategy, it did not work. Jessie was admitted to the Poorhouse again on 12th April 1927. Liz had been summoned to appear at the Sheriff Court on 8th April, but did not appear, and a warrant was issued. When she finally appeared on the 19th, she was charged with neglect under the Children Act 1908, pled guilty and was admonished. The Inspector reports:

> As I already intimated this woman's girl Jessie has been admitted to the Poorhouse, and yesterday, in Elgin Sheriff Court, her mother appeared on a charge of neglect, when she agreed to allow the girl to be removed to a home until she attains the age of 16 years.

Jessie was enrolled at the Central School in Kirkton of Skene, Aberdeenshire, five days later. As Lynn Abrams points out, 'Institutions were used as places of safety for children removed from cruel or neglectful parents'.[6] Left alone, Liz eventually found a house in the Moycroft area of Elgin, and appealed to the Inspector for 10/- to pay a month's rent in advance. Apart from one appeal at Pluscarden for 5/- in May 1928, no more is recorded of Liz until she was admitted to Craigmoray Institution in Elgin in January 1937.

Meantime, the AGM of the RSSPCC, as it became in 1922, is reported in the *Elgin Courant and Courier* on 1st April 1927. 'Drink was still one of the main causes of children's suffering'. Cases brought forward from the previous year had improved:

> with the exception of one, whom the Inspector had found necessary to report for prosecution and petition for the custody of the child concerned owing to the persistent neglect and lack of control on the part of the parent.

The story outlined here is different in events and in impact from that recorded in *The White Bird Passes* and other treatments of the early years. However opaque, it seems to give the lie to the newspaper allegations that Jessie exposed her mother to public shame in her novel: she has left a great deal out, with deliberation.

Clearly, Jessie was brought up in filthy, squalid slum conditions. She herself was habitually dirty – water was in short supply. She had only one set of clothes and could not go out when they were being washed. She was frequently humiliated at school by being singled out for treatment for headlice and being made to sit apart from the others. Daily life in the Lane included countless 'swears'. Women had physical fights, and were imprisoned for these, and frequently for drunkenness. Children died, and the 'Cruelty Man' was always investigating how the survivors were treated. Officers of the RSSPCC formed a key agency. 'In 1913 the Local Government Board for Scotland admitted that but for them some clauses of the 1908 Children Act "would be practicably inoperative"'.[7] The inspectors 'were vigorous in rooting out neglect, acting on tip-offs from neighbours and initiating visits to "problem" families'. Jessie's mother was often drunk and engaged in prostitution, and Jessie understood this, her worst fear being that Liz would like one of these men better than her. Perhaps worst of all, Jessie told film director Michael Radford that she had been sexually abused by one of her mother's clients, a deformed dwarf. This could help to explain her far from physically active adult love life, and her aversion to deformity. This is illustrated, for example, in *The White Bird Passes*, when Janie shrinks from the legless Thoomikies, or in 'Until Such Times', when the girl is appalled at the notion that her 'Aunt Ailsa' might marry a man with a wooden leg, or in the *Scotsman* interview with Colette Douglas-Home:

'I remember a mannie gave me a doll one day. It didn't have shoes but its shoes were painted on. I remember taking that doll, flinging it from me and breaking it. I didnae like the mannie because I knew why he was there and he looked like a deformed mannie'. She fell silent and gazed through the window of the room where we were having lunch, but it was obvious that she was looking far beyond it, back through the years.[8]

The above is the starkest example of the dilemma of anyone attempting Jessie's biography. Almost all the extant evidence of Jessie's life is in her own papers, her writing, her letters. The biographer is forced back on this 'evidence' and must cite it: even when not reliable in a strictly factual sense, it is all evidence of the vision and/or the psychology of the subject. But this example has been placed first as a warning against undue credulity, and an example of the inherent impossibility of the biographer's coming up with a triumphant exposition of 'truth'.

Some things were held back in some need for privacy even while she was apparently walking naked. It was a long time (1987) before Jessie told the story of where she was born – that when she went to Inverness to be married she learned that the 'big hoose' where she was born was in fact the Workhouse. It was 1990 when she told Colette Douglas-Home that her very early years were spent in a Model Lodging House. She never publicly acknowledged that her grandfather's anger over her own birth was made worse by the fact that Jessie was not Liz's first 'mistake' but her second, the first illegitimate daughter having been taken into the grandparental home some years before, and brought up as one of the family, or that she was pretty sure that she knew the identity of her father, having learned it in her fifties from an aunt.

So she had to work over and over her early years, to make a story at once in important senses true and yet omitting a great deal of detail, something like Edwin Muir's distinction between the Story and the Fable. Her early work almost all centres on her childhood and teens, and she seems simultaneously to work psychologically through her need to centre herself by what she writes and to teach herself the craft of writing. Although she was lucky to receive the education she did receive from her beloved gifted 'Dominie', the Headmaster of Skene School, she was artistically alone in many ways all her life, and almost all her lessons are self-taught. The early magazine pieces about 'The Makar in Miniature' and 'Anybody's Alley' and the early radio pieces on other versions of the same stories all involve constructing a myth by trial and error, and finding an appropriate attitude to her most challenging subject, herself. Of course she had good friends and inspirational help, from Dominie Murray, from novelist and poet Nan Shepherd, from radio producer Elizabeth Adair, and many others, but none of them had been where she had been. In the one relationship where she might have been able to share her most painful experiences most intimately, her marriage, she found she had married a good and supportive man who had no talent for words and was not very articulate, and who had no comprehension of the inner life of the wife he loved loyally and devotedly for 58 years.

Her strategy for coping with this situation came to be a matter of living different lives at the same time. She worked all her life at hard, demanding jobs; she wrote with a commitment and urgency that might sometimes leave her children out at elbow or less than shining clean. She had a lifelong commitment, which she tended to deny, to helping youngsters disadvantaged as she had been, writing or working behind the scenes on their behalf. And she formed a vast number of important relationships, which for a lot

of the time were held rather apart from each other. As a young
woman living in a cottar house, for example, she wrote for *The
Scots Magazine* and *North-East Review,* and for the humbler
People's Journal, and she soon had a partial life of her own with
the BBC in Scotland, as she would later in London, with another
circle of friends and colleagues with whom, chameleon-like, she
could glitter and perform. She not only wrote for radio, she
performed, sometimes in her own programmes, but also, for
example, in James Crampsey's famous radio version of *Sunset
Song.* Later, from London, she kept up relationships with landed
gentry, with former cottar neighbours and with a wealth of others,
often quite unknown to each other. Life was less daunting if
relationships could be sorted out and kept discrete.

Kesson never knew a father, and her relations with her mother,
while at bottom loving, were problematic. She went from institution to institution: insecurity was the element she occupied.
Perhaps one reason she married Johnnie Kesson was that he was
11 years her senior, almost a father figure. The whole pattern of
her life is filled with significant and usually lasting friendships
with both women and men: the women include Miss Bella
Walker, Nan Shepherd, Elizabeth Adair, Marilyn Imrie, Thelma
Shuttleworth and, perhaps closest of all, her daughter Avril. The
men with whom she significantly corresponded, or whom she
regularly saw, included librarian Lindsay Simpson, poet Shaun
Fitzsimon, writer John Keir Cross, publisher Peter Calvocoressi,
radio producer and writer Stewart Conn and Scottish academic
Dr William Donaldson. If Johnnie did much to supply the place
of a father, some of these men provided an intellectual or
emotional interest he could not supply.

THE EPHEMERAL NATURE OF RADIO

Another factor which makes the task of Jessie's biographer
particularly difficult is this: she has a misleading reputation for
producing a very small oeuvre. She published just four slim
volumes of fiction. But she was a very accomplished and prolific
writer in a field which remains resolutely closed to most of us, her
writing for radio. Again, her subject matter for the most part

remains childhood experience. Radio was enormously important for her as a listener, supplementing her reading in cottar houses across the North East of Scotland, mainly magazines and library books. Many Scottish writers contributed regularly to the BBC in the '30s, before she began. Their input must have formed a significant part of her cultural experience. They include Edwin and Willa Muir, Eric Linklater, Compton Mackenzie, C. M. Grieve, William Power, Joe Corrie, Donald and Catherine Carswell, Ann Scott-Moncrieff, Janet Adam Smith, J. R. Allan and Ian Macpherson.[9] And Neil Gunn, her favourite writer, was a radio institution. The history of these years and the next decades needs to find a way to be told.

In Jessie's case, her radio work has effectively vanished, for the time being, at least. The question of whether the public would be willing to tackle reading radio scripts in their unique format has never been settled: very few experiments have been made, and none until now in Jessie's case. This means that her public is deprived of the chance to read a huge proportion of her work. So there is here a double loss; the loss of the radio work itself, and the impossibility of recovering the novels we have in the rich and varied context of their evolution. In Jessie's case, and with other fine radio drama, there is also a third loss, that of the heard experience of the play, the collaborative creative end-product of author, producer and cast. This last could only be remedied by collecting especially fine productions on cassette or CD. In that case, a whole lost experience could be recaptured, and another art form, the completed sound play, could be made available. Her last producer, Marilyn Imrie, suggests that 'her most successful medium is writing for people's voices'. Asked whether she sees Jessie as an important writer, she replied in the affirmative, saying her work was most exciting because 'she wrote for the ear'.

Virtually none of Jessie's radio work has been published: most of it languishes at best in the archive at Caversham, where scripts which survived the BBC – particularly the new leaner BBC – have been entombed. Legend has it that she wrote 90 plays for radio. I have so far been able to trace five poems, more than 40 talks, reviews and discussions, about 20 shorter plays and features (up to

30 minutes), and about 20 longer plays and features, some on television. A selection has recently appeared in *Somewhere Beyond: A Jessie Kesson Companion*. On the whole I will have to be descriptive rather than analytic about the nature of Kesson's radio work, as little of it is in the public domain, but Stewart Conn, himself a noted writer, who also produced much of her work, has called her 'one of the finest of for-radio practitioners'.[10]

Some of the peculiarities of Kesson's life pose particular problems for the biographer. The so-far near-secret history of radio, as indicated above, is a very major one. What has been called 'the golden age of radio' has been variously located in the late '30s, the late '40s and the '50s, the war years narrowing the scope of radio, as all the relatively independent 'regions' were amalgamated into one for the duration.[11] It was during the late '40s that Kesson established herself first in Aberdeen, and later in Glasgow and Edinburgh. But this golden age, however interpreted, did not last long, and the work done for or in it currently seems especially ephemeral. The history of radio has received some attention, from Asa Briggs's four-volume *History of Broadcasting in the United Kingdom* (1961–79). The Third Programme over 50 years is the subject of Humphrey Carpenter's *The Envy of the World* (1996), and the more specialised field of Scottish broadcasting has been traced by W. H. McDowell in *The History of Broadcasting in Scotland 1923–1983*. There is even a *Literary History of the Third Programme* by Kate Whitehead (1984) and a volume by Val Gielgud called *Radio Drama 1922–1956: A Survey* (1957). But there is so much ground to cover, and most histories are so London-based, that few writers gain mention in any of them, and even fewer Scots: Kesson's name appears in none. Any recent work on broadcasting has tended to consist of personal accounts by broadcasters, or historians or sociologists, not literary critics.

In this prevailing obscurity Kesson is by no means unique. Some 'for-radio' writers have at least for the moment vanished without trace and, as indicated above, sound broadcasting appeared as a great opportunity for writers, including Scottish ones, both for those who saw creative opportunities here and for those who saw some much-needed fees in it to feed the family. Literary critics and historians are going to have to find ways of making some of the best of this material available, and of integrating the study of broadcast material with that of the more traditional media, if we are not to present distorted views of these writers and their lives. Until some of this is accomplished, it is going to be hard to assess Kesson's achievement in the full context of her time. My claims for her technical innovation and originality must be muted to some extent because of the general lack of availability of both Kesson's own radio work and that of her contemporaries. What is more, historians of child care in Scotland, for example, are necessarily unaware of her radio work about boarded-out children and the furore which followed it, and the enquiry to which Jessie gave evidence, outlined in Chapter Five.[12]

But Kesson is likely to remain, at all events, a very special and unusual case. She is a writer who largely concentrated in every available medium on ways of describing and presenting one of her own selves, or choosing and constructing which mythical self to define. Typically, she wrote versions of her childhood traumas in *North-East Review* and *The Scots Magazine*, and not much later adapted these for radio. The radio version(s) could eventually be subsumed in the production of a printed novel, the outstanding example being *The White Bird Passes*. It was published in 1958: the first brief published attempt at that material dates back to 1941, with versions shown to sympathetic readers even further back. Or the radio version might in the end also become a film, simultaneously with the publication of the novel, as with *Another Time, Another Place*. Her own favourite novel, *Glitter of Mica*, underwent similar processes, but here she persisted in planning radio and television versions after the novel's publication in 1963, and she never achieved the long-desired film script which she believed could do justice to the subject matter of the novel, the oppressed and imprisoned lives of cottar workers in the North East this century.

Radio remained Kesson's second-favourite medium. Her love affair with the word is above all celebrated in print, and the four slim volumes published in her lifetime would be more than enough on which to rest a great reputation. But radio came a good second, as she told me in an interview when we first met in 1985:

> First of a' as I've aye said, in the beginning was the Word. I hinna said it, the Bible says it, but I repeat it. And for me the words has always been the purest – the actual written – the word! Always. Because you see Isobel, whin you write a thing it's in a way private, it's between you and the anonymous reader – you're illuminating an experience for this person – you'll never see them probably, you know: in the normal way o' things you'll never know them. But when you're writing even a radio play, you write it, and then it's somebody else's job to give their interpretation of it; that is the director and she gives her interpretation and then the actors give theirs. Now this applies to any form . . . but next to the printed word I love radio and I'll tell you why. Because words mean so much to radio and words and the sound and the meaning of them is *my* thing. I love radio.[13]

She was right. The intensity of her writing comes from her lifelong love affair with the word. And she was right to mention both sound and meaning. Jessie was raised at an unusual tangent to the oral tradition, learning vast amounts of poetry first orally from her mother. Memory played a crucial part in all she wrote. She was formed too by the 'words and music' she heard, from street songs and popular lyrics on the Green with the Chairoplanes and the hearty hymns of the Salvation Army in Elgin's High Street to the grave beauty of the traditional hymns at Skene. She always remembered the Minister giving a solo rendition of Blake's 'Jerusalem', when words and music together produced a transcendental experience. Her radio plays rarely lack music, and the heroines of *The White Bird Passes*, *Where the Apple Ripens* and *Another Time, Another Place* each have poetry and song, 'sound and music', integral to their consciousness.

This is surely one definitive characteristic of Jessie's work, often combined with the experience of vivid sensuous memories. She often quoted Wordsworth's 'Tintern Abbey' on 'wild ecstasies', and her love of Neil Gunn's novels owes much to the 'moments of delight' so central to his writing. The personal impression she made on others, even strangers, was very strong: 'the Lady in the Train', Nan Shepherd, had the sense of 'life gushing out in all sorts of ways', and the vicar who met her before Johnnie's funeral recognised 'her overwhelming sense of awe and wonder in the beauty of language', and said 'the loveliness of words allows her a glimpse of the radiance of eternity'. These qualities are permanently captured in her writing.

Chapter One: Elgin

Jessie Kesson died in 1994. It is too early to hope to present an objective 'historic' life, and because of lack of outside evidence it may never be possible. For now, many of the other characters in her several stories are still alive, and sensitive to comment or criticism which they could rightly claim was unfair. I have had a lot of help from many people, but in the end it remains partly accidental which witnesses I have found and what papers survived and have surfaced. But I *can* hope to preserve some of the freshness of the impact Jessie made on others, and some of the complexity and multisidedness of the woman and the writer. And her understanding of this. Her relative lack of education and the longed-for university degree may have left 'spots' of unawareness, such as her refusal to understand what even her beloved Virginia Woolf meant by 'feminism', and she strongly resisted suggestions that she was herself a feminist. But later we will see that images of great women of the past, discovered in the course of her own reading, were central to her own drive and aspiration. The word 'feminist' continued, for her, to carry connotations of being feminine, in an older, rather derogatory sense: inferior. Understandably, she wanted to be a writer, not 'just' a woman writer, although her work consists largely of expert analyses of the oppression of poor people, farm workers, and especially women, with great understanding and penetration. She hero-worshipped great women, such as Emily Brontë, George Eliot, Marie Curie and Virginia Woolf, and she understood and portrayed the situation of women as she experienced and observed it, brilliantly.

And she did understand the lessons she taught herself by painful experience. One of these was a uniquely complicated one: as already shown, she spent her writing life largely on a fine line between autobiography and fiction. And she never claimed *The White Bird Passes* as definitely either. She 'covered' her two childhoods in *The White Bird Passes*, the 'sma' perfect', after many earlier attempts at some parts of it, but inspection of the long and caring correspondence with the very supportive but sometimes perhaps overdirective directors of Chatto & Windus show how they all wavered about how fictional it was to be, and how much of 'Janie's' life it should cover. The directors were at some disadvantage here, for she kept them in the dark on many issues.

When later she considered writing her autobiography, she encountered grave and indeed prohibitive problems. There was the simple feeling that to write an autobiography would be to 'sign off'. Then there was the technically almost insuperable problem that she had 'done' her childhood in a way in *The White Bird Passes*, on that fine line between fiction and autobiography. How could she repeat this, or find an appropriate style for an autobiographical sequel? And there was her awareness of the impossibility – and probably the undesirability – of trying to reach a single truth about anything, when everything one writes changes because of mood, audience and motivation at the time of utterance. She wrote to Dr William Donaldson, whom she asked in 1986 to write her biography, if one was considered necessary:

How in the Name *can* you understand, when I don't understand me, myself?

It would take me all my life – and longer – to 'understand'. And it's no use looking back at what I'd describe as the tangents of my life as I do often – to say: '*that* was the right reaction . . . *That* was the right – or wrong way to "cope".' No use at all trying to work out whether you did the right or wrong thing. You do what you *feel* like doing *at the time*. It seems *inevitable* to you to do so then, the choices being limited.

That, I think, is why the biographer's job is so difficult. He can only *ever* know in part. Even with a *thousand* letters of his subject on his files. Because one writes to suit the nature, the relationship of and with, the recipient. I can write the *same identical* news to six different people, and in each letter it will have a different colour, a different accent. The closest letters to the truth are the ones which take on the aspect of what is really a letter to myself.

Her career also proves she can write what she calls 'the same identical news' at different stages of her life, in different moods and modes, and every time produce something essentially unique. And memory is another imponderable, as the girl who perpetually watches the weather muses in the radio play *Friday* of 1966:

No one has ever watched the sky longer or closer than me. But for as long and for as close as I watch it, I know, even now, that I will never be able to look back afterwards and remember exactly how it looked. I will remember only the threat and promise on its changing face and the threat and promise of all the Fridays under it.

This first biography of Jessie Kesson will pay particular attention to the subject's own warnings, and not attempt to find '*the* truth'. It will quote the writer's papers freely, indicating where possible the occasions and relationships involved, and displaying some facets at least of the kaleidoscopic person and writer Jessie Kesson was, often using her own words. It will not be uncritical in parts, and will use whatever outside evidence can be adduced. Most of all, it will resist the temptation of accepting all the subject's 'autobiographical' writing as strictly, in any ordinary sense, true. More than any 'ordinary' women of her time, she experienced particular difficulty in trying to 'write herself', to construct a life for herself in a world where the writing was done on the whole by men, and women writers were expected to defer to set patterns of experience. Jessie's main strategy for survival and for creative writing was to write her own life, but what she constructed was a necessary myth of her life, and from the start of her writing life she omitted or suppressed some areas of her experience.

ELGIN, MORAYSHIRE

'As capital of the Province of Moray, cathedral city, county town and heart of the diocese, Elgin has always been favoured.'[1] Cut off from strife-torn central Scotland by the Grampian mountains and the swift, and for many centuries virtually unbridgeable rivers of Spey and Findhorn, it was the centre of peaceful and plentiful farming country. Architectural historian Charles McKean chronicles the 13th-century cathedral and 'successive waves of rebuilding', given growing prosperity over 300 years of persistent redevelopment, so that by the 1850s it was 'a stately neoclassical town'. A local historian, Herbert B. Mackintosh, writes rhapsodically about one area in 1914, two years before Jessie's birth. On the site of Elgin Castle, near the middle of the town, is Lady Hill, formerly Castle Hill, its summit now crowned by a 'Tuscan column' raised in 1839 in memory of the fifth and final Duke of Fife, also referred to as the Duke of Richmond and Gordon:

> Among the many delightful spots that nature has scattered with a profuse hand around our good city, none is more lovable to the eye or beneficial to health than the Lady Hill . . . This green mound has remained unchanged for generations. The same green braes dappled with the gowans – the ruts down which the children slide in the summer evenings – the nettles within the Castle enclosure – the hoary ruins, not a stone vanishing – wear now exactly the same face that they did in our great-grandfathers' time.[2]

Jessie's nostalgic love for Elgin and the area round about it was as proud and comprehensive as Mackintosh's:

> The areas surrounding Elgin Cathedral 'fan out'. Pluscarden, on the site of the old Benedictine Abbey, Maisondieu, Bishop's Place, Lady Hill, Lady Lane. Like tributaries of the Cathedral, so that the source seems to 'live on' in the minds of Elgin's inhabitants.[3]

She learned her way round all of this barefoot, with her mother.
And remembered it:

> Surely it is landmarks that first define direction for the child.
> As long as Lady Hill remains and the Duke of Fife stands
> high on his column – I'd know from two miles distant in any
> direction that I was on 'the right road' to Elgin. My
> Grandparents' house, demolished now – still has its founda-
> tions – a stone's throw from Coxton Tower. And if the main
> road to Lossiemouth were to disappear – I'd take the short
> cut – in the shadow of Spynie Castle.

One of the most distinguished buildings in the vicinity is Ladyhill
House. A Regency villa, it was bought and transformed in 1853 by
Thomas Mackenzie, one of the most respected of Scottish
architects. Mackintosh says that Mackenzie took a keen interest
in everything pertaining to 'Old Elgin', and collected and re-used
heraldic and sculpted stones as old houses were demolished. His
son, A. Marshall Mackenzie, later of Aberdeen, was responsible
for further alterations to Ladyhill House, for the Town Hall,
Elgin, 'and many fine buildings in the north'.[4] Mackintosh goes
on:

> The present proprietor, Mr J. Cooper Clark, has carefully
> preserved the best, having built a piazzaed summer-house
> with them.

By the time Jessie and her mother moved into the adjacent close
at Ladyhill Lane, at 295 High Street in 1921, the house
belonged to John Foster, the Sheriff Clerk and, in a small
way, a writer.

But for ordinary folk in Moray, country life was hard at the end of
the 19th century:

The collapse of the rural linen industry due to competition from the south affected many parts of Moray, but the greatest exodus from the upland areas occurred in the period of economic depression in agriculture from 1880–1910 . . .

Many of the people leaving the upland areas settled in Elgin . . . where there were more job opportunities, a range of occupations and better pay. Small industries in Elgin in 1915 included woollens, tweeds, leather, breweries, sawmills, cornmills, nurseries and ironfounding. The population of Elgin increased from 6286 in 1881 to 8250 in 1911 (+31pc) . . . In 1913, 1500 people left Moray for the USA, Canada, South Africa and New Zealand.[5]

In 1913 the population was 10,192, and the average number of regular poor was 160. Rural depopulation would increase after the First World War, and in the 1920s '121 crofters and 339 agricultural servants left farm-work in Moray'. (This is to anticipate, but underlines the plight of a couple going into farm service in 1939, as Jessie and her husband Johnnie would do.)

Meantime, the incomers would crowd into the narrow wynds and closes off High Street and other main thoroughfares. These have to a great extent been restored of recent years, and the restored Lady Lane (now renamed Hill Terrace) bears little resemblance to the place Liz and Jessie moved to in 1921, just one step up in respectability from the Corporation Lodging House. It could be exotic: their 'lenient' landlord was a 'Coloured Gentleman', Herbert Gordon Stuart, who built himself 'a strange crow's-nest-shaped house at the top of Hill Terrace', wrote letters to the Prime Minister, and fed the children hot curry and sweet beans[6]. But mostly it was squalid. As a few of Jessie's writings make clear, there were two lavatories to serve the whole Lane, and all water had to be carried some distance and sometimes up many stairs (Jessie and her mother had an attic room). Mice were unremarkable; some houses had bugs and were reported; some children, like Jessie, were treated at school for headlice. There

were some terrible smells, including cats' urine. In her contradictory, self-defensive way, Jessie often later denied that the Lane
was a slum, although it was her own writing that had, surely justly,
established it as such.

THE FAMILY

In 1984 Jessie was prevailed upon by Maurice Lindsay and her
long-term friend Alexander Scott, the editors of *The Scottish
Review: Arts and Environment*, to contribute. People who knew
of her, from newspapers, radio or *The White Bird Passes*, most
likely knew that she was short of relations. But it cannot be a
simple accident that in her piece called 'My Scotland' Jessie spent
some space on a hitherto unknown subject, her great-grandfather,
and more on her unforgiving grandfather. She also displayed,
despite a light tone, a mature understanding of her mother's
situation, and the same kind of commitment to questions of
landownership that pervades *Glitter of Mica*, and which in other
circumstances might have led her to a more political career.

From the age of six it was impressed on me that I had my
roots in the soil of Morayshire – albeit that discovery was
made gazing down on the six feet of earth – that ultimate
heritage of all men.
Every Sunday, rain or shine, I went with my mother to
Elgin Cemetery, 'the dead' she always reminded me, 'are
quiet folk', acknowledging in passing the 'quiet folk' she had
known in their lifetimes. But the purpose of her pilgrimage
was to the grave of one

JOHN GRANT
FARMER
BURNSIDE

to whom she laid claim – first claim! . . . 'My Grandfather' –
before allowing me a *lesser* kinship! 'Your Great Grandfather'. She also bequeathed me with his surname as an
extension of her own to atone perhaps for the fact that my
natural begetter remained forever . . . nameless!

With maturity and hindsight I realise that our weekly visits to the grave of John Grant were for my mother an affirmation of her own roots – blurred sometimes by what must have been to her an alien way of life in a tenement room in a slum 'close'.

My Grandmother – a farmer's daughter, married a farmer – a Tenant farmer – with 'a Place'. In the North East farms are referred to as 'Places' – Crofts as 'placies'. The right word for them, 'Place', something to which we are all entitled, and which becomes to each his own.

The Landowner, casting a possessive eye on my Grandfather's rented land, decided that he'd like it back for himself, and served an eviction order accusing my Grandfather of being 'A Bad Husbandman'. An accusation which greatly distressed my Grandmother, her priorities were concerned with her family, not with their possessions; so that she kept on impressing on her children . . . 'It doesn't mean that your father is a – bad Husband – Husbandman is a different thing.'

My Grandfather fought the case in the Court at Edinburgh, and won it, vindicating his reputation as an Husbandman. A hundred years ago for a small farmer to 'take on' a Landowner needed both courage and conviction. My Grandfather had both.

I share his conviction . . . in that Morayshire seems to me to be *my* Scotland.

Jessie's stress on these forebears is proud and significant. Great-Grandfather was the only male relative of whom she could boast. He was the father of her beloved Grandmother, Jessie's love for whom is clearly shown in *The White Bird Passes* and shorter stories and radio plays. Here she boasts also about the unforgiving grandfather. In one of those 'letters to herself' that survive in the form of draft letters she wrote to friends, but did not always send, she wrote:

The vindication was what *mattered* to my Grandfather. He gave up the farm of his *own* accord rather than stay in 'ill grace'. Built Badentinnon – kept only a cow, pigs and his horses, and took on the *Wood* contract from Jones Brothers, Stirling. Overseeing the cutting, planting, etc. of all those woods – Darnaway, Inchettle, Nairn, employing (Cawdor) the wood-men from different parts of the country. When he paid them, weekly, he (non-union days) *first* set aside an amount which he forwarded to those whose wives, families, etc. were not living in the area. He made sure they didn't drink it. And those *tough* men accepted that!

She went on to claim proudly that his 'walking funeral' stretched six miles, from Badentinnon to Lhanbryde Cemetery. She added sadly that Badentinnon, 'that small house on the road to Rothes', was no longer a homestead.

Grandmother was born Jessie Grant on 1st October 1856, daughter of John Grant, farmer, and Jane Littlejohn. According to one of Jessie's 'letters to herself', she was 'a farmer's daughter Rothes/Craigellachie way', and her family thought she had married beneath her. She and Robert McDonald, who left farming for forestry, had a large family of eight children, four boys and four girls. Most of these will not concern us unduly, as they were not concerned with Jessie or her mother, Liz. The eldest was Robert, born in December 1880. He became a policeman. Next came Archie, born in February 1883. Family gossip mainly recalls Archie in a slightly scandalous liaison, which I will come to shortly. He was to die in 1954. Jessie's mother Liz (Elizabeth) was the eldest daughter. She was born on 12th February 1885. Brother John, born in February 1887, did not get on with his father. Of him we know that he returned from Canada with typhus, that he went to visit his sister Liz at Moycroft, and that he died in 1940. Brother William was born in 1889, and Jane in 1892. Jane was the Invalid Aunt always found in Grandmother's house, whom the young Jessie obsessively disliked and envied.[7] Jessie McDonald, the mother of Mina Skea, to whom I am indebted for much of this family detail, was born in July 1896, and died in 1977. Neither

Jessie nor her cousin Mina, who became close friends in later years, ever knew why Mina's mother Jessie and Jessie's mother Liz had not spoken to each other for 40 years when Jessie at last persuaded her aunt to attend Liz's funeral – but Jessie respected her for making no pretence of grief! The last daughter was Minnie [Williamina], born in 1898. We will come back to Archie, Jane the Invalid Aunt and Aunt Minnie.

Part of Grandmother's achievement, then, was to raise a respectable and often successful family in extremely cramped conditions: enough of the family stayed at home as adults to make this a considerable achievement. Mina Skea recalls the vanished house at Badentinnon as having stone floors, a living room, two bedrooms, a porch, a dry lavatory outside, and a well for water.

Jessie spoke and wrote of the ironies of the family tree – how one first cousin was Town Clerk of Elgin when she and Liz lived in Lady's Lane, for example, and how Liz was abandoned by her respectable family, while her youngest sister Minnie became very socially superior and wealthy. She married Raymond Gray, of the family of John Gray who had founded Gray's School of Art in Aberdeen in 1884, and moved in elevated professional and academic circles. Jessie wrote: 'I've often been intrigued by the contrasting destinies – and lifestyles – of my mother and her youngest sister'. Minnie trained as a nurse and it was in this capacity, Jessie reported, that she met her future husband, when she nursed him at the Edinburgh Royal Infirmary. Jessie told a friend in a letter that once and once only Aunt Minnie wrote to her in the orphanage, asking if she needed or wanted anything: Jessie did not need anything she could have offered. She died in 1982, somewhat disappointing some family members who had hopes of inheriting her tea plantations, by leaving her body to medical research, which did not require it, and her money largely to nursing charities.

Very little evidence survives about Jessie's mother Liz, except what Jessie herself wrote or said about her. Colette Douglas Home writes, 'As a child she loved, but was slightly in awe of, the tall, moody, strong-willed, auburn-haired woman, who wore a

shawl and smoked a small clay pipe'.[8] Jessie got on well enough
with Aunt Minnie when she was older, and she was grateful to her
for precious glimpses of Liz as big sister:

> I owe Minnie her memories of my mother. How she took
> Minnie to see her first play – 'Bunty Pulls the Strings' at
> Keith. Minnie – 'They spanked along in the pony and trap'.
>   How my mother who was working while Minnie was still
> at school in Elgin, bought her a 'Birthday Frock' for 'Birth-
> day Parties'.
>   Yes. My mother *would* have done that.

Liz's life story is a tragically lonely one, which begins in the
nurturing, caring centre of a loving family, leads to expulsion from
family and 'decent' society, and ends, all too slowly, in a combination of hospital and Poorhouse, with the appallingly destructive
symptoms of chronic/tertiary syphilis. Any attempt to understand
or feel for her will come back to *The White Bird Passes*, where it is
easy to miss the careful wording of every detail concerning her.
Jessie had thought endlessly about every word. When the novel
came out, one tabloid newspaper screamed about the daughter
who would submit her mother to open shame and label her a
prostitute.

**Mother's secrets told
Daughter Shows No Shame**
(*Daily Record and Mail*, 10th July 1958)

While this did not budge Jessie in her determination and need to
find and tell a truth of her own, it did leave her sensitive: she had
already concealed a lot, as we have seen, and after that she
concealed a number of details for many years, such as having
been born in the Workhouse in Inverness or initially raised in a
Corporation Lodging House. It also made her defensive: had she
betrayed her mother? In later years she used to wish she had
dedicated the novel to her mother instead of her beloved Dominie: readers had missed the carefully crafted words of love for

Liz. When I interviewed her in 1985, having myself momentarily
forgotten some of them, she reminded me with some asperity, and
a perfect memory:

> It was my mother, great credit to her, she was the one that
> had the poet in her – she really had – it wis her gave me my
> great love for all o' it, my mother . . . You have another read
> at telling the story of the cathedral and the singin' the
> ballads, and where the girl says 'Liza in one of her rare,
> enchanting moods'.[9]

We have to remember that she did have these enchanting moods,
but also that they were rare. In the context of the novel, an
unexpected narrator or commentator underlines this for us.

> Those rare moods of communication between Janie and her
> Mother more than made up for the other things lacking in
> their relationship. And yet, if these moments had never
> existed, it would have been so much easier for Janie in the
> years to come. (66)

But I think her narrator was wrong, great though Jessie's unhappiness at missing her mother was to be. This can only be
measured by extreme and unhappy comparison. Elizabeth McKay
was seven years Jessie's senior, and her autobiography was published in 1980 as *A Discarded Brat*. These two young people
suffered comparable agonies in institutions, were both boarded
out in villages outside Inverness, were both awkward and unhappy
in 'service', and even lived within a few yards of each other in the
early '30s, when Elizabeth was in service at St Margaret's Convent
in the Spital, Aberdeen, and Jessie was unhappily housed under a
hostile matron at a Home for Working Girls across the road.

But in one respect Elizabeth's story puts Jessie's in the shade.
Her six-year-old half-brother was violently and inexplicably
murdered some ten days before her birth in April 1909 in
Tollcross, Edinburgh. The new child's father, not the mother's
husband, was unknown. Her mother rejected her violently and at

once, 'unhinged with grief', and only enters the story twice more, on both occasions kicking her child, and on the second attacking her with passionate fury. However briefly and imperfectly, Liz Macdonald gave Jessie a love and security that Elizabeth McKay was never to know.

And Jessie was right to tell me that Liz's essential qualities and characteristics *are* given in the novel. Liz was essentially a countrywoman, rather trapped and out of place in Ladyhill Lane. She was romantic, and imaginative, and could bring history to life for Jessie. She loved poetry, and taught Jessie reams of it by the time she was eight – sad, elegiac poetry about lost or lonely children, for the most part. Jessie often detailed poems: Words-worth's 'Lucy Gray' and 'We are Seven', Colley Cibber's 'The Blind Boy', Felicia Hemans's 'The Better Land' and 'The Child's First Grief'. To Dr William Donaldson she quoted 'The Orphan Boy', which is credited to Mrs Opie:

> Poor foolish child how pleased was I
> When news of Nelson's victory came
> Along the crowded streets to fly
> And see the lighted windows flame.

. . . *my* favourite, since *I*, too loved to 'fly' down the 'crowded street' and see the 'lighted windows'.

And the ballads she taught me: she was awful fond of Mary Queen of Scots! *Her* love was verse.

Jessie's most moving tribute to her mother is in *The White Bird Passes*, when the suffering, syphilitic Liza (Liz) has come to the Orphanage to try to get Janie out to care for her, as she is going blind. She does not present herself attractively. The girl fails to find words to tell her mother she loves her, but leaves the reader in no doubt:

All the things I know, she taught me, God. The good things, I mean. She could make the cherry trees bloom above Dean's Ford, even when it was winter. Hidden birds betrayed their names the instant she heard their song. She gave the nameless little rivers high hill sources and deep sea endings. She put a singing seal in Loch Na Boune and a lament on the long, lonely winds. She saw a legend in the canna flowers and a plough amongst the stars. And the times in the Lane never really mattered, because of the good times away from it. And I would myself be blind now, if she had never lent me her eyes. (129)

Very much later Jessie wrote a poem, ostensibly for the Italian Luigi to say for his mother in a radio version of *Another Time, Another Place,* but she wrote to her daughter and son-in-law, 'I think to be honest it grows too out of my own feelings for my "Mama Mia" in *White Bird.*' It did not survive into the script: the tone is too serious for the volatile Italian.

> Not always does time cancel beauty
> Nor wars and sorrows rob it of its flowers.
> My mother has not an accent
> A look, a smile, an act,
> That does not sharply touch my heart.
> Ah! If I were a painter
> I would not ask of Raphael
> His divine brush
> I should like to exchange life for Life!
> To give her all the vigour of my years.

Liz was raised in a respectable if crowded household, and she was her father's favourite, as she tells Janie in the novel (64). But her love for Mary Queen of Scots is significantly contrasted with his outlook later. She tells Janie:

Your Grandfather will never allow mention of that. His religion lay in a chield by name of John Knox. Him that put the dampers on Mary Queen of Scots. She was Queen of Bonny France. (84)

The almost fated outcome is indicated here. Grandfather could not forgive his favourite daughter for her disgrace, and refused ever to speak to Jessie, or acknowledge her existence. She had been christened Jessie Grant McDonald, after her Grandmother, but Grandfather objected to the use of her name. Young Jessie was reared as Ness: Liz wryly explained that she was born in Inverness, and a town could not object![10] Cousin Mina remembered Grandfather telling her: 'Put your toys away. She's coming from Elgin'.[11] He was a hard man, but there was perhaps some excuse for him in his day and by his own lights. Jessie, it transpires, was not Liz's first 'mistake' but her second. Her first child, a daughter, was born on 13th January 1907, when Liz was 21. This daughter, Margaret Elizabeth McDonald (Peg), was taken into the family and raised with the others. Grandfather must have hoped and decided that Liz had 'learned her lesson'.

It is in connection with Peg that Liz's brother Archie caused gossip. Peg eventually had children, whose supposed father was an invisible Mr MacLeod. But Jessie believed that Archie was the father: there was a strong family tradition to that effect, if no direct evidence. Family gossip records some animosity between the half-sisters, and when Jessie and baby Avril were later to stay with Peg and Archie at Cawdor while Johnnie went to work on Skye, Jessie soon left to pursue her husband and escape their home. But things improved somewhat: the unsent draft of a letter to an Elgin friend in about 1980 tells a little more about Peg:

> When I lived near Elgin, cottared, I always got my stamps, envelopes, etc., from Sub-Post Office Bishopmill, and became fairly friendly with the two 'retired' ladies who managed it – I forget their names -
> Anyhow
> One of them said to me, 'I believe you are Margaret McDonald's sister.'
> Me 'Yes. That's right.'
> P.O.L. 'She was the best nurse I ever had.'

The elder of the two sisters had been Matron of East
Fortune Hospital, East Lothian, and my sister worked there
for years. In the years when it was much used for war-
wounded men, and Tuberculosis.

She trained in Glasgow . . . and I know, quite apart from
P.O.'s opinion, she was a fine nurse.

She died about six years ago in Elgin. [January 1974]

There is one other story about Peg, who fostered children. When
Jessie was cottared at Linksfield, she had a confidential friendship
with the Elgin Children's Officer, with whom she often discussed
his problem cases. On one occasion a young mother left husband
and baby in a temper. Husband deposited child with Welfare
Officer and demanded it be fostered. A good home was found,
and the baby stayed two days, until the couple reconsidered and
demanded the child back:

WO: What on earth am I going to do?
Me: Give them their baby, of course. They're just young and
silly – not old and wicked. They've plenty of time to learn to
be wise.
WO: I know. I know they must get their child. It's the
Foster Mother I'm thinking of.
Me: Explain to her.
WO: I wonder if you'd explain. You see your sister took the
baby.

Jessie thought Peg would rather not have had Liz as her mother.
Jessie never felt that way. When Liz became pregnant for a second
time, nine years after Peg, it was too much for Grandfather. This
time she was on her own, and had her baby at the Workhouse at
Inverness, more recently the Hilton Hospital, and now offices.
Jessie told a touching little story about the Matron of her
orphanage years. She needed a birth certificate to show before
she sat her 'Qualifying' examination at school: when it came, it
had her birth address. Matron was asked to look for the address
when on holiday, and tactfully came back to report only that it was

a big house with flower gardens. Child Jessie was well pleased, and did not discover it was the Workhouse until she was in Inverness to get married, when it did not worry her at all. Liz disappears from the record after this, until the remembering child is old enough to register her in Lady's Lane. In two interviews, one with Colette Douglas-Home in *The Scotsman* in 1990, the other with Edi Stark on Radio Scotland in 1991, Jessie said that the two lived until she was four at Elgin's Corporation Model Lodging House. This institution, North Lodge, 'Handsome and Comfortable Quarters for Weary Wayfarers', was opened for the purpose in 1906 in North Street, and continued until 1959, when it was demolished and the new town hall was built on its site.

> During the two months in which North Lodge has existed as the 'model', there have been no fewer than 2108 sleepers. Of that number a good few are regular customers, some of them having 'dossed' there nightly since the opening, but the majority consists of that class of people who are here today and away tomorrow.[12]

Colette Douglas-Home writes:

> Jessie Kesson started life in a corporation lodging house (our nearest equivalent would be a down-and-out hostel). 'At that time I got my sense of direction by a sense of smell mair than anything. There was a sweetie shop where they made tablet and had my favourite sweets, jelly beans. I used to smell my way there.
>
> My earliest memory is of sitting outside the lodging house on a section of kerb with my feet in the gutter. It was an awfa' hot day, that hot my bum was burning. Knickers really were superfluous. I mind I played with the sweeties, made patterns with them in the dust, before consuming them. They served a double purpose. I must have been under five then because when I was five my mother found us a room in the Lady's Lane [Ladyhill Lane], Elgin'.[13]

The ecstasy of early sensuous experience is conveyed in both interviews, with particular reference, in Stark, to the potent smell of rabbit skins from a nearby rag-and-bone shop.

BEGINNINGS OF CONSCIOUS INVENTION

This helps to date another of Jessie's stories that was clearly very close to life. It could explain a time at Rothes Primary School. Readers of 'Until Such Times' will remember that the child, missing her 'Aunt Ailsa', is staying with Grandmother:

> 'Until Such Times', Aunt Ailsa had said on the day she took you to Grandmother's house . . . 'Until Such Times as I can find a proper place for you and me to bide. For you should be at school. But the authorities would just go clean mad if they found they had a scholar who lived in a Corporation lodging house. And spent most of her time in the Corporation stables. Sat between the two dust cart horses! So you are going to school. And biding with Grandmother . . . Until Such Times'. (*WAR* 107)

Evidence that much of this is based on fact is provided by an early draft among Jessie's papers. Roughly written, it would be ruthlessly pruned before publication. In this Cousin Alice (Mina) and Emma (Jessie) are joined in the wood by Tresta, an imaginary friend of Jessie's in whom she confides. It is hardly surprising that the isolated child should manufacture such a 'friend': these things often happen; but here we see the child consciously inventing, and setting limits to her fiction. Tresta, we are told, 'could only be conjured up into life outside the house': she shared the city child's unease at times, although 'Tresta and me always knew what to do when we lived in the town'. When Cousin Alice cries because she is frightened in the wood:

> She's frightened, Emma confided silently to Tresta. She's got shoes. And a new wooden pencil case. And blue ribbons. But she's still frightened. And you and me are not frightened.

Tresta cried once when she got lost in the Wood, Emma remembered. But that was a long time ago, she added silently. She began to shout for Grandmother.

At one point in this draft Uncle John says of the girl, 'She'll *never* be a scholar.' She muses: 'The first time I've ever heard the uncle's voice. The first time. Ever.' Grandfather speaks too, although not of course to his granddaughter. When 'Aunt Ailsa' writes to say she is coming to visit, and the Invalid Aunt predicts this will be in order to 'cadge', Grandfather replies: 'Either that. Or she's gone and lost this other job too.'

More evidence of the secret friend Tresta follows:

You maybe *could* come with me to meet my Aunt Ailsa, Emma informed Tresta reluctantly when she'd escaped outside again. I'd love you to see her, just once. She might be wearing her blue costume, with her white blouse outside it. Her hair hangs down in curls all over it. She's got a blue ribbon in a bow at the back. She's got silver buckles on her shoes too, Emma remembered. Maybe you *could* come with me. But her doubt increased. For Emma, Aunt Ailsa and the secrecies were far too personal to share, even with Tresta.

Tresta could come just as far as the station, Emma decided at last. So that we can play at that. Bumping into the trees, all the way there. On the way back, Emma knew, bumping into the trees wouldn't matter. Nothing bad *could* happen.

In *White Bird*, we were told, 'Janie had learned to enjoy the prospect more than the reality' (65). This seems to me a key insight into Jessie's own psychology. So now she fantasises over the prospective visit, preforming the event into story:

She stood moulding the pattern of the day to come, into the small distinct remembered details of Aunt Ailsa's last visit. She would start the song. Just to show Aunt Ailsa she hadn't forgotten

> There was Mary Beaton
> And Mary Seaton
> And Mary Carmichael
> And me.

She would know Aunt Ailsa was really listening. Because she would start to sing the bit *she* knew

> O often hae I dressed my Queen
> And put gowd on her hair
> But noo I hae gotten for my reward
> The gallows to be my share.

> There was Mary Beaton
> And Mary Seaton
> And Mary Carmichael
> And me.

They would sing together. Bumping into all the trees in the wood. And not caring.

'It was Mary Fleming was the Mary that wasn't there any more,' Emma would say quickly, before Aunt Ailsa could say it first.

'You still remember that, then?' Aunt Ailsa would stop sudden, and look at Emma with a smile that was small and pleased and surprised. 'You still remember.' Spurred on by such appreciation Emma would remember something else.

'Weep not for me, my good Melville.'

'That's it! My, but that's good.' Aunt Ailsa's surprise would stretch her smile. Until suddenly, they'd both start to laugh, about nothing at all, and, both in chorus, would go singing up through the wood.

This unfinished, much corrected and scratched-out manuscript would be all the evidence there was of the imaginary Tresta, were it not for the evidence of Isabel Baird, who was a classmate at Skene Central when Jessie arrived there, and who heard rather a lot about a certain Tresta. Mrs Baird told me in August 1996 that, when the new girl came to Skene, she was forceful and wanted to impress: tales of an Elgin paragon called Tresta Soutar were intended to put the Skene girls in their place. Jessie was deliberately using her invention. In an undated letter full of reminiscences of early days, Jessie wrote to her, showing how the relationship had been purely fictional, even if the girl had a real-life counterpart:

> No wonder, as you will now realise, I tried to hold fast to memory in Skene playground a la Tresta Soutar!! Tried to impress *her* superiority on my new contemporaries!
> The curious thing is – I don't suppose she knew of my existence!!! Her sister Lesley was in my class.
> I was ever, of course, a Hero – or rather a Heroine Worshipper. I wonder what happened to some of my West End School 'Heroines' – *none* of whom I ever spoke to. Or they to me!!!!

Jessie remembered the West End School with affection – 'Skene never took its place' – and described one teacher, Miss McLaren, who always dressed in purple and figured in rude playground rhymes.

MOTHER AND CHILD

But mother and child together form the lasting image of these early days. The complex relationship between mother and child in the time at Lady's Lane is ultrasensitively explored in *The White Bird Passes*. Sometimes it seems almost the reverse of the traditional picture, with the small girl taking care of and looking after her mother, who is still a countrywoman bewildered in the city slum. She even spends half of Mysie Walsh's last largesse on tobacco for the small clay pipe Liza regularly smoked, like the traveller 'Beulah', and the whole company of travellers described in Betsy Whyte's autobiographical volumes, *The Yellow on the Broom* and *Red Rowans and Wild Honey*.[14] Much though she missed her mother in the orphanage, the writer acknowledged the relief of no longer being always a 'small Martha'. Their relationship was not physical: the child wistfully wishes they could hug – and yet in 1985 Jessie told us that her own relationship with her children lacked physical warmth: these things often tend to perpetuate themselves. When Mysie Walsh commits suicide in the novel, Janie's mother brusquely refuses to grieve:

> 'There's nothing to cry for.' Liza didn't look at the child. And didn't slacken her stride. 'Nothing at all. Death's the poor man's best friend. Burns said that. And do you know something? He was quite right.' (37)

But her incomprehensible attitudes never negate the joyful times. The bad times are clearly indicated in the novel, but never spelt out as clearly as they were in the uncharacteristically open interview with Colette Douglas-Home referred to above:

> She knew it was poverty that reduced her mother to bartering her body to local men in return for coal, tobacco or the money for food. Kesson never uses the word prostitute. 'She didnae go out and pick up strangers. She kent the men . . .'
>
> But, young though she was, she knew how her mother earned her daily bread. 'I knew instinctively but I never saw. There is a scene in the film of *The White Bird Passes* when the child looks into the room and sees a man in bed with her mother; that never happened. Certainly the men were there and I knew what they were there for.'

Back at the respectable West End School, which, according to the simplified chronology of the novel, she had first entered in December 1921, Janie daydreams about being discovered to be the Headmaster's daughter, but is summoned, instead, to have her head deloused. She is given an ominous note for her mother, but excitement about the essay prize competition dominates Janie's attention: she knows her mother will help, and she does. But the 'Cruelty Man' (also greatly feared in Betsy Whyte's accounts) has called for them three times – about the Headmaster's note? – and Liza fears the worst, while neighbours prophesy a Home for Janie (85–86). In Chapter Seven, 'the worst had happened': Liza received a blue summons declaring 'that Janie was neglected, and in need of care and protection':

> To Janie it seemed that Liza, numbed and white and bewildered, was really the one who needed care and protection. Janie found herself able to provide both. (97)

Some version of the desperate flight from the Lane chronicled in the novel may also have happened in fact. Together Liza and Janie run away to another 'Diddle Doddle' (Model Lodging House): many years later Jessie said it was in Keith, some 17 miles from Elgin.[15] In another version they just spend one night in a wood. But the important truth is that Liza is increasingly helpless and hopeless and terrified, and they give themselves up, and Liza is resigned to losing her daughter. Little is known for sure about Liz's subsequent lonely time in the Moycroft district of Elgin, where young Cousin Mina, for example, knew her by sight and was afraid of her, in her black coat with the fur collar. Some time after the fruitless journey she made to the orphanage to reclaim her daughter when she was going blind in the course of her illness, in 1937 she was admitted by the Inspector of the Poor in Elgin to Craigmoray Institution. It had formerly been the Morayshire Union Poorhouse, where Jessie had been taken twice as a child because of her mother's 'neglect'. Now it had 24 beds for chronically sick patients. It was there that Liz died in 1949.

GRANDMOTHER

Both in the novel and in fact, by far the most important person in young Jessie's life, after Liz, was her Grandmother. The Grandmother was a wonderful and unique person for her. Both capable and strong, her sure hands were in demand to dress local corpses, but she had a lively side too, kept hidden from the rest of the family. In *The White Bird Passes*, Liza describes her playing her new piano in the wood, before anyone came to move it inside: 'it was such an odd thing for Grandmother to do. She was always so tall and strict and busy.' (72)

Grandmother's eye was penetrating: in a 1953 broadcast Jessie said, 'Grandmother could see beneath the surface of things, right through my frock to where the buttons of my liberty bodice were missing; and right up past the line where I usually finished washing my legs.' But as a memorable scene in the novel shows (72–73), she showed her secret playful other side to Jessie and their farmyard companion, the black pig, singing and sedately capering in a romantic, fairy-tale world. Even the thought of walking barefoot from Elgin to Grandmother's, five miles away, left the girl weak with excitement – 'I got my love for gardens throughout the long walks from Elgin to Redbog,' Jessie told of her in 'Memory Portrait of a Grandmother' in the *North-East Review* in 1944. Grandmother had a gift for happiness and secret powers of enchantment, speaking sometimes in Gaelic when she was weary: 'Her very words and their intonation drift down the years because they transcended the commonplace.' When the girl was jealous of her Cousin Alice's shoes in 'Until Such Times', wanting 'ankle-strap shoes' like hers, Grandmother replied, 'Sorrow be on shoes! The lark needs no shoes to climb to heaven' (*WAR* 113). Cousin Alice in real life was Mina, with whom Jessie would eventually be close friends. Jessie wrote to Peter Calvocoressi in January 1958:

This cousin and I are very fond of each other. It was not always so. As children, our visits to Grandmother sometimes coincided. We are the same age. As a child she was very beautiful. Very fair and Nordic, always very beautifully dressed. But best of all, she had patent leather shoes. I envied her those shoes more than anything in the world. Once the envy became so strong that I flung the mud pies we were making over her. Her screams brought Grandmother to the door, terrifyingly tall and severe looking. 'I want shoes!' I told Grandmother. 'Shoes like Mina has got!' I thought Grandmother would be furious, but all she said was . . . 'Sorrow be on shoes! The lark needs no shoes to climb to Heaven.'

This is a good example of how close 'fiction' and 'autobiography' can be in Jessie's writing.

In *The White Bird Passes*, Grandmother's magic and importance are clear: similarly with the earlier treatments, and everywhere her enthusiasm for song and dance and rhyme. The early story 'The Shadow', about the death of the Invalid Aunt, is remarkable for the straightforwardness with which it records the girl's triumph and delight in the death, but it shows too the child's delight in at last receiving the pick of the Aunt's hoarded 'treasure' box. Granny has 'sensed Jane's cruelty' and enjoyment over the years in grudging the child a treasure: it is she who now gives the child her choice, understanding and forgiving her crude feelings, so that:

> Charlotte sang and skipped the whole five miles home at the thought of all the tomorrows to be spent with granny in the red house undarkened by the shadow in the window-corner and the shadow in the porch.[16]

This makes an interesting blend of 'truth', wish-fulfilment and fiction. It was published in November 1946, when Jessie was no longer the child 'Charlotte', but a woman of 31. The BBC was to teach her to avoid using real names and places wherever possible but, astonishingly here, although the child's name is disguised, there is no attempt to disguise the uncles and aunts, here named. And Jane had only died in January of that year.

One last early treatment of Grandmother is in *The Scots Magazine* in 1949. Again the walk is important, as also in the novel:

> The whole world lay in the five-mile walk from our tene-ment to Grandmother's house, for I thought that where the

sky sloped down to meet the black, furrowed fields marked
the end of the world. But Grandmother's house stood safely
in the centre of the world. It stood on a hill. We could see it
when we were four miles away from it. Grandmother's house
looked down and over the whole world, and the whole world
looked up to see Grandmother's house.[17]

Here a grim gathering is discussing the disposal of Grandmother's
house after her death. (Like the previous example of Aunt Jane's
death, chronology is 'stretched' here. Grandmother had, in fact,
died in 1933, when Jessie was at Auchronie, and this occasion must
be imaginary – or wish-fulfilment – although the emotion is
certainly 'true'.) The talk is all of the price perhaps to be got for
the house, and of Grandmother's strict and hard Christianity. The
narrator's memories are quite different, like those of Janie in *The
White Bird Passes*, and she affirms: 'Grandmother was the glow that
kindled and lit up all my childhood in a slum' (21). Her home was
demolished in Jessie's lifetime, but even the address had magic for
Jessie, as she recited it to Joy Hendry for her *Scots Magazine* article,
'Badentinnon, Redbog, Orbliston, by Lhanbryde.'[18]

THE ABSENT FATHER

There has been endless debate on the question of Jessie's pater-
nity. The story went that Jessie had only to go 'up the town' in
Elgin to be offered up to five different fathers on one trip. People
in Elgin are still curious, still ask. I was offered different solutions.
But Liz never told her secret. It survives in a draft letter Jessie
wrote a friend in October 1987, telling the story of her elder half-
sister Peg. In this draft, she also gives the story her Aunt Minnie
told her of her parentage, for the first time ever outside the family,
clearly accepting it as true. But she left it out of the letter she
finally sent.[19]

   She never told even Dr William Donaldson, whom she had
asked to write her biography, and to whom she told so much else.
It is interesting to remember what she wrote to him, above: 'The
closest letters to the truth are the ones which take on the aspect of

what is really a letter to myself.' In the unsent draft above she writes 'letter to myself' . . .

When I was grown up, I got on fine with Aunt Minnie. She it was who revealed to me the man who fathered me. John Foster of Ladyhill House, Elgin, who wrote *The Bright Eyes of Danger*. According to Minnie, '*Everybody* knows who your father was: you're so like him – in looks, in everything. In your manner, movements.'

'Everybody' – except *me* – and then not until I was in my fifties. My mother took *that* secret to her grave.

(And you are the first 'outsider' to know. For you, too, I trust, to keep it.)

Until and *if* and *when* I write the autobiography Chatto keeps clamouring for.

The idea of John Foster as Jessie's father is ironic. He had been Sheriff Clerk of Elgin since 1901. She did not know he was her father until her fifties, when he was already dead (he died in 1946). But she 'knew' him, in a sense, from very early on. Ladyhill Lane was adjacent to, a stone's throw from, his wealthy residence, where Liz, it is suggested, had been housekeeper. Family rumour has it that she went to a solicitor every month to collect money, but this hardly squares with the pauperdom and prostitution.

It is an ironic conjunction too, because John Foster was a writer himself, in a small way. He began publishing stories, usually adventure yarns, in *Chambers' Journal* in 1909. He made his way alongside other contributors such as Jeffrey Farnol, John Oxenham, John Buchan, J. J. Bell and D. E. Stevenson: one could almost say the magazine developed a house mode of romantic fiction, often historical. His first publication, 'The Luck O' The Spey', in three parts, was a particularly clumsy historical tale of 100 years before, where Celt loses out to Lowlander, and – a constant feature, this – there is far too much set description. The story was coyly labelled as being by 'Sheriffs Clarke'.

The pseudonym was dropped as he went on, improving somewhat with practice, to 'On Old Speyside' and 'The Forgotten

Rock', each in seven parts. The latter is somewhat in the manner of Conrad:

> Wherefore the bronzed fishermen of the North-East, well-nigh useless ashore, are when afloat of the breed of men, grave, resourceful, steady-eyed, as those whose sailing-orders often lead them to look without falter on the grey face of the Enemy.

He continued with 'The Bernardine', 'The Black August', 'The Other Passenger' and 'The Moaning Bay', all with relatively slight plots, lengthy descriptions, styles reminiscent to some degree of others, and awkward framing devices. They began to get longer: in 1913, 20 chapters of 'The Ship of Shadows' were serialised, but it was in December 1914 that *Chambers'* began to print his best-known work, *The Bright Eyes of Danger*, in 40 chapters and an Epilogue. Published as a novel, it went into several editions. As late as 1937, Chambers reissued it with a gaudy cover, comprising Prince, fair lady, attendant soldier and swathes of tartan. The novel is a fairly passable attempt in a well-known sub-Stevensonian mode. Here is its full title:

THE BRIGHT EYES OF DANGER:

Being a Chronicle of The Adventures of Edmund Layton of Darehope-in-Liddisdaill in the Troubled Years 1745 and 1746; How he Rode from The Border to The Lothian and what Befell him There; His Quest on The Moray Seaboard; and his Personal Dealings with The Young Pretender; All of Which came of Meddling in Other Folks' Affairs; Written by Himself, and now edited by

JOHN FOSTER.

The short title, of course, is from Stevenson's *Songs of Travel*:

> The untented Kosmos my abode,
> I pass, a wilful stranger:
> My mistress still the open road
> And the bright eyes of danger.

We are reminded of the epigraph to *The White Bird Passes*, also, of course, from Stevenson's *Songs of Travel*, and addressed by the orphaned girl to her Dominie:

> Bright is the ring of words
> When the right man rings them
> And the maid remembers.

Foster published one other novel, *The Searchers*, in 1919. It is a modern-day romance and adventure story, somewhat in the mode of John Buchan.

But for a half-century, until long after his death, Jessie would be perfectly indifferent to him, except as part of the landscape. In 'A Childhood', published in *The Scots Magazine* in 1945, she outlines it:

> The Duke of Fife's Hill, willed as a playground for the inhabitants of the town, became peculiarly our possession. It loomed above the Wynd; the stone effigy of the aristocratic Duke gazed down on us with an indifferent eye. [She describes in detail the one-armed man who guarded the tower.] His power of instilling terror diminished only when the apples in John Foster's garden at the side of the hill ripened . . .

And in *The Child's Christmas*, a radio play in December 1947, in which Jessie was both author and narrator, one little boy is afraid the police won't have him to the traditional free Christmas dinner:

> Wullie Smith's wintin' tae ken if his name's doon! He disna like tae ask hissel' after bein' catched pinchin' Foster's aipples bit he'd jist like tae ken if he's gettin' the Christmas denner!

Foster's real life was elsewhere, as a solid, sociable, upright citizen. He was born in Galloway about 1868. He was the son of John Foster, a draper, and Helen May Dixon. He came to Elgin in 1894, as organising secretary of the Unionist Association.

He began practice as a solicitor in 1897 and soon made a reputation for himself. His smooth, disarming manner, especially in cross-examinations, was often the undoing of truculent or disingenious [*sic*] witnesses and he gained considerable fame as a pleader. He accepted the Sheriff-Clerkship in 1901 . . .

Apart from his professional duties, Mr Foster took a prominent part in the social life of the community. He was connected with a number of local organisations and was a pioneer of the Moray Operatic Company of long ago. He was for thirty-three years secretary of the Elgin Burns Club, and was himself an enthusiastic Burnsite. He was a former captain of the Moray Golf Club and secretary of the club for eight years . . .[20]

He was mildly celebrated as a local author. When he retired in 1937, the Christmas number of the *Northern Scot* described him in light-hearted vein:

A man who is witty; a man who is wise;
A man who lights laughter in other men's eyes;
Whose old-time romances of mountain and glen
Have sprung from an effortless, versatile pen.

He lived at Ladyhill House until 1940. He had no legitimate children, and his wife, Isabella Glen Mitchell Balfour, predeceased him by a few years. Latterly he lived in Lossiemouth, at the Rockybank Hotel. He died in Bilbohall Hospital on 13th May 1946, and was buried in Elgin Cemetery. The cause of death was given as senility.

CHILDHOOD IN THE LANE

No one who has read *The White Bird Passes* needs further persuasion of how much Jessie/Janie loved Lady's Lane [Ladyhill Lane]: the novel concentrates to perfection the excitement of the child and her interaction with the Lane. But, of course, the work of art does, deliberately, concentrate: it deals with the child's Lane experience as the events of one week, and her years in the Orphanage essentially in one day. The other, earlier treatments of the Lane, thus, do have an interest as biography, filling out the life, covering Christmas, and Halloween, a powerful sense of smell and a fascination with the colours of jelly beans, messing about on the River Lossie catching 'bandies' (minnows), going to the West End School, the children's holiday rush to earn 8/3d a week weeding or picking cabbages.

> Life was: eating when there was food; fighting when there was drink; and . . . 'all along a dirtiness, all along a mess, all along a finding out rather more than less'.[21]

Jessie's identification with gypsies or tinkers is familiar from the character of Beulah in *The White Bird Passes*, as well as many generally favourable references. In her first four years in the Lodging House, she probably knew more gypsies and travellers than non-gypsies. Even in the crisis atmosphere of the Diddle Doddle (Model Lodging House) in *White Bird* (99–105), the child Janie is enraptured with the life and vitality of it all: it is her mother who is afraid. Jessie's first recorded story was the one that won a 'Sangschaw for Makars' competition run by the Aberdeen Scottish Literature and Song Association, called 'The Sleeping Tinker'. She later adapted it for radio in Scots, and took part in the broadcast herself (May 1947). This play, in comic vein, admits a tinker wife to Heaven, acquitting her in turn of idleness, dishonesty and wasting her life as a tinker. The travellers already in Heaven are all a little wistful for Earth, and prefer the music of the old melodeon to the perfection of golden harps. Jessie wrote more than one version of the short story. Another early radio play was entitled *No Fixed Abode*. In *North-East Review* in 1946 she published 'Vagrant: A Scottish Profile', in which she continues to visit the Beulah character, here called Johan, who has now been living not in her caravan but in a council house for 12 years. But Johan still conforms only outwardly to the image of the ordinary housewife. She'll read your hand, 'for a silver consideration, of course', and dilate on her past, an 'ancient tale of fundamental things'. Like Beulah, she 'made the best whole-rice in the world', which was mainly eaten by hand – 'no plates . . . and insufficient spoons': her caravan 'was my foster-home'. She collected rags, 'choosing the whole family's wardrobe from the bag's contents': one is tempted to suggest she was the figure Jessie wrote about to Peter Calvocoressi, who shamed her, dressed up, in the street, offering her cheap used clothes for her family, and knowing the family sizes.[22] Her frequent drunkenness, indicated also in the novel and dealt with by the law, was harder for the children to cope with.

So 'The Years Between' shows an older heroine, uncertain 'whether she loved or hated' the Lane, and remembering that 'one couldn't see much of the sky at the top of it; and washing, endless washing, that never looked clean somehow, hung from one side of the close to the other'.[23] An early poem, 'Blaeberry Wood', recalls trawling through the (posh) West Road of Elgin, searching in dustbins:

> Excited, plunging headlong in
> How carefully I'd search each bin,
> For a broken doll or a coloured tin . . .
> Life at the child must often smile –
> The rich folks' dustbins a Treasure Isle![24]

In 'Triumphant Day' she remembers hurrying through the West End to school, where she often had to sit separately from the rest because she 'wasn't clean' enough: the other children called her 'Beastie heid!' and she had to go to the clinic. Just once, she told her mother of the teacher's sarcasm, and Mother came up to school, strode up 'with an old scarf wound round her head'.

> The scene that followed was painful; Miss Sim was sarcastic, and Ness's mother, too honest to resort to sarcasm, became abusive. At last the headmaster intervened, and after many threats involving policemen and Inspectors of Cruelty, her

mother withdrew, squashed – but still shouting abuse till she
was out of hearing.

Miss Sim had won. Ness couldn't quite understand why
her mother – who could easily fight any woman in Lady's
Lane – was so easily beaten by small, young Miss Sim.
Perhaps it was because Miss Sim was a 'toff' and spoke
'swanky'. All the people Ness held in awe – nurses, cruelty
inspectors, policemen – spoke 'swanky'.

Ness felt terribly ashamed because her mother had sworn
at Miss Sim, but another stronger feeling, a fiercely protective feeling had surged up inside her: 'Hit her! Hit her!
Dinna mind the things she's sayin' tae ye. She disna hae tae
cairry her water up a lang stair like ye hae tae dae, and she's
nae puir like ye; it's easy for her tae tell ye fat tae dae.'[25]

In the story, this immediately precedes the cathedral essay prize
familiar from *The White Bird Passes*: hence the title. But this story
suggests that Liz's misbehaviour at the school directly contributed
to Janie's eventual removal from her care. An early draft of 'Until
Such Times' also has the child dreading the 'sudden inexplicable
angers' of her 'Aunt Ailsa'. But the novel is concerned to present
Liz more as victim and as spell-binder in the scenes immediately
preceding the summons. It makes no mention of the confronta-
tion with Miss Sim, although the teacher's name remains the
same.

In August 1945 Jessie contributed a piece to *The Scots Magazine*
called 'A Childhood: The Riches of Poverty'. Inspired by another
writer's bitter and self-pitying account, Jessie here celebrates
methods of acquiring money, 'most of them legitimate'.

We stole bundles of sticks for the stick-man. We queued up
at Fishy Jimmy's barrow for herrin's for the wifies that didna
like stan'in' themsels. Alas! We were usually recompensed by
these ladies with a herring, or a promise, neither of which is
exciting when you're under ten.

Our greatest harvests were gathered in on Saturday
nights, when bare feet proved an asset. We'd collide with

wonderful reality into a sufficiently drunk man, and, holding
our 'injured' foot, howl piteously. The man, if he'd reached
the rose-coloured stage, never compensated us with less than
sixpence for injuries rendered by his tacketty boots.

When I glimpse down the tunnel of the years a slum
becomes enhanced, its greyness shades from rose pink to
vivid gold, and people cease being people and tumble out in
rich assortment – characters from all childhood's story-
books.

Jessie sometimes chose to differentiate her youthful experiences in
Elgin and Skene by contrasting descriptions of worship: one such
is 'The Near Kingdom', where she tells how she waited in line at
the wee Mission Hall in Elgin to win a penny by correctly reciting
the parable of the Prodigal Son. And worse:

Not even a white frock trimmed with lace and fixed round
me with a wide blue ribbon, plus a proud-looking mother
with a scarf round her head sitting with other mothers with
scarves round their heads and shawls round their shoulders,
could inspire me to fulfil my promise, and add song to a
temperance social held in that same Mission Hall by singing
solo 'Jesus Wants Me for a Sunbeam'.

My contribution was not to be given till the latter part of
the evening. After I had consumed two baps and a mugful of
tea, I slippit oot at a wee side-door leading on to the street.

Alas! The episode did not end there. I got a lickin' from a
naturally irate mother. Between the thumps she expressed
the reason for irritation.

'Efter me peyin' three bob tae Beenie Stewart for a frock
tae ye, ye wadna sing "Jesus Wants Me for a Sunbeam"!'[26]

Another treatment of contrasting worship is found in *The Child's
Christmas*, a radio script from 1947. This follows mother and
child to church: on a bet that, hidden upstairs and without hymn
books, they will know all the words of all the hymns. They do!

In 'The Lost River' it only takes the sight of an excited small

boy to remind the writer that she used to see the River Lossie
much more vividly than now, and to understand, retrospectively,
the parents' reactions:

> How our mothers must have disliked the river! Mine did. I
> see long successions of jars of bandies being ruthlessly
> captured from under the kitchen sink and thrown onto
> the garbage bin.
> One could never explain to an enraged mother that the
> bandie gasping its last on the top of the tattie peelings was
> not just *any* fish, but the very biggest bandie caught that day
> after hours of infinite patience.

Surprising gamblers was another riverside activity:

> I see the minor fortunes won and lost on the banks of that
> river; and I remember – rather ashamedly – the gold mine it
> proved to us bairns. We would creep up upon the absorbed
> Crown and Anchor players, and announce: 'We're gaun tae
> tell the bobby on you anes!' As a result of this genial
> announcement, we were often given a penny 'tae keep
> oor big mou's shut'. This we did, for one never killed the
> goose which laid the penny for the pictures.

Even the happiest evocations of the Lane tend to be tinged with
the child's desperate insecurity. The recurrent fear expressed in
The White Bird Passes, that Liza might die, is surely associated
with another ironic paragraph from 'The Lost River':

> I see the white 'Mother Die' flowers which we pulled in
> defiance of superstition. We would run home with them,
> hoping all the way that our mothers wouldn't die because we
> had plucked the flowers. Yet we always had a vague sense of
> disappointment when we saw that our mothers were alive
> enough to be in a temper because we had gone to the river
> instead of to the gas-house for cinders![27]

But there is a clearer source for Janie's morbid fear in 'Anybody's Alley'. This fine 'dry run' for *The White Bird Passes* records a real death in the Lane, that of one of Janie's schoolmates: 'Unable to believe that Dolly was really inside the white box they carried out. Frightened because if Dolly could die, your mother could die.' Another script records that a man committed suicide in fact, and the child learned that someone could *choose* to die. The biggest fictional leap in the novel is surely the masterstroke of having the suicide be Mysie Walsh, the only 'working girl' in the street apart from Liza, a warm, exciting figure to the child: this underlines Liza's own unhappiness and bitterness.

'Anybody's Alley' is otherwise a celebratory piece. It deals with Annie Frigg and her endless promises to the child of rewards that never materialised, as in the novel, but it pictures her more in the round:

> Annie Frigg was a witch, but a good witch; a little, curly, grey-haired woman with black eyes, and a yellowish complexion. Under her nose was something brown that looked like a moustache. It wasn't a moustache. It was snuff. She aye had a wee walking stick slung over the crook of her arm . . . A man lived with her. I never heard him called Mr Frigg. He was just aye 'the dummy'. He could only speak one word, a big oath, he made good use of it. I was terrified of him.
>
> Annie Frigg was a good witch who owned the moon, and would verily have given it to me, if she hadn't been so busy 'takin' wee pinches o' snuff oot o' her mullie'. Only once did my witch fall from her eyrie. I came into the lobby one day, to find Annie lying at the bottom of the stairs, stick in one corner, mullie in another, and the dummy at the top of the stairs, shouting the only word he could speak. I was very angry, because in spite of my frenzied entreaties to 'Come on! come on! Missis Frigg's gettin killed!' nobody seemed the least bit worried. So poor Annie lay at the bottom and the dummy stood at the top of the stairs and swore down at her.[28]

This short piece goes on to give details about life in the Lane for a child that necessarily were omitted from the novel, where the time-scale is unobtrusively limited to one week. The excitement is wonderfully conveyed:

Summer holidays – and Wiseman's! Racing up the street in the early mornings, the 'Kelbie's Closers' trying to be there before the 'Moycrofters', kicking over any ashbucket that happened to come in contact with your right foot; delighted to hear the clatter; and see the stoor flying; relieving a few customers of their morning bottles of milk, also of their 'butteries', if they were stupid enough to leave them out, or too lazy to take them in. Kneeling in single file, weeding, not quite sure what you were weeding, wondering if it was carrots or young trees; getting a kick from the one behind you for being too slow, duly passing the kick on to the one in front, for being too fast. Glad to get off your knees to go and pull bunches of cabbage plants. 'Jist fifty tae the bunch noo,' the gaffer would shout, but, as he was aye kept too busy tying them to have time to count them, forty to the bunch was the maximum.

Running home – slower – at night. Brave enough, now that it was quite bright, to stand up on the dyke opposite the asylum and shout over to the inmates, who were walking in the grounds: 'Dafties! Dafties!' Fascinated by their big, white hats, and long coats; jumping down, and running faster than ever in case one would maybe escape.

Saturday! Getting an envelope with your name written on it, and the magnificent amount 8/3d written too. Gripping on to it, not opening it for anything in the world, till you gave it to your mother; getting the threepence to yourself. Great discrimination in the spending of it; changing it into six maiks;[29] deliberating in front of Mr Robertson's window, for most of the afternoon. Then blueing it . . . a lucky tattie; a sherbet dab; a cake of toffee; a lucky bag; a ha'penny's worth of jelly beans.

Enough material in this one piece to have filled that autobiography she never could face. The lack of main verbs adds a touch of breathless haste and excitement to it all:

> Halloween! Running through the streets shouting: 'Eellie o' lo. Gie's nuts.' Scrambling with fifty others to catch the nuts the shopkeepers threw out. Greetin', nae sure if ye wis greetin' because the loons stood on your taes, or because they stole yer nuts.
>
> Delighted to go to Mackenzie's shop for a tin of condensed milk, explaining that your mother hadn't a tin-opener, would he please open it for her? Sookin' the milk a' the wye hame; giein yer best pals a sook as well; your mother beginning to get cute too. Going to Mackenzie's another time for a tin of condensed milk; horrified to discover he didn't believe your mother hadn't a tin-opener.
>
> Sitting on the summer seats at the foot of Ladyhill; crocheting a 'bedcover' with rainbow wool; very interested till all the colours were in; changing your mind about the bedcover; making a doll's hat instead.
>
> Listening to the big girls singing 'Peggy O'Neill'; watching Dolly Munro and Vicky Stewart, jazzing on the pavement to the others singing; wishing you were big; dancing under the street lamp with Teenie Burns,
> 'We're two little dusky diamonds, real gems you know.'
> The other kids shouting: 'Dae't again! jist this once!'

Jessie adapted this piece for radio in October 1947, playing the part of the storyteller herself, in her element.

ROAMING MORAYSHIRE

But it is clearly misleading to think of the Jessie of the Elgin years as a Lane child only. I have already stressed how Jessie and Liz wandered the countryside, enjoying both its beauty and its freedom – and as often as not reciting poetry. Jessie confirmed this in

1990, when she wrote about the countryside aspects of her childhood for *Country Living*:

> The first eight years of my childhood were spent in a small room in a city tenement. My mother, country born and bred, was alienated from her family, so that springs and summers were spent wandering through the highways and byways of her Morayshire roots. We haunted that wide landscape. Rarely able to afford public transport my feet became as tough as new leather.
>
> Most people have a specific destination in mind on their weekend journeyings. A point to their travels, a stately home, a garden open to the public, an acquaintance whom they might 'drop in on' in the passing. Not us. Never us. The countryside itself was the magnet that drew us.[30]

Jessie was thrilled in 1946 when Neil Gunn, her favourite author, suggested her to *The Scots Magazine* as his successor for the monthly feature 'Country Dweller's Year'. She was thrilled; not only because of her admiration for Gunn and delight in his praise, but also because of the opportunity of writing about wild natural things. Split yet again, the slum child was also a devoted country lover from early on. She elaborated in the *Country Living* article:

> It was our journeys to The Oak Wood that remain so vivid in my mind. A wood that stretched for five miles on either side of the road. You could get lost within its immensity. With the passing of each spring I became old enough to venture further into its depths. But I was stopped dead in my tracks one morning by what seemed a great blue loch shimmering under the trees. I was grown-up before I could put into words the mirage effect that sudden appearance of thousands of wild hyacinths imprinted on my mind. In the few springs that were left to me there, a return to verify that loch of hyacinths became a compulsion:

Down on the wet grass on my knees
Plunging my face in the hearts of these
No smell I know is half so good
As hyacinths' tang in a morning wood.
I always saw them with new eyes
The heart runs out so swift to meet surprise.

In the 65 springs that have passed over my head since then,
that oak wood still holds for me the essence of a different
spring. Not for me the trumpeting yellow blare of daffodils
that heralds ordinary springs or the regimental crimson of
tulips. But just the small 'flowers made of light' that nestled
beneath the great trunks of the oak trees. Myriad. Translu-
cent. White Stars-of-Bethlehem, frail primroses, windy
anemones, yellow-eyed dog violets, and wild aconites
snuggled deep in their green chalices. Like candles lighting
us to bed.

With the move to Skene, Jessie lost not only her mother and the
excitements of the Lane, and all her friends, but also this roaming
freedom in the wildness of nature that meant so much to her.

Chapter Two: Skene

When Jessie arrived for her new life at the Orphanage, she was bald. On top of leaving mother, home and all the life she had known, the authorities shaved her head, which had often housed troublesome nits. A major mortification. In 'Railway Journey' she wrote that she 'wasn't too happy':

> My hair was cut off and to cover this deficiency I wore a large straw hat of many colours. I was conscious that I looked odd in my heavy boots and summer hat, but nothing could persuade me to take my hat off in school. It was my helmet against ridicule.

Nevertheless, the boy she was to sit beside asked the others 'if that was a loonie or a quean'. In a controlled, reflective piece she wrote for the centenary of the Orphanage almost 70 years later she described the scene:

> My long, navy-blue frock touched the toecaps of boots that were too big for me. My cropped head was covered by a large straw hat decorated with vividly coloured raffia flowers.
>
> The effect, on my first day at Skene School, as I walked through the boys' playground to the girls' section, was even more dramatic. The boys' silent, bemused contemplation was broken loudly and suddenly by one who had come to a conclusion: 'It's an American donkey.'[1]

Readers of *The White Bird Passes* may recall that the child's anguished mortification is there balanced against her other great loss:

Her new hat lay safely. So huge that it hid her small bundle
of underclothes. She felt her head, still with a small sense of
shock, although it had been shaved hours ago, after she left
the Courthouse . . . If I got one wish I'd just ask for all my
hair back again. No, I wouldn't. I'd just ask to get home to
my Mam again. Not having any hair wouldn't matter if I
could just get home again. (110)

Skene was a small village with a population of 1310 in the 1931
census. It is described as 'purely an agricultural community of
small farms and crofts'. The origin of Jessie's Orphanage is
outlined in the *Third Statistical Account*, with some indication
that things were harder in Jessie's day:

> The Proctor Orphanage at Skene was built in 1893 with a
> legacy of £4,500 left for this purpose by Mr Proctor of
> Kirkville, Skene. Boys and girls, usually 10 to 12 in number,
> are brought up there as a family, under the care of a house
> father and mother, and attend the Skene School . . . In the
> past few came into the parish: the latter were for long
> regarded as strangers.[2]

The limitation of numbers, usually up to eight in Jessie's time,
was an advantage. It is instructive to compare Jessie's accounts of
her Orphanage and her life there with that of an almost
contemporary writer, Dorothy K. Haynes. She was sent to
Aberlour Orphanage in 1929, where she was one of 500
children. Although her aunt encouraged her that it would be
'like a big boarding school', Haynes writes, 'I never once stopped
wanting to get away.' But her book *Haste Ye Back* (1973) shows
that in many ways Aberlour *did* work for her, and became in later
life a very secure foundation. Aberlour was in some ways the
same kind of establishment as Proctor's; the difference being in
scale. Both institutions were good of their kind; both trained
children for lives in service. Haynes and Jessie were dazzled by
similar details, displays of flowers, the annual trips to Lossiemouth; each learned at least surface obedience, and each har-

boured literary ambitions. Haynes's situation was less precarious than Jessie's: she and her twin brother were sent to Aberlour together when their mother died after a long illness which had left their father temporarily unable to cope with the ten-year-olds, but home and family remained realities for her, although far away in Lanarkshire.[3]

But the biggest difference is a striking one. From the start Haynes writes as 'we', and seems to be happy to do so, to participate in the community, and not to mind having to label her clothes with her number, which reflected how many orphans had gone before her since the founding in 1875: she was Number 3659. Jessie never writes as 'we'. She may be Janie, or Cassie, or 'the young woman'; even on occasion 'I', but her character is usually alone, singular, distinct. As she told us in 1985, she was born to be an 'ootlin':

> Every work I've ever written contains ae 'ootlin'. Lovely Aberdeenshire word. Somebody that never really fitted into the thing . . . Now, I know mysel at last and it's just in one line in that book where fowk were oot who never had any desire to be in.[4]

She did not want to be part of an 'us' who lived at Proctor's, and chose her friends predominantly from local children.

Jessie's feelings about her time in the Orphanage varied enormously in the different tellings. In a letter to her publisher when she was struggling with *The White Bird Passes*, she spoke of the whole time at Skene as a kind of waiting room, 'the "lull" in life', until her life could really resume, but other accounts are glowing and passionate. One true feeling was clearly desolation and loss. Getting the age wrong as usual (she was 10½), she wrote in *Leopard Magazine* in December 1992:

> For myself, total exile and the pain of it lies in the enforced expulsion from Eden. Not that my actual Eden was paradisiacal but all roads out from it led to the wide Morayshire countryside which I began to know so well in all its seasons

with a companion who 'minted her words from a fund of thought, seeing it good'.

The tales told on our long travels, the ballads sung together, the wonder of words in verse learned on the road (words remembered after a mort of years, needing no confirmation from books) and just the joy of being alive itself.

I was eight when I was forced out of Eden and to this day there's a vacancy − a kind of hole in my heart that nothing can fill.

But in the 'My Scotland' piece she began with a suggestively different use of the same image:

I wonder whether Eve grew old enough in Eden to realise that its green chlorophyll was not sufficient; that her veins needed the red blood of life; to be found in a wider world. If so, perhaps she walked out into exile . . . without regret.

I was a child when I was dragged protesting, out of my Eden, Elgin and its county of Moray.[5]

And later in the piece she reflects that in this 'bleak locale' words were few but dependable: 'with the passing of time, I began to realise that words, in their Aberdeenshire brevity, had the merit of truth'. And that the Dominie's reiteration of 'No padding', and the discipline of the Orphanage had been indispensable in her development as a writer.

It is clear that she was deeply ambivalent, and also that she threw herself into, and made the most of, every situation she found herself in. And there was a lot to love about Skene, starting with enough to eat and clean clothes to wear. Her joy is illustrated in the radio play *Friday* of 1966:

Isabel   Years ago, when I first came here, and got so excited when I got my clean vest and knickers, that I danced around the Dormitory in them. And something came

into my mind that matched the cleanness of them, and
I danced to the tune and words of it:

> When He cometh, when He cometh
> To make up His jewels
> All the pure ones
> All the bright ones
> His loved and His own . . .

Matron   Hymns of Praise are for singing in Church, Isabel.
Not for cavorting about to. I can see that I am going to
have difficulty with you. Not only do you get yourself
excited, but you get the other children all worked up,
about nothing at all.

Isabel   (to self) Not about nothing at all. Never about
nothing at all! But the truth only came when the time
for telling it had passed. And you were left with only
yourself to tell its words to . . .

. . . It isn't about nothing. It's because I love my clean vest
and knickers. I'm never afraid now of the School Nurse
catching me in a dirty one. It's because I feel as clean as
everybody else now.

There was a real sense of security, of an austere kind, and an
education she really loved. And it was a small orphanage. Its total
complement was eight, but at one stage she was the only one, and
began to feel very possessive about it. 'Railway Journey', written in
1941 briefly describes the beginning of the orphanage years.

I shall never forget my first impression of the Orphanage. I
thought then, and still do, that it was the loveliest place I
had ever seen. There was nothing of the institution about it.
In structure it was like an old English mansion and it was
approached by a long tree-lined avenue. In front of the
house was a large lawn bordered with lilies. I never saw so
many lilies! And I can never think of the Orphanage without
thinking of lilies. Above the front door was the inscription:

Proctor's Kirkville Orphan Training Home 1891. I remember
it well because I was marched round to read it every time I
forgot to dust beneath the beds.

The inside proved as much of a joy. A big range glowed,
big windows shone, and the woodwork was spotlessly white.

But what Jessie had written to Dr Donaldson (above, pp. 16–17)
about writing the same news to different people and ending with
different sets of news also applies to different accounts she wrote
of the same thing dependent on age, perspective or circumstances.
'Railway Journey' celebrated both what she loved in the Lane *and*
what she loved in her more ordered life at Skene: the girl is
travelling to find out 'which is the real me – Ness of the
Orphanage, or Ness of Kelbie's Close':

> Has everything changed, or is the change just in myself? I
> haven't forgotten; it's all too vivid. The years don't bring
> forgetfulness.

She never did forget, and she never fully resolved the questions. But
she gave many meticulous, moving and varied accounts of the split
childhood that produced a uniquely gifted writer. In 1991 the
orphanage celebrated its centenary, and Jessie wrote a quite different
account of her second chapter then, for the *Press and Journal*:

> I arrived at 'The Orphanage' as Proctor's was then known
> (and still is by the older generation of Skene residents),
> when I was eight. That was 68 years ago. My first two years
> were spent in the care of an English Matron and her
> husband. They were childless, in their sixties.
>
> That Matron could well have been one of the first
> Matrons. I remember an afternoon when a man in his
> forties arrived on a visit, introduced by Matron as 'one of
> the first orphans'. In the photographs of some of the
> children who had been in her care, the boys wore belted
> Norfolk suits, the girls lace-up boots with long pinnies
> covering their frocks.

Proctor's, then as now, was an imposing building. But its interior was bleak. Drab fawn and green walls; stone floors in all utility departments; drab linoleum in the two dormitories and public rooms. The 'Recreation Room' – never used for recreation – was covered in black linoleum of a rubber texture. I *know*. My specific 'duty' on Saturday mornings was to wash the floor – for some unexplained reason – with skimmed milk.

The only whiff of Recreation in that room was a large mahogany bookcase. An ethos of Victorianism contained in the books on its shelves. Books suitable for children were on its lower shelves, to be perused on rainy Sunday afternoons: *Christy's Old Organ; Jessica's First Prayer; Eric: or Little by Little; Eyes and No Eyes* – books that implied it was better to die young but saved than to grow old and become a sinner.

As I grew older and taller and could reach the higher shelves of the bookcase, I managed to get swift illicit peeps into the *adult* attitudes of Victorian times . . . *John Halifax, Gentleman; Mrs Haliburton's Troubles; East Lynne.* O! *Forest Lovers!* My favourite book.[6] The little verses above each chapter easily assimilated . . .

> In a garden fair I met you
> And you told me all your woes,
> Love to me had captive brought you,
> I bestowed on you – a rose.

. . . The religious ethos that pervaded the Orphanage in those days was not simply confined to Sunday afternoon readings of religious books. Nor to compulsory attendance at Church and Sunday School. Matron had a store of saws and biblical texts which seemed to punctuate ordinary moments in ordinary days. So familiar was she, herself, with these texts that she never felt it necessary to complete them. I never got their *full* meaning until I became familiar with the Bible:

'Train up a child . . .'
'Whatsoever thy hand findeth . . .'
'What's bred in the bone . . .'
'Who steals my Purse . . .'[7]

The hardest, as she became aware of its meaning, was of course,
'What's bred in the bone will not go out of the flesh', that
accusation of hereditary taint, for both the prostitute and her
bastard. (When Jessie was 17, she would be subjected to a very
unpleasant psychological persecution on these lines by an ex-
missionary Hostel Matron. This finally galvanised her to a
physical attack on the Matron of St Katherine's Hostel in
Aberdeen, and led to a nightmare year in a mental hospital.)
    The initial regime at Proctor's was stern but not unkind. It did
not offer much to an emotionally deprived child:

> In the early days of initiation, I was taken to the front of the
> house to read the plaque above the door, the plaque that
> confirmed the Orphanage's purpose and its age: Proctor's
> Kirkville Orphan Training Home 1891.
>
>   I became familiar with that plaque, now gone. Whenever
> my work was not properly done, I was taken to refresh my
> memory – with emphasis on training.
>
>   The next thing was to read and memorise Table Manners,
> printed on a large tract on the wall beside the kitchen range
> and surely a relic of Victorian times:

> In silence I must take my seat
> And say my grace before I eat,
> Must for my food with patience wait
> Till I am asked to hand my plate.
>
> My mouth with food I must not crowd
> Nor while I'm eating speak aloud,
> Must turn my head to cough or sneeze,
> And when I ask say 'If you please'.

I must not talk about my food
Nor fret if I don't think it's good.
I must not speak a useless word,
For children should be seen not heard.

When told to rise then I must put
My chair away with noiseless foot
And lift my heart to God above
In praise of all His wondrous love.

Jessie was right. A longer but only slightly different version can be found in Iona and Peter Opie's *Oxford Book of Children's Verse*. Anonymous, it is said to date from c. 1858, and is entitled 'Table Rules for Little Folks'. The ban on criticising food was not a problem, with one exception. Jessie was thrilled with wholesome food and regular meals, and dependably clean underwear. She particularly loved the Saturday dish of pease brose, which others did not, perhaps because, as she later declared, it looked like babies' nappies! The narrow line between autobiography and 'fiction' is again illustrated by comparing the story 'Stormy Weather' in *Where the Apple Ripens* with this letter to Peter Calvocoressi about the one food she could not stomach:

We never dared complain about our food. I had other ways of dealing with it, though. I couldn't then, and can't now, eat porridge. But, if we didn't eat *all* our porridge, we got no tea. I had formed an erratic alliance with one of the boys, who could eat anything. Matron always said: 'Albert has never been bottomed.' A good thing for me, too. For our bargain was that Albert would eat my porridge as well as his own! He did. With the swiftness of a conjuror. Alas, on the many occasions when we 'fell out', Albert got his own back, by refusing to eat my porridge! I always hoisted the White Flag before him, at the end of about three tealess days!

But even under the early regime, there was more bark than bite. There was a legendary cane of which Jessie often writes, but she never knew of its being used on any of the children: indeed, she never even saw it:

> Our faults were faults of omission – not wiping our feet, not washing properly behind our ears or, in my case, polishing the tops of the lockers but turning a blind eye to anything that lay under the beds . . . But in my early years in the Orphanage, I – accustomed to the warmth of dust and clutter, to Sturm and Drang, to the closeness of common humanity – took badly to its clinical bareness, its objectivity. I could not expand emotionally.[8]

There could be wounding unimaginative oversights. Once a year, the Trustees visited, and presented each child with a book and some sweets. Each child, that is, except Jessie. She did not come from Aberdeenshire, so did not qualify. But the Matron saw to it that all the others gave Jessie some sweets, and Jessie saw to it that she read all the books. Typically, she made the most of it. She survived.

Luckily for her, Jessie experienced more than one Matron's regime at Proctor's. Both were kind, but very busy and tending to be baffled by their Elgin child. The first was Mrs Gerrie, and the Minutes of Proctor's Trustees confirm what Jessie says below about Mrs Gerrie applying 'for the custody of Margaret Hunter'. The second matron, Mrs Elrick, was the wife of 'the Mannie' in the novel.

> One morning, three years after my arrival at the Orphanage, Matron did not appear at breakfast. She had suffered a stroke during the night.
>
> She took a long time to recover before retiring to a cottage in Montgarrie, Alford, taking with her as companion the other older girl whom she had brought up from a small child.
>
> My second matron was also in her 60s. She had a grown-up family of her own. She and her husband were country folk. He was a retired farm grieve.

For a few months, I had the Orphanage all to myself and felt possessive about it, so much so that when a full complement of children arrived, I felt my nose slightly put out of joint.

The house was never refurbished during my time there. But with the coming of the new matron, the atmosphere changed. The Recreation Room became more recreational, with the arrival of a gramophone. We listened to the songs of Harry Gordon, the well-known Aberdeen entertainer, and to the songs of Harry Lauder.

Music was always of crucial importance to Jessie, as all readers of her work will know, and she associated certain songs or hymns with specific times and places: they brought it all back. Music at Proctor's was not confined to the gramophone:

> From Matron's husband, who often sang as he worked around the byre while I milked the cow, I learned the whole of the tragedy of Tifty's Annie, often followed by a rousing encore: 'Duncan Gray cam here tae woo . . .'

It is clear from the novel that 'the Mannie' was important to Jessie, for all that she says he 'hovered on the fringe of Orphanage life' (134). There, he enriches her musical experience, and tries to teach her that she might find it 'easier to work your thinking in with your other jobbies': these words later help a bit (137). There is a nice additional story about the mannie called 'Judgment' in *North-East Review* in April 1946, some phrases of which survive in the novel. As there, he is 'kindly and humorous'. The children explore a forbidden loft, quaking lest the famous 'cane' be inside.

> The day they stood accused on a charge 'o' kennin something aboot the broken biscuits that aince war in a sack abune the loft' was one of the rare occasions on which the bairns had public dealings wi the mannie. Indeed the experience was such a rare one that the six bairns felt awe, for the mannie was an unknown quantity, even though

the twinkle was still in his een. 'Fa wist,' he speired, 'that first suggested comin up here?' . . .

'We aa cam up thegither' . . . 'Aye: we thocht first the divil bayde here'.

'We aa ate them, bit it wis Janey that said biscuits warna good for hens, corn wis best.'

'So,' said the mannie, 'ye thocht the biscuits wad be gweed for you, like! Weel, I ken the divil fine, him and me's gweed freens, and I'm pittin him up here tae bide.'[9]

Jessie was hopeless at indoor tasks. She could not maintain interest, but turned aside from floor-polishing and dusting to composing poetry. The indoor tasks were repetitive and relatively pointless. She put this to Dr Donaldson in October 1985:

When I was in the Orphanage, my Saturday morning job was to dust the iron-wrought work – very intricate design – which supported the stair-bannisters. I escaped its tedium by planning all the different menus, the things I'd cook for my mother when I got home. Strange, that – the nearest we ever came to cookery in the Orphanage was podding peas.

But Matron, if uncomprehending, was not unkind. In 'Makar in Miniature' Jessie offers one reading of their mutually baffled lack of relationship:

The Makar never made the moment, but seized it when it came. She would be sweeping the library with the best intentions in the world when, like some secret telepathy, the signal would flash through the cool dark room that it was hyacinth time. The library could be swept another hour; explanations to the Matron could wait; but the Makar must go *now* to the Ducks' Wud, for hyacinth time is so brief that, if you dinna catch it, it's gone.

Fortunately, she seldom met unkindness. The Matron might puzzle over the unswept library and the swift disappearance of the sweeper, but she was never anxious nor angry. Another bairn would be sent in search of the missing Makar. 'Mrs Elrick sent me tae look for ye, she said ye'd either be in the Wud or speaking til yersel in the lavvy.'

Time had no significance for the Makar since she never said goodbye to any place, person or incident that touched her. She carried them all within herself and could recall them at any moment in their pristine vividness.[10]

When it came to outdoor life, and to school life, there were more compensations. Jessie much preferred working outdoors, and there was plenty of work to do:

> With a former grieve in charge outside, the fields attached to Proctor's became fully worked, losing some of their bleakness, becoming like a well-run, almost self-supporting croft.
>
> We grew our own potatoes, turnips, curly kale and corn, milled by Mr Davidson, the local miller, and returned to us in bolts of oatmeal. Our cow supplied us with milk, butter and a kebbuck of cheese. When the pig farrowed, the sale of its piglets added a little to the Orphanage's income.
>
> At one side of the house was a large fruit garden. Its blackcurrants, white currants, redcurrants and raspberries kept us in home-made jam.
>
> One of our most pleasant duties was picking the berries, exhorted by Matron, half-jokingly, half-seriously, to 'sing while you pick'. I think she overlooked the natural devious-ness of children. We took it in turns to sing. In that way, each and all of us found time to consume some of the fine berries in peace.
>
> When the grocer's van visited us once a week, it was simply to supply basic needs – flour, sugar, tea, partly paid for in kind by the eggs from our hens and ducks.

Jessie's short article 'My Country Childhood' gives an overview of her life at Skene:

The next eight years of my childhood were spent in an orphanage in agricultural Aberdeenshire. A harsher country, a bleaker landscape. For all that, the genes of generations of my farming forebears stood me in good stead. I could milk the Orphanage cow night and morning, before I was nine. I turned the churn once a week, my ear becoming finely attuned for that 'plop, plop!' – that precise signal which sounded: the butter had come! I became young Ruth amid alien corn. Making the bands of straw and binding the corn into sheaves as it fell from the reaper. I was given what Matron always seemed to imply was a prestigious task – plucking the hens for the Orphanage Trustees' Christmas dinner, 'because', she explained, 'you never tear the breasts'.

I became Officer Commanding Ducks. A joyous job that meant I could – legally – escape from the Orphanage walks by simply going about on my lawful occasions: racing up through the fields to the ducks' wood and calling them to their supper of kippled maize. 'Dilly, Dilly, Dilly! Eenie, Eenie, Eenie!' After the meal, the drake took command, tail high, leading his plump, douce wives home, without any help from me. There could, to this day, be a relic of mine up in that ducks' wood.

Every year, the Orphanage children were allowed to go to the village Summer Show. The Minister of the parish always treated us to a free Lucky Dip from the bran tub. I was just into my teens. The right age for my delight with, and appreciation of, the gift I withdrew from the bran tub. A golden powder compact, complete with mirror. I knew I would not be allowed to use it. Vanity was not encouraged in the Orphanage. I had never seen my face properly; I wouldn't have known it if I passed myself on the road. I hid the compact in the ducks' territory, where I would always have access to it. In this way, as the song has it, I became 'accustomed to my face'.[11]

These ducks became important in themselves, and in what the child felt she shared with them:

> The home-taking of the ducks ceased being a duty and
> became a vocation . . . 'You' (ducks and drake) 'and me kens
> far the wild pansies grow' . . .
>   'Hame' was strangely remembered and interwoven with
> Orphanage life. Phemie completed much of the weaving in
> this wood. She viewed the time between 'here' and 'hame'
> with urgency. There was so much to be taken from here to
> 'hame'. Phemie sometimes felt terror lest she'd forget to take
> all the things 'hame'.[12]

I find it almost uncanny sometimes, the knowledge that the young
woman writing at 30 had of the struggle she had to keep her life, or
character, or reality somehow whole, or at least not totally disintegrated, when she was ten. Another such story, more fictionalised,
dates from 1942. Again the young woman is looking back:

> Eight years ago she had been the champion bandie-catcher
> of Murdoch's Close. Was it really eight years ago? Of
> course, it was. She was eighteen now. Pictures flashed across
> one's memory!
>   Flamer wasn't quite sure whether she loved or hated
> Murdoch's Close; it was long, and narrow, and cobbled;
> and one couldn't see much of the sky at the top of it; and
> endless washing, that never looked clean somehow, hung
> from one side of the close to the other. One was forever
> running to the pump at the top of the close for pails of water;
> Flamer hated that side of Murdoch's Close.
>   But there was the other Murdoch's Close that Flamer
> loved; the friendliness of the kids; the fun of it all; the lamp-
> posts you climbed up playing at 'Reliever!' . . . And then the
> chip shop, with the smell that made one hungry; its constant
> hum of voices; its brightness and laughter, and the gramo-
> phone in the corner playing 'Let the Great, Big World Keep
> Turning'. ['The Years Between']

Jessie talked in *Country Living* about being dragged, protesting,
out of her Eden, but saw it as maybe necessary. By the time she

had to leave Skene, she could think of the time at the Orphanage as 'the golden years', and when Flamer/Jessie gets to the hostel in town, she cries herself to sleep. Her roommate asks why she's crying:

> 'You surely can't be homesick. I've heard orphanages are terrible places' . . . A muffled sob came from Flamer's bed. 'My orphanage wasn't. It was a lovely place'.[13]

CHURCH

Church was an important aspect of the new life at Skene, after the cheerful clamour of the Mission Hall in Elgin. The Christmas hymns there had made Jessie and her mother happy, but in Skene there was something new, an ecstasy of appreciation. In the reflective 'Makar in Miniature' Jessie wrote:

> When she was ten the Makar left the Wynd to live in a country orphanage. Two new elements began to have their influence upon her – words and Nature.
>
> 'Ye mountains of Gilboah' was the phrase responsible for the Makar becoming a Minister at eleven. But when Masefield's Ned came along, she doffed her clerical robes and became a teacher. There was little privacy in an orphanage in which to practise being a teacher, but mind always conquered matter with the Makar, and so 'Softly along the road at evening' became perfectly modulated in the lavatory.
>
> With the approach of her teens, the Makar no longer consciously *became*, she simply *was*. She was Spring, Summer, Autumn, Winter – each in its season. She could see them so vividly, hear them so acutely, become so immersed in them that she knew she was part of them.[14]

In 'The Near Kingdom' there is a fairly lengthy description of the kind of new 'religious' experience the child was having. I want to quote it nonetheless, as it conveys so perfectly the sensuous awakening of the young girl, as well as her reaction to word and ritual and solemnity:

Unlike the jumping, thumping evangelist of the Mission Hall, the minister of the Auld Kirk had the mien, the slow gait, the quiet kindness of dignity. God was easily conjured up then. He was just our own Minister with black robes embroidered with white.

There was reverence in the very atmosphere of that Kirk. When the service was by-ordinar long, scanning the Bibles helped to hasten the last paraphrase. 'Thomas Skene, 1843', easily emerged from a pale scrawl in the yellow flyleaf of a mouldy Bible to take his place in sober blacks in any of the faded pews in the musty, dim-lit sacred place, that the Minister desired to call by the name, St Bride, but which still remains, fittingly, the Old Parish Church.

When it was the season for singing 'Summer suns are glowing', the Kirk's dimness became less profound; the sunlight crept through in patches, and anent the stained glass windows the dust of centuries was gathered and reflected in long coloured rays, green, red and blue.

When it was the season for singing 'By cool Siloam's shady rill', thick, yellow Himalaya cowslips sent their incense from the pulpit to mingle with, and overpower, the foostiness. And when we had to forsake our own familiar pew to sit up amongst the cobwebs in the gallery, then it was time for singing, ''Twas on that night when doomed to know', and, because we were very young, then the gleaming communion cup in the Minister's hand really contained blood, for a' that the aulder anes maintained 'it's wine that's in there' . . .

Moses came alive in the old miller, who, over eighty, was as much part of the Kirk as the pulpit itself. When winter proved too severe for younger folk to attend, the old miller was all the choir there was, and all that was needed. Like somebody out of another generation, he stood alone, oblivious to the empty choir seats round him, a unique figure in his sweeping tailed-coat that years of Sundays had faded from black to dull green. His great white beard swept over his chest, and from somewhere under it, arose filling the Kirk with volume and beauty, 'I joy'd when to the House of God'.

We outlived the miller. We saw him carried into the kirk for the last time, and listened to the Minister confide to God of the virtues of 'Thy servant, William Laing'. We sang the miller's favourite hymn, 'The sands of time are sinking', and the kirk itself seemed to wait and listen for his voice, as had been its wont, swelling out with lovely assurance, 'and glory, glory dwelleth in Immanuel's Land'.

The old man was never quite dead to me. When I was about thirteen, I sat where he used to sit, and though I could not sing 'Jesus Wants Me for a Sunbeam' in the Mission Hall, I was not afraid to sing 'Kilmarnock', 'Winchester', 'Martyrdom', 'Duke Street', in the Auld Kirk where echoes of the miller's mastery and perfection of those airs still lingered.[15]

The Minister, a keen gardener, was responsible for the Himalayan cowslips, and other wonderful flowers. While he was remote with grown-ups, like Grandmother, he was closer to children, and taught them in the woods to sing 'Clementine' and 'Shenandoah'.

SCHOOL

School was in many ways the centre of Jessie's life in Skene. The years there made a refreshing contrast to the hectic wanderings to and from West End School in Elgin, with erratic intervals at Alves and elsewhere. She made friends with local children rather than fellow orphans, on the whole, rather condemning the other orphans for lack of spirit. She was the only one from the orphanage who chose to become a Girl Guide, and to go off to camp for ten days each year. She found herself in a small, rather closed community where status was acutely important, and much later wrote to an old school friend:

What sticks to mind about Skene School days is the fact that
one of two things was necessary for the happiness of a child.
Status or Brains.
I got by because I had some of the latter. Not so my
Orphanage colleagues. They disliked school.

Tension between native children and orphans or boarded-out
children was not confined to Skene. A few miles away, at Finzean
School, Chrissie Gibson reports an elaborate 'class' system of
incomers:

> The greatest change at school was the introduction of new
> children to our area, who were strangers to life in the
> countryside.
> Orphans were boarded out to people in our area. We were
> told they weren't really 'Home Bairns' . . . Some of these
> children would eventually be going home to their mothers or
> other relatives. They didn't wear the usual rough grey material,
> which reminded people of the old Workhouse or orphanages.
> My mother never dressed us in grey. She said grey was for
> clergymen and 'Home Bairns'. We were told not to call these
> children orphans, they were called 'Boarded-out Children'.

Chrissie reported they were unpopular.[16]
Jessie's recall of Skene school days was extraordinary, but it was
matched by many of the others. Evidence for that is clear in the
many letters she got after the televising of *The White Bird Passes* in
1980, and on later occasions when she got wide exposure: many
old classmates wrote in, shared memories, discussed school
photographs with manifest enthusiasm. John Duthie was puzzled
by one: 'I certainly don't recall you as the shy sad uncertain little
girl in the photo. I would say you were pretty extrovert, if not
downright bossy, when we sat in the same classroom listening to
Dominie Murray.' Although some I have talked to lamented that
they did not have many of her letters because she was such a user
of the telephone, still quite a heap of correspondence remains.
All the evidence suggests the importance of the teachers, both

Dominie Murray and 'Missy Crook' (Miss Cruickshank). Missy
Crook could be stern:

> Miss Cruickshank – 'You Orphanage Children' – I was
> luckier than most, in that I formed an 'armour' round myself,
> becoming a kind of Court Jester. I was well aware of this, but
> it helped me to 'get by'.

But she was respected:

> 'Missy Crook' . . . a *fine* teacher. She rarely showed favour-
> itism. She used to call me 'the girl with the lisping voice' –
> I've *lost* that lisp!
> But 'Time and Tide', you know, 'a' comes ben' – She
> wrote to me in after years. She had been asked to give 'The
> Immortal Memory' at a WRI Burns Supper – would I write
> it for her? I did. With great pleasure. She *was* a fine teacher.
> Tending times to sarcasm . . . I was never very good at
> Drawing. The conversation would go something like this:
> Miss C (surveying my effort with an assumed bewildered
> air) 'And what is *That?*'
> Me 'The Object, Miss!'
> Miss C (parting thrust, as she moved across to next desk)
> 'It *is* an Object!'

But Missy could also be restrained, as another of Jessie's reminiscences records:

> I don't know whether you remember, but one of my most
> lasting memories of 'Poetry' in Crookie's room . . .
> One of the loons, easing himself up out of his desk. Red
> faced. Red knee'd . . . in his brown corduroy breeks and
> reciting an *English* verse that, in his accents, sounded some-
> thing like this:
> The sulver birch is a denty Leddy
> Miss Cruickshank didn't even smile.[17]

Dominie Murray was special, however. He was a splendid teacher, a great communicator of his love of poetry, and a very kind man. The first really important man in Jessie's life, he had an incalculable influence on her and great ambition for her. She told Dr Donaldson that she was very much 'teacher's pet' and that the Dominie only once gave her the strap – one stroke – 'after she had put some disagreeable substance mischievously on the end of a disagreeable girl's nose – causing a small hole'. He singled her out for praise: it was always her essays that he read out to the class. (Years later, at Maud, when another of the Dominie's pupils voiced ambitions about becoming a writer, he showed the boy some of Jessie's essays, to show how good you had to be. The boy in question, the late Arthur Argo, turned out a fine and talented folklorist.) He was totally generous with his time, when it came to suggesting private coaching for the University Preliminary exams, and with his money – he offered to buy all the books she would have needed.

It distressed Jessie considerably to learn that he died just a few months before the publication of *The White Bird Passes*, and never knew that she had not only justified his faith in her, but dedicated the book to him. He did know that she had become a writer: he wrote about one of her contributions to *The Scots Magazine*, 'Even if it has happened but *once* in my lifetime, it has been worth it.' Jessie cherished a note from his widow Molly, written in May 1958, which went in part:

> I write this with an overwhelming pride. I couldn't have any greater tribute paid to my husband than your dedication of your book, *The White Bird Passes*. Thank you, Jessie, from the bottom of my heart. I only wish Donald were here, to see his name on one of your books – books he firmly felt you would write some day.

As late as 1988, in a radio programme called *Just Three Wishes*, Jessie's second wish was that the Dominie could have known the novel and its dedication. (Conversely, with typical self-contradiction, she often regretted that she had not dedicated the book to her mother.)

The Dominie's kindness was not restricted to Jessie. In March 1993, for example, she had a letter of thanks from an old schoolmate, John Duthie, who was thrilled to see the illustrated piece by Joy Hendry in *The Scots Magazine*:

> The picture prods my memory and I recall moments long forgotten. I think it must have been Empire Day 1930 when we all paraded in the playground (there must have been a flagstaff then) and I had to march up to the flagpole and salute on behalf of us all. (I remember cursing myself for taking too short steps – very difficult to change once embarked upon.) In the autumn term of 1930 my brother Lindsay and I stayed with Dominie Murray and his wife in the Schoolhouse because there was no room for us at the house at Dyce to which my mother had moved. They spoiled us dreadfully, and I remember being in distinctly two minds about just how anxious I was to return to the bosom of my boisterous and altogether too numerous family.

This elicited further memories from Jessie, which do something to colour in her school life there. She writes in a draft reply:

> Harking back to a previous letter from you, re Empire Day a la Skene Central School. Our Dominie was a genuine Imperialist. Under Missie Crooks's thumping piano fingers we sang our Empire Day Song before setting out for the Play Ground Parade:
>
> > On the Twenty Fourth of May
> > Our Royal Empire Day
> > With banners true red white and blue
> > We'll march along quite gay.
>
> *Fired* with Patriotism, garbed in my Girl Guide uniform as Second Patrol leader of 'Fuschia' section – we were all flowers then – I felt as proud as an NCO with a Corporal's stripe.

'The sun never sets on the British Empire', the Dominie always reminded us on Empire Day.

The Dominie's favourite poet was Rudyard Kipling, also a great Imperialist:

'Gunga Din'
> Though I've belted you and flayed you
> By the Living God that made you
> You're a Better Man than I am
> Gunga Din!

How he *belted* out that! And Kipling's 'L'Envoi':[18]

> It's down by the Lower Hope dear lass
> With the Gunfleet Sands in view . . .

> They're all old friends on the old trail
> Our own trail, the out . . . trail

> O the blazing tropic night
> When the wake's a welt of light
> That holds the hot sky tame

Dear Dominie! he could always infect me with his passion.

Elsewhere, and many times, she chronicled his favourite poems: 'Poetry was mainly anthological, and nearly always heroic – "The Battle of Blenheim", "Burial of Sir John Moore", "Of Denmark and the North", "Our Bugles Sang Truce", "Marmion" – and so on.' Or, again, she listed Southey's 'The Battle of Blenheim', 'Young Lochinvar' and Campbell's 'Hohenlinden'.

English was Jessie's subject, but mathematics was alien to her. She told Dr Donaldson she was weak in this area, although she passed her exam. The Dominie always used to write at the bottom of her sums, in his beautiful hand, in red ink, things like 'Very Neat Work'. He either avoided reference to the contents, or added '0 out of 50'.

But

He had what I thought was a slightly ironic sense of fun. I
was a perfect idiot when Maths came into their period.
Having an excellent memory I could memorise every word of
every theorem.

Invited out to the blackboard to 'prove' the theorem was a
different matter. With one swipe of his duster, the Dominie
would wipe the ABCs and DEFs from the sides of the
triangles; replaced them with *unfamiliar* symbols XRS etc. I
stood wordless before such strange symbols to the amusement of the class, for I was seldom wordless!

Yet

I felt no malice towards the Dominie. Au contraire. I felt
in league with him, feeling he probably felt bored, or
fascinated by my reaction to triangles under a change of
symbols.

'Do you follow?' was his frequent query to a somewhat
bemused self. I didn't. He *knew* I didn't, and I knew that he
knew – a kind of game it became.

In a 1987 letter to her old schoolmate Isabel Baird, she wrote:

I floonered helpless through triangular mysteries . . . To this
day I don't understand *how* parallel lines *can*, according to
Dominie Murray, 'meet at Infinity', that inaccessible place.
Or did he simply mean that they *never* meet! If so, why not
say so, straight out – and not bewilder *me*!!!

Although Jessie and Dominie Murray had set their hearts on it,
and the Dominie was offering help free, it was never likely that
Jessie would be allowed to proceed to university. H. M. Paterson
argues that such a career was getting ever harder:

The main effect of the Scottish legislation of 1872 was to
threaten the traditional Scottish ladder of meritocratic
educational advancement via the parish school and the
universities . . . The arrival of state legislation . . . resulted

in the breaking down of that important ladder for meritocratic advancement which the tradition of the Scottish
parish school had represented.[19]

He characterises 'a twofold division of children and schools', one
for the academic and one for the 'non-academic' child. Skene
Central School took pupils in primary, covered the 'Qualifying'
exam and offered up to three more years of education, leading,
if parents did not require their children to leave school to work,
to the Day School Certificate (Higher). Jessie wrote to Anne
Downie, who was dramatising *The White Bird Passes*:

> School was the District's Central Secondary School. Going
> up to Third Year Advanced. Three teachers. Roughly 100
> pupils. *No* further education in *those* years for Orphanage
> girls or boys. Domestic Service for girls, farmwork for boys,
> irrespective of scholastic ability.

Proctor's was an 'Orphan Training Home', after all. The normal
earliest leaving age was 14. Potential university candidates would
have to transfer to a school which taught five-year courses: 'Children had to stay the full course to seventeen if they were to obtain
the Leaving Certificate.'[20] In this case it would mean going to
Aberdeen. The chances of the Trustees financing such a thing
would have been very low indeed, even if Jessie had been a boy.

Jessie was not alone in her ambition. You did not have to be an
orphan to have few career choices, depending on your economic
background. In an oral-history study of 80 women around Jessie's
age, nearly half of them expressed the desire to have remained at
school to obtain qualifications: 'But for all but a handful . . .
"staying on" was impossible . . . By far the most common starting-
point was domestic service.' Another, Lowland, study summarises
the typical fate of even the brightest children: 'Like the rest of
pupils and parents from her background she took school-leaving
at the minimum age for granted.' This study describes 'those who
wanted to stay on at school but "had to" leave' as 'an important
minority'.[21] This was Jessie's destiny too, although the Day

School Certificate (Higher), which she passed was not insignificant. It was a group certificate, awarded on the basis of performance in all the subjects taken. In 1932, the year after Jessie probably completed it, regulations were modified, and candidates were for the first time able to offer only four subjects, instead of a minimum of five, but Jessie passed in seven – English, Geography, History, French, Mathematics, Science and Drawing. She expressed surprise that she had ever passed Science, but boasted proudly that she passed English 'with excellence', and that Dominie Murray had been told her English papers were the best in Aberdeenshire. Naturally, she also came top of the school. But no one else in her small world seemed to share her joy in her achievements. When she took home her prizes, Matron would say, 'That's nice, Jessie. Now put it in the bookcase and go and change out of your good frock.' In one manuscript scrap she has the prize-winner seeking to impress a shepherd:

> The shepherd appeared through the gap in the dyke.
> 'The rain's on its road. My word!' he exclaimed, bringing his gaze down from the sky to the books cradled in her arms, 'But that's a fine hantle of books you've got there.'
> 'They're Jane Austen,' Chris told him. 'They're all the books Jane Austen ever wrote.'
> 'Grand things, books,' he said.
> 'The covers are leather. Real leather,' she emphasised, handing them over, imploring deeper examination. 'And the pages are edged with Gold,' she told him, watching his rough hands encompass the soft texture of the books' covers.
> 'Aye. Grand things, books,' he said, handing them back. 'That's if you've got the time.'

Just before she left the Orphanage, Jessie had yet another unsettling experience, as she explained to Grassic Gibbon expert Douglas Young:

> A school friend lent me a copy of *Sunset Song* when I was [almost] 16, at the Orphanage. Ironic, isn't it? It was taboo

in the North East at that time. (It would have been even more taboo in the Orphanage.)

To read it, I 'snecked' myself inside our outside dry lavatory next to the pig's sty. And although I had 'written' bits and pieces ever since I could *spell*!!! it was then I had my first conviction that I'd be a writer, in my reaction to *Sunset Song* – in the dry lavatory.

'That's MY book,' I protested to myself. 'He's written MY book!

I so identified with Chris Guthrie.

So Jessie had to leave school; Anne Downie, who dramatised *The White Bird*, says it was a week after her 16th birthday, in November 1932. When the Dominie sent her on her Day School Higher Certificate, to the farm where she was working, he 'enclosed a wee letter':

'My efforts were unavailing. But you will get over this. You have the Gift. But Festina lente . . . Festina lente.'
I didn't know for many years what Festina lente meant – Nor did the Matron when I asked her!

A part of Jessie remained angry and bitter all her life about this, as can be seen, for instance, in the interview in *Scottish Writers Talking*, but when she wrote about it to Dr Donaldson she made light of the whole thing, and a comedy of it all. She had told him how an almost annual performance of the same musical play, Gavin Greig's *Mains' Wooing*, was the high point of the calendar in her early teenage years:

The Premiere was always on Friday evenings. The night of cars, disgorging farmers and their wives. We, at the Orphanage, also was part of Friday Night, for a dastardly reason which you will soon appreciate.
Saturday night now – ah! a morte of difference! Bike night – young farm servants and kitchen deems. Congregating in swarms in the Milne Hall. Not so much out of theatrical

appreciation. Lured there by that compelling advert in *The People's Journal* – under 'Forthcoming Events' declaiming: 'All roads lead to the Milne Hall on Saturday night' – for a dance always followed *Mains* on Saturdays.

I think I would have given my soul to have been a Saturday Nighter.

This is the context in which she told him in 1987 about her theatrical hopes just before leaving the Orphanage in early November 1932, and the humiliating disappointment of her return to the Milne Hall as a 'Saturday Nighter':

In October – birthday month – fate was decided: I went to work as 'Kitchie Deem' in a local farm.

Strangely, what upset me most was that *at the time* 'Missie Crook' (Miss Cruickshank) was casting for her annual Christmas Play cum Musical. That year it was to be *Princess Chrysanthemum*. She had already cast the Chorus:

> Long live the Emperor
> Bow down before him
> Mighty and proud is he
> Subjects adore him
> Long live Great What for Why –

So, only Principal parts remained. In the previous play, I was the Gypsy. Dancing with a beribboned, be-belled tambourine, with brass curtain rings for earrings; a nifty velvet waistcoat, wide red paper skirt. I also sang solo my Gypsy number:

> Hark I hear the blackbirds singing
> In the woods of yonder grove
> Loud and clear their notes are ringing
> Banishing all grief and sadness
> Banishing all fear and pain
> Rising high with notes of gladness

> Much I love their cheerful strain
> Pum! Pum! Pum!

So you see it was *not* unnatural for me to anticipate self in role of Princess Chrysanthemum!!
   But
On the great first night a potential Princess sat anonymously in the audience – Full House audience!
   Worse: on the Second Night (Saturday), I went to *The Dance* which always followed play. That Dance I'd looked forward to being free to go to since I was fourteen – the Apex of desire!
   I wasn't ten minutes in the Hall before I became instantly aware of my *diminished* status in the eyes of my erstwhile school colleagues. I literally – and also in the context in which the phrase is now used – 'got on my bike' and pedalled my way back to the farm.

But the orphanage was not easily left behind. It was all she had to offer continuity to her life, and while at some times she felt excluded from Skene and its life, at others it exerted a powerful if mysterious attraction. A letter to Mr and Mrs Baird in 1980 shows how real and somehow urgent all these conflicting feelings still were for her nearly 50 years later:

> I spent a long time in Skene Kirkyard when on location for *The White Bird* – saw the graves of some former school acquaintance, Evie Youngson, Sandy Taylor, and names of adults high in Skene's hierarchy . . . But the tombstone that stopped me in my tracks
>   The Reverend John McMurtrie
>   for thirty-eight years
>   Beloved Minister of this Parish
>   I had a sudden small feeling of protest – 'He was *my* Minister too.' Then I realised something. I was *not* nor ever had been 'of this Parish'. That hurt in a way, because Skene meant a *lot* to me, but I really meant nothing to Skene.

I also realised why. Although the foundation stone of the Orphanage was laid down – 1891 – 93 years ago, going on for a century, I knew that I should not find the grave of even *one* of decades of children who had been brought up there.

The irony is – and was – en route to the Orphanage I – and I'm sure all the other bairns – were being assured that we were going to a home (with a small h). A new start. A new life. But of course it wasn't like that. We had 'no continuing city':[22] we never became integrated in the life of the Parish.

Chrissie Gibson again implicitly confirms this:

When orphans, known as boarded-out children, came to our school they became very unpopular. Some children resented the strangers, who seemed to get preferential treatment. Some of the boarded-out children seemed to expect trouble and overreacted to any problems they encountered. I found it was better avoiding these children.[23]

For all that, the Orphanage exercised a powerful magnetic force, even when Jessie was in a Hostel in the city. In a draft she writes:

It was only when I began to 'break a rule' that the girls began to accept me and confided in me. But I didn't break the rule for that reason. It was broken for no reason that I can give words to. I'd smelt the spring. A different thing altogether from knowing it was there. I smelt it almost before it came, as if it had told me it was coming. I'd walk for miles, always on the road to the Orphanage, as if it was there that spring began. I'd walk along the back way, Tyrebagger Hill walking with me, brushing through the small thin woods on the slopes of Cullerlie till I came within sight of the Orphanage. But I never went closer than that. Then I'd walk the ten miles back to the town. Untired and comforted, I think, by things that I'd almost forgotten, the sting of the Spring wind, with the thin rain in it. Unafraid of that dark that is never really dark in the country. Nearing the city, lying

within the glare of its own light, blinding the bright eyes of
Heaven and blotting out the Milky Way.

'*That's* where you've been, is it? You might at least have
told me,' Matron would snap in justified irritation. 'I cannot
understand anybody being homesick for an Orphanage.'

I wasn't homesick for the Orphanage. But I *was* homesick
for something I couldn't name.

Chapter Three: 'Chronicle of Failure'

Jessie's history from the time she left Skene Central School in 1932 to, say, 1935 is again somewhat unclear in detail. This is not so much because we find difficulty telling fact from fiction, as is sometimes the case in the Elgin years, but because she wrote very little about this time, and published less, and she tended to dwell on some subjects and omit others; almost deliberately, it seems, muddying the waters. Serious lying about her age in retrospect sets in when she writes about this period. It is not surprising that a displaced child who has had two names and then discovers, when she is about to sit the 'Qualifying' exam, average age 11+, that she has two dates of birth – it is not surprising that a child in this situation should get confused or careless about her age. In different accounts she claims to have left Elgin when she was eight, in others nine – once, ten. As shown in the Introduction, she was, in fact, ten years and five months. These two missing years are surely significant. But now a cover-up really seems to begin. In part, perhaps, it was vanity. She admitted to Julie Davidson, for example, that she had lied about her age so often that she had made both her children illegitimate.[1] She consistently lied, but her lies were not consistent! On one occasion she claimed to have been 18 when she first met Nan Shepherd in 1941: she was 24. Conflicting claims about age and/or dates dog her accounts of her life.

But vanity is not sufficient explanation. I am more persuaded by a passing remark in *Another Time, Another Place*, with reference to the young woman's cottar friends, Kirsty and Meg: 'It was as if the whole chapter of their youth had been torn from their book, and they had turned the page from childhood to middle age' (36). Her own resistance to such a situation is patent. That novel shows all too convincingly that marriage has ended choice and opportunity for the young woman: 'She had thought she could go anywhere. Go everywhere, do anything. Do everything . . . It's all different now. Being married, I mean' (11). Jessie was married at 20, to the first man who asked her, after she had spent a priceless year of her teens in a Mental Hospital, and was desperate to make up for lost time. She was on probation from the mental hospital, in the country, and some friends have suggested she married partly because she could thus end her period of probation, with Johnnie Kesson as her 'responsible adult'. I can find no evidence for this suggestion, and find the parallel situation in the novel more convincing: in this world marriage, in reality, brought women no liberty, no broadening of experience, rather drudgery, poor housing and a draggle of children. The young woman in the novel has no choices, no freedoms, is more a prisoner than the transient Italians. Jessie's marriage was happy enough at the start, but still she had lost irreplaceable time and heedless youth, and now her normal youthful freedom was dramatically curtailed. Her family began with daughter Avril when she was 21. Although Johnnie, 11 years her senior, understood she needed some youthful 'space', and patiently stayed at home with the baby when she went drinking with friends, she did miss out on the phase of youth she writes so movingly about, with the consciousness of being on a threshold, and untold possibilities ahead. She never totally ceased to yearn for the freedom, frivolity and heedlessness of youth, confiding in Peter Calvocoressi in 1956 that she wanted an occasion to wear an evening dress before she was too old to enjoy it.

And she seems to have needed to perpetuate the myth. Jessie told her intended biographer, Dr William Donaldson, some imaginative versions of her life, and omitted to tell many true things. Her writing had got her into a situation where there were too many discrepancies between the myth and the detailed history to keep control of. Whether she was always conscious of this or, indeed, remembered better her history or her myth, cannot now be established, but her determined if apologetic refusal to be interviewed by Dr Donaldson on tape indicates great uneasiness.

Of course, when she came to write about it retrospectively, she was having to reconstruct this phase of the past, after the culminating anguish of her young life, a year in a Mental Hospital suffering some illness and great unhappiness, and loneliness. Factual truth was perhaps not the most important thing for her to try to recover: continuity, a personality which is not wholly 'disintegrated', as the Orphanage Trustee Minister had it (*WBP* 147), is perhaps more urgent.

I have not managed to pin down much detail about three episodes of Jessie's life between leaving school and orphanage and her breakdown, episodes to which she referred rarely if at all, and about which she wrote little. Her usual story was of being sent from school into service as a 'kitchie deem' (kitchen maid on a farm), but sacked after six months because her heart wasn't in it, and she could only concentrate on reading or composing poetry. Then comes the breakdown, and the year in a Mental Hospital. This makes a good stark myth, if chronology and detail are not required. But there were two other short chapters in here too. After the debacle on the farm at Auchronie, she went on to the Central School in Aberdeen to do, not a Leaving Certificate for university, but a commercial one for some kind of secretarial work. Letters survive from schoolmates to prove it, and 'Flamer', one of Jessie's alter egos, does the same thing in 'The Years Between', before going on to train as a nurse. In fact the records of the old Central School, now Hazlehead Academy, show that she was registered there on 4th October 1933, one year after leaving Skene. I suspect that this third school experience is generally sacrificed for the clarity of her personal myth. And there is written evidence of another unsuccessful job, in a big store in Aberdeen. Elsewhere she was prone to 'neaten' stories, such as the tale of her lone, pioneering journey to London for the first time.[2] When she told us this story we never doubted it: I was very surprised when her daughter Avril Wilbourne mentioned in conversation that as a child of about 11 she was with Jessie all the time. I doubt if Jessie remembered it that way, by the end. So we may set what evidence there is for this time in what seems most like chronological order.

Mrs Letta Williamson, who was one of the two Youngson

sisters of Auchronie, remembers that she and her sister enjoyed Jessie's time there more than anyone else did. Jessie helped the Youngson girls with their homework, and told them wonderful stories. This was the first six months after she was dux at Skene. Mrs Williamson remembers Jessie being sent to the commercial course, in Aberdeen, *after* her time at Auchronie. When Jessie yearned for opportunities, Mrs Williamson's uncle, John Mac-Diarmid, an advocate in Aberdeen, arranged for her to be admitted to Aberdeen Central School. Mrs Williamson thought she was not there for very long, and suggested she was not an outstanding student in subjects other than English. And, as Jessie wryly recorded, English Literature was 'a once a fortnight extra' in the Commercial curriculum. Her great ambition had been to be an English teacher.

Something like this outline might fit and even partly explain the slightly ambivalent ending of *The White Bird Passes*. There, although the Trustees have turned down the idea of university education for a gifted but 'disintegrated' personality, and Janie is going to the threshing and will soon be 'ready for the knife', as the sniggering male farm workers have it, the Mannie persists that she will only thresh this summer: 'Janie's going to Kingorm [Aberdeen]. They've decided to mak' a scholar oot o' her. They have that!' No doubt a well-intentioned attempt to find a 'middle way', a school Commercial course with shorthand and typing would prove no answer to the girl who wanted to write poetry 'as great as Shakespeare'.

If Jessie's 'forgetting' or ignoring of her time in Aberdeen, either back at school or working in the store, may have become deliberate, it was not so early on. In 'The Years Between', published in 1942, Flamer, the Jessie figure, is a lot more conventional – and conventionally successful – than Jessie, but much of her life experience is directly comparable.

Thus the golden years passed, and the time came, when she was a little over sixteen, for Flamer to leave the Orphanage, and because she'd done well at school, the authorities were granting her a business training in the commercial side of a

secondary school in the nearest town, and she was going to
live in a girls' hostel there . . .

Flamer wasn't commercially minded, and so the commercial classes never initiated her into the mysteries of
book-keeping, but she gained an average speed in shorthand
and typing.[3]

Thereafter Flamer becomes a nurse, 'on the strength of her school
certificates'. Five years after she wrote 'The Years Between', in
1947, Jessie was interviewed by Frances Hall for the *Elgin Courant
and Courier*. This apparently factual account is open about her
commercial training – though it is now a 'college', not just a
school, and the exact status of her school-leaving examinations is
blurred. (No new certificates are, in fact, recorded.) This account
is already blurring the truth, but here it seems she was more
inclined to hide the Mental Hospital than the commercial
training, and obsessive about holding on to her teens, at the cost
of whatever experience:

A brilliant scholar, Mrs Kesson was dux of her school and
took her Higher Leaving Certificate. But for her penurious
and lowly circumstances she would undoubtedly have completed her education at Aberdeen University. As it was, she
received from the institution a commercial training at an
Aberdeen college with a view to her taking up a business
vocation.

At seventeen years of age she left Skene to earn her living,
but about twelve months later she met and married Mr John
Kesson, a native of Glasgow.

FAILURE ON THE FARM

First came the move to Auchronie, with the loss of status she had
experienced at the dance. She had come top, but was in a menial
job. The two sisters at Auchronie, both younger than Jessie and
less academically gifted, were being sent to a fine school in
Aberdeen. She must have been agonisingly lonely, with no peers

and a job she hated. She worked a 90-hour week for 10/-, with a 'Sunday off' once a month. Her nearest approach to companionship was 'unofficial minutes off' at the Kirk Brig with other servant girls who yearned for more glamorous service in town, where there were boys to meet. Her best friend from school, whom in writing about it she calls Bertha, had insensitively and repeatedly lamented that by coming first in the school Jessie had deprived her of the bicycle her father had promised her. Bertha was going to a Commercial College in Aberdeen. Jessie often wrote scraps about their inarticulate farewell on the last day – yet another parting of the ways. There were no words to express the finality, the friendship past. It must have been her intense mortification that led Jessie to cherish a grudge against 'Bertha', and to enlarge a small incident of misunderstanding to tragic heights. She wrote to a friend in the late '80s:

> One afternoon I got a few hours off from Auchronie, and was walking down the brae. Coming up it towards me was Bertha, on her way home from college. I hadn't seen her since we left School, and was so pleased to do so, thinking we'd walk a bit of the way together, and have a fine 'news'.
>
> 'Aye, aye,' Bertha said. And walked straight on past me. I couldn't believe it.
>
> I never saw her again. And I never forgot such an appalling snub. I couldn't believe it. Not Bertha, whom I knew so well – or thought I did.
>
> So – and I'm sure you'll understand this – the only kind of triumph, if you like, that I *ever* feel about achievement is in relation to *that* afternoon.

For once, this story has a happy ending. 'Bertha' was told of her imagined offence, which had been quite unwitting, and she and Jessie were reconciled, and became old friends who happily reminisced in correspondence. In 1987 'Bertha' wrote: 'Do you remember the time we took refuge in the toilet to escape Mr Murray's wrath for trespassing in the schoolhouse garden and using the swing. We sat in holy terror while he rattled the "sneck"

of the door.' But the insecurity reinforced by a lifetime of new
situations, new friends and sudden farewells helped to make Jessie
prone to fall out with and hold grudges against people in a rather
rash way. This readiness to take offence was to last her lifetime.
And sometimes, sadly, there was no reconciliation.

In the ruefully funny letter to Dr Donaldson already quoted,
about the school play and the dance, she gives us some insight into
her life on the farm:

> O, I did get *one* Dance, a 'duty' kind of Dance!! from 'Saps',
> my own mental name for my working colleague on the
> farm. The Horseman, about five years older than myself.
> There was a kind of intimacy between us. He lived in the
> Bothy. A bleak place for a man to live in. Just iron bed,
> wooden kist, hard wooden floor; his mattress filled with
> chaff from the threshing – prickly, harsh stuff. His bothy's
> sole adornment, cut from magazines, Janet Gaynor, Madge
> Evans, Colleen Moore – so he, too, must have had his
> fantasies . . .
>
> I also made his morning brose – he ate in the kitchen. A
> quiet, lumbering chiel, all hands, he seemed. Front teeth
> missing, so that his brose oozed out between his remaining
> teeth – hence my name for him, Saps. I also served him his
> denner but never ate with him: his squelching put me off.
> Strange, isn't it. I would sit down and eat with him *now*, it
> wouldn't bother me. It's when I was young that physical
> defects were so off-putting.
>
> Mind you, my wee bedroom next to the kitchen wasn't
> much cop either! I did have a wee better mattress, filled with
> 'flock', which got all lumped up together.
>
> But this I *do* know, flock or chaff, Saps and me were
> always tired enough to sleep sweet and sound.

Jessie parted with the Youngsons on good terms, and never
wrote directly about her time there, apart from the above. But
she used the circumstances and the conditions to produce a
Gothic little tale called 'Ferm Deem', which is reprinted in

Somewhere Beyond: A Jessie Kesson Companion.[4] In the story, Rose is not very intelligent, but flourishes under a first mistress, who treats her like a human being. But, almost inevitably, she 'gets into trouble', and returns to the Workhouse to have her baby. Her second mistress is hard, mean and unsympathetic and, in retaliation, Rose finally deliberately burns down all the haystacks and is removed to a home for poor craiters like herself. Her mistress triumphs, having got a new piano out of the insurance money. The story is dark and dramatic, but it succeeds because of the writer's thorough knowledge of the life of a 'ferm deem', and because it is so economic and understated. Jessie played Rose in a radio version in February 1948, produced by Elizabeth Adair.

Jessie left two neatly typed versions of her post-school employment, one of which she entitled, 'The Useless One: Chronicle of Failure'. Both may be sketches towards the long-promised autobiography. Neither mentions school in Aberdeen. One is in the first person, while the other continues the 'Janie' mode of *The White Bird Passes*. One of them begins with a sort of postscript to the story 'Stormy Weather' in *Where the Apple Ripens*, where the girl schemes to go to the Band of Hope, a children's temperance association, on Friday nights, to see a boyfriend. Jessie *did* attend the Band of Hope, which was described thus by Thomas Johnstone in his *Memories* (1952):

> One great institution of our childhood was the Band of Hope. It met on Friday evenings and provided an occasion for the appearance of old gentlemen with magic lanterns showing entrancing pictures of mice being poisoned in beer, and of dipsomaniacs, wife and child beaters, being ultimately buried in paupers' graves, or hanged for murder committed under the influence of the Demon Rum.[5]

This 'boyfriend' plot recurs, and clearly had a basis in truth, as indicated in other treatments of the story, as well as in a letter from 'Bertha', in 1987:

I cannot visualise your life in London, because you were so much at home roaming the countryside around Skene, scheming on how we could meet George Bain and Alec Cooper at the Band of Hope at Lochside Church.

The radio play *Friday*, directed by Stewart Conn in July 1966, is another especially poignant version of the story. Confronted by the Orphanage Matron who has found her letters, Isabel, aged almost 16, answers on two levels, Matron's factual 'truth' and her emotional truth.

M   How long has this been going on? Well? How long?
I   (recollecting; to self) A hundred summers! Can it be? Over the fields and far away. Beyond the night, across the day -
M   I'm waiting, Isabel!
I   I don't know exactly how long. But it was all the Fridays, of all the winter.
M   Who is this boy?
I   He goes to Gordon's College in the town.
     (to self) And he's my lad. Someone of mine. My own someone.
M   Yes?
I   He lives with his grandfather.
     (to self) And they think of us together. 'Beldie Milne and Alan Cooper.' That's what they shout. And I'm more than me now because of that –
M   And . . . ?
I   He wears blue stockings with yellow tops.
     (to self) Our names are cut out together on a tree; and scratched out together on my desk –
M   Anything else?
I   (to self) Everything else . . . I can smell the wind now. And the morning stars and the setting sun are not just things I see any more. I feel them, as if I could reach up and touch them, because I'm within them. And I can

sing sweeter. And run faster. And I can feel my eyes
brighter and my hair softer –
M – so you know nothing else about him?
I No. Nothing.

In *Friday*, Isabel tells the girls the official story about dressmaking, but hears a Male Voice giving her own account:

Taken the east from you. She has taken the west from you.
She has taken what is before you, and what is behind you.
She has taken the moon from you, and she has taken the
sun . . .

In the prose account, when the girl leaves, clearly not long after, the Matron returns the letters she confiscated on first finding them.

Both versions of the 'Chronicle of Failure' feature the last letter from the Dominie, who had failed to persuade the Trustees about the appropriateness of higher education for Jessie. She had it by heart but did not have enough Latin to understand it fully for a long time:

. . . My efforts were unavailing. But you have the Gift. You
never know what the years will bring to you yet. But . . .
Festina lente . . . Festina lente.

In both versions of the story, we cut from a scene where Matron is packing the aprons the Trustees had provided for her job on the farm and the Bible the Minister had given the girl 'in the lugubrious hope that "God's Grace" would go with me'. The next scene has the girl's Mistress overseeing the girl's packing to return six months later:

'You was just never cut out for Service.' My Mistress tried to
console me, when I packed my tin trunk again, after six
months' working on the farm. 'Just never cut out for it.'
I silently agreed with her. My first and earliest ambition

was to be a Tinker. Maybe I should have stuck to it, for Outdoors had always had such a powerful pull on me.

It had taken so little to entice me away from scrubbing the kitchen floor, or doing the weekly wash. A stray dog barking at the back of the house. The whiff of burning gorse, and the men laying it to waste on the slopes of the brae. A hen, slinking past the back door, with the proud but furtive looks of having returned safely from 'laying away'. And I would be up and off, on a voyage of discovery.

Bent over the ironing board on lamp-lit nights, lost in the book of poetry the Dominie had given me. Oblivious to the smell of scorching . . .

> Quand tous renait a l'esperance
> Et que l'hiver fuit longue de nous
> Sous le beau ciel de notre France
> Quand l'hirondelle . . .

My Mistress, justifiably enraged, had pointed out that she 'paid me Twenty-six pounds a year to do the housework! Not to improve my French. And singe the best tablecloths!'

There had been no ill-feeling at parting. But, the more my Mistress tried to console me, the more a sense of failure assailed me.

The next scene is one Jessie returned to many times, in stories and radio plays. The Return [to an Institution] in Disgrace. The confusion of feelings experienced by the self-conscious subject. The most likely reason for such a return occurred to all: she saw 'the speculation glimmering in the other girls' eyes'. And needed to say two things, almost simultaneously, that she was *not* pregnant (which was true) – but that she *had* had 'plenty of chances!' (which was *not* true). As late as 1991 she produced a story version, 'Cold in Coventry', for the celebratory volume *A Writers' Ceilidh for Neil Gunn*, edited by Aonghas MacNeacail, and a *Thirty Minute Theatre* for Radio 4 with the same title, directed by Marilyn Imrie. The story is reprinted in *Somewhere Beyond: A Jessie Kesson Companion*, and the play, perhaps the most effective of all, will be dealt with in its place.

ABERDEEN

Jessie had been living since she was ten in the small country village of Skene. Aberdeen must have been yet another challenge to her experience and adaptability. Aberdeen in the early 1930s was the major city of North East Scotland, a kind of local capital to a prosperous hinterland of farming, fishing and light industry, long before the advent of North Sea oil. And it was a university city, the one she had desperately longed to attend. But in her 'Chronicle of Failure' she is not disappointed, rather triumphant at the new job, and the prospect awaiting her, being employed as a Sales Assistant:

> I strutted through my last days in the Orphanage. No more
> Domestic Service. The *Town* for me! From now onwards, I
> would be called 'Miss'. No more sack apron. Nor caps of
> servitude . . . I started with the best will in the world.

This has a ring of truth, perhaps. The next episode was probably a brief spell of employment in a large Aberdeen store, Isaac Benzies in George Street, which lasted perhaps another six months, to summer 1933. Then came school in Aberdeen, from October 1933, with the intervention of Letta Youngson's uncle. Very little is known about this latter, because Jessie chose to ignore it after 1947. As far as is known, Jessie acquired no new qualifications at the new school. But she was spotted by Miss Stewart, her English teacher, and the Headmaster, 'Jock' Robertson. John W. Robertson was Headmaster from 1926 until 1954. The Central School had been a kind of ad hoc training school for would-be teachers until 1921, when the Education Authority decided to admit pupils who had no intention of becoming teachers. The school hall was a former church where young Mary Slessor had worshipped as a child: Jessie would remember this.

A former schoolmate, N. L. Harvey, had been in the same class and wrote in 1985 that he remembered her coming in late! Another, Mrs Elizabeth Cameron, had something of the same type of correspondence with Jessie about the old days at Aberdeen

Central as Jessie had with several others about Skene Central. Mrs
Cameron wrote to me in March 1997:

> I was a school friend of Jessie's. We used to walk home
> together and my earliest memory of Jessie was a remark she
> made when she left me one evening to go to the Aberdeen
> Women's Christian Association Hostel in the Spital, where
> she was living.
>
> On parting she said to me, 'You're right lucky you have a
> home to go to.'
>
> I never forgot it, and from then on I appreciated the fact
> that I had a home and parents. I don't think she was very
> happy at the YWCA Hostel . . .
>
> Many years later she told me of the kindness of her
> English teacher, Miss Stewart, who used to invite her to
> Sunday tea, and who took a great interest in her welfare. She
> also spoke highly of Mr Robertson ('Jock', as we called him)
> who encouraged her to go on at school.

When I asked Mrs Cameron if this interlude at Aberdeen Central
could have been after the time at Auchronie, she replied:

> You could well be right that Jessie was employed at Auchronie
> before going to the Central School. I could never understand
> why her age was given as being a year or two older than mine. . .
> I think it would have been either 2nd or 3rd year when I first
> knew her. She was in a different class but the same year. I was in
> the 'A' class and she was in the 'B' class and would have gone on
> to the Commercial Class which was 4C . . . It would be 1934–
> 35 when we would have been 4th year pupils. I only knew her
> because she and I went home from school together as we lived
> in the same area of town . . . Jessie would have left the school in
> 1935 when she finished her commercial training.

Mrs Cameron's help is invaluable, but the number of times she
uses 'could' and 'would' indicates that she is not sure, for example,
that Jessie ever finished the training.

Jessie lived in a hostel at the Spital, which at that time was known as St Katherine's Hostel for Girls, and owned by the Trustees of St Katherine's Club. (It was later the YWCA.) Jessie probably stayed there throughout this time in Aberdeen, and it seems clear that it was the Matron of this establishment, Helen MacCrimmon, who precipitated the crisis which led to Jessie's breakdown. Jessie records bitterly that the Hostel was for girls on probation, which she was not, and that she was sent there because it was the cheapest place to send her. Both these assertions seem fundamentally true. Miss Bella Walker, co-founder of the Club, is described in her obituary in 1962 as a pioneer of probation: 'She supported the first local efforts to introduce a probation service, becoming herself a voluntary probation officer, and early recognised the necessity of adequate training for youth leaders'. Jessie was befriended, in particular, by Miss Bella Walker, who ran the Club with her lifetime companion Miss Elsie Moffatt.

But yet again, inside the Hostel, Jessie was made to feel an object of charity by the Matron. Many years later, in a *Woman's Hour* discussion on gratitude, she said:

> When I was in my teens, I went to school, and I'd come from an orphanage and everything I got was charity and I stayed in this hostel. A lot of the clothes were given by wealthy patrons of the Hostel, and I used to be clothed from the same gifts. I used to be taken down to a basement and there I was fitted with a pair of shoes and the Matron of the Hostel, who gave the charity given by other people, she gave it to us as if she herself had personally given it to me − as if it was a million pounds she was giving . . . wasn't I a lucky girl and shouldn't I be grateful and humble and goodness knows what all: and you see I didn't feel grateful. It sounds terrible, but I didn't, and I said 'Thank you' and in the last analysis − if somebody saves your life or saves your soul, there is nothing more you can say than 'Thank you', but she expected so much more, and it was very hard, and I think *that's* what's meant by 'charity is murder'. That's from the receiver's end . . . It all depends on how you give it, you see.

Here first is an account Jessie sent to her very trusted friend and
publisher Peter Calvocoressi, when in 1957 Chatto was still
hesitating over whether to publish *The White Bird* as it now
stands, or to continue Janie's career further. The reader should
bear in mind that Peter Calvocoressi was among the people Jessie
was eager to deceive about her age:

> The early teens in the early thirties, in a city under the
> apathy and depression. The Trustees reconsidered, Janie
> went on to a secondary school in the city, sent to a 'Hostel
> for Working Girls' – a home for girls on probation, because
> it was cheap. None of them, I discovered, were fundamen-
> tally bad: like Janie herself, they were the children of slums
> in the twenties, now adolescent in the sort of 'futile' thirties.
> Tough and crude and moulded so, I'm sure, by the tough,
> crude times. The Matron was a person who, in her nature,
> did *not* like to see them become 'better' girls. Almost like a
> person who recovers from an illness, and hates to lose her
> illness, isn't pleased when you say, 'My word, but you're
> looking better today.'
>
> Her attitude was more emphasised towards Janie, be-
> cause Janie was there for expediency, and not as a
> delinquent. She also, I feel, resented the 'further educa-
> tion' of Janie. One of her favourite 'readings' at night was
> a very curious – in the circumstances – text: 'I have piped
> unto you and you have not danced, I have mourned with
> you and you have not wept.' But how willingly any *one* of
> the girls would have danced, if ever she had piped. She
> never did.

Jessie's fullest and most open account of that traumatic occasion
continues:

> In the end Janie physically attacked her, and then attacked
> herself: hence the Mental Hospital, although never at any
> time was Janie insane. In the end, the Matron was asked to
> resign. They realised that *all* the girls – probation or not –

couldn't be wrong all the time. But that of course was too late.

Miss Bella Walker made a special protégée of Jessie, at least up to a point. Jessie became a habitué of St Katherine's Club, the leisure and community centre run by Miss Bella and Miss Elsie. This seems almost inevitable, given the temperament and hostility of the Matron at the Hostel, and Jessie's consequent desire to avoid her. St Katherine's began as a social club for a handful of girls living in a crowded area around the Castlegate, in the city centre. By Jessie's day, it was rather like a non-residential YWCA, in a fine building in West North Street (now the Lemon Tree). It had meeting rooms and a chapel, with a well-attended weekly religious service. It was supported by the Pilgrim Trust, with grants from the Scottish Education Department towards staff salaries and classes. In 1944 the membership was divided between 14 clubs: Junior Girls' Club, Thirteen Club, Intermediate Girls' Club, 'Senior Plus' Girls' Club, Tuesday Senior Girls' Club, Wednesday Senior Girls' Club, Young Women's Club, Junior Boys' Club, Intermediate Boys' Club, Senior Boys' Club, Young Men's Club, Mothers' Association, Married Members' Club, Good Neighbours' Club, 1942 Club and 1944 Club. 'Each Club is run on the plan of one attendance at "Club night", choice of one educational group, choice of two social activities (dances or "Rendezvous"), and religious education'.[6]

Jessie got a great deal out of the Club and the sense of community she found there, and wrote a nostalgic piece, 'I'll Walk Beside You', about the girls and Miss Walker, in 1942. Here she is very positive about Miss Walker, and the reverse towards the woman she mentions towards the end, who was surely the Matron of the Hostel:

These girls taken at random, each possessing in a high degree the courage and gaiety common to most St Katherine's girls . . . held down their jobs well, put a lot into life and got a lot out of it . . .
Sunday Fellowship was the most impressive aspect of

Club life. Don't misunderstand me. St Katherine's girls aren't 'goody-goody' – they'd be terribly dull if they were! They are intelligent and they won't accept 'Gentle Jesus, Meek and Mild', dished up in Sunday School fashion.

A straightforward Christ, who disliked hypocrites so much that he got angry and styled them 'whited sepulchres', a humorous Christ, who with twinkling eyes could conjure up a picture as absurdly amusing as that of a camel struggling to get through the eye of a needle, a young, strong Christ, who by the sheer force of his personality could attract strong-minded fishermen like Peter. Him they can understand and respect, but never an insipid Jesus!

It is a striking tribute to Miss Walker that the girls, without compulsion, come to Fellowship in numbers that ministers only dream of.

At Fellowship with the girls, singing with them:

Be Thou my battleshield, sword for the fight,
Be Thou my dignity, Thou my delight -

I always got a feeling that I couldn't tell anyone about; because I lived with some of them and knew how hard they worked and how gay they were, I used to feel my throat getting tight.

A woman who disliked me – the feeling was mutual – unwittingly put into words the secret of Miss Walker's success as Club leader. This woman resented the fact that I liked Miss Walker, and at every opportunity went to the Club and reported my defaults. Returning one day from a clyping excursion she said, baffled: 'Miss Walker is still your champion.' Almost I cocked a snook at her.

But that's just it: Miss Walker never breaks faith with her girls; and St Katherine's girls rate loyalty very high. That's why Miss Walker *is* St Katherine's Club – she's still their champion![7]

But much remains unclear. It is implied in the 1962 radio play *Somewhere Beyond* that it was Miss Bella ('Miss Erskine') who became Jessie's 'guardian' and oversaw her life in Aberdeen. Was it Miss Bella to whom the unhappy girls at the hostel complained so long in vain? Miss Bella was and remained an important figure in Jessie's life, whose approval Jessie seemed to seek, but details about the relationship are very sparse. Clearly, it was flattering to be picked out for special attention from a membership of up to 100, but Miss Bella is another person who features very little in what Jessie wrote about the relevant period of her life. We have letters from her which Jessie kept (rather unusually at that time), and evidence from Avril Wilbourne about how much Jessie wanted to please her: although Avril was never baptised, her name was registered as Avril Walker Kesson, and it was understood that Miss Bella was her godmother. But Avril remembers deliberately smashing a fine doll Miss Bella sent her. Miss Bella's letters are kind, and anxious on Jessie's behalf: but is it my imagination that the relationship was nonetheless a little uneasy?

By the time she got to Aberdeen, Jessie had experienced one mother, two matrons at the Orphanage, one mistress and many teachers. Now at the Hostel she had a difficult and non-comprehending Matron whom apparently she could not criticise to Miss Bella, and, at the Club, a much-respected and very respectable mentor in Miss Bella, who was accepted by prominent circles in the city. Perhaps in succeeding years she showed herself too anxious to achieve a similar acceptance on Jessie's behalf. In later years when Jessie was working, not entirely happily, at the Cowley Institute in London (1955–60), Miss Bella was repeatedly thrilled that she was working directly under the Hon. May Ammon, daughter of the Fabian Labour peer Lord Ammon. Miss Bella and Miss Elsie had a mutually fulfilling emotional relationship, which may have left Miss Bella uncomprehending of some of the needs of her girls. She may have been loath to think ill of the Matron she had presumably employed. Moreover, the unmarried Miss Bella seems to have cherished some thwarted desires for motherhood: she gave special encouragement to some girls and developed special relationships with them, and ambitions for them. She offered to adopt Grace Law, who was a secretary at the Club, in the 1940s, and encouraged her to aspire to a career in teaching, which latter she successfully undertook. As late as 1960

Miss Bella took on the 'equipment for life of a girl of 15 years. She lived at the foot of our drive at Greystones.' It is important to remember that Jessie's mother was still alive, and Miss Bella may well have hurt Jessie by in some way seeking to supplant her.

Most puzzling and suggestive of all, although I have to stress that its reference to Miss Bella is quite unproven, is a passage in a letter to Dr William Donaldson in 1986, where Jessie was writing about Nan Shepherd and her understanding:

> To me it also opened up an *old* pain of my young teenage years, for no one knew the ups and downs of those early years as did Nan Shepherd. For there was another at that time who cared much for me, as I cared in return, but who never understood me, with painful results for me . . .

Interestingly, it was Nan Shepherd who wrote gently to Jessie in 1962 to tell her Miss Bella had died – 'Miss Moffatt will miss her very badly, and I am sure you will be far from the only one who will remember and spare a thought or two to the old days when she made a mark on your life.' And Nan Shepherd's last letter to Jessie, written shortly before her death in 1981 and extremely hard to decipher, comes back at some length to analysis of Miss Bella:

> Now I must answer a letter I had from you about being Miss Walker's guest in Torphins. I can quite appreciate how much the visit meant to you. Being an honoured guest isn't always easy! But both you and she had been able[?] for the past.
>
> And the saddest part – yes, one must have margins. She was a great woman in her day, and her whole-hearted devotion to her cause altogether admirable. No, not altogether. Appreciating you, you queer kid, alive at so many odd corners, was the saving grace for her. If she had been *all* standardisation, she couldn't have seen what was in you (not of course that she saw it all, but enough to realise how far you were from orthodox, and to appreciate it, even if she didn't understand it). So being a gracious hostess to you was

at least a crumb of life. But she hadn't you long enough or often enough to be graced by you. Still, you did something there!

In my reading of *Somewhere Beyond*, I feel I can detect a hint of betrayal at the point when Jessie has attacked Matron and may be going to sign herself into a Mental Hospital. The 'Miss Bella' figure listens to her unhappiness, her homesickness for the past, and says: 'I think, you know, Mary, what you really need is a rest; a real rest; away from everything for a while.' Moments later, the Narrator comments on 'that rest which was to stretch into a year' in Mental Hospital: did Miss Bella give misleading advice, deliberately or not? Shortly after that, 'Mary' tells someone, 'But I'm only in here for a rest. That's all. I'm not mad, or anything like that. I'm just here for three months for a rest.'

Not surprisingly, Jessie never managed to find a coherent tone or a wholly coherent narrative for the months immediately preceding her breakdown. She left no account of her time back at school, and her account of the foredoomed job in the department store is typically jocular and self-mocking. She began her second job as a Messenger, delivering mail to the Buyer in Garden Implements, in the basement, already plagued by the same kind of engrossing fantasies that had interfered with her career as kitchen deem.

'Call me *Madam!*' she snarled, grabbing the Mail. Without setting eyes on me. As if it was just one of the Garden Gnomes, clustered round her feet, that had handed over her Mail.

The idea was ridiculous. But, all my life, I have suffered from sudden attacks of ridiculous ideas. The Garden Gnomes. And 'Madam'. And the situations and relationships which might occur between them down in the vast secrecy of the Basement intrigued me, and kept my mind off my work for the rest of the day.

But she did achieve a first promotion, to Lift Girl, which she found exhilarating. The next step up would be to 'Junior Sales' in a

particular department. Where other lift girls dreamt of Perfumery
or Mantles, Jessie longed for Window Dressing:

> Who knew *Who* might chance along and join the crowd that
> always clustered round the Windows when Transformation
> was taking place before their very eyes! 'It's just the nude wax
> models that draws them,' one of the Lift Girls pointed out,
> 'the dirty-minded things!'
>   But I felt I could outmatch any nude wax model, in a
> brightly coloured smock, and wide, black skirt.

Instead she was promoted to the dreaded China Saloon, where
the Madam was 'a Martinet and a Perfectionist'. The hapless
Jessie never progressed beyond 'Goldfish Bowls'.

> I sold few Goldfish Bowls, and, in a desperate attempt to
> wrap both quickly and perfectly, cracked more than I
> sold . . .
>   It was only natural for Madam to serve me a week's notice.
> I *was* 'A Financial Loss' to the Department.

But the intimidating Madam, like Mrs Youngson of Auchronie,
had clearly developed a soft spot for Jessie: having sacked her, on
her last day she bought her a new dress, and the day following
took her to Crathie Kirk to see the Royal Family, who were at
Balmoral. Jessie responded with characteristic gratitude: when she
heard 'her' Madam confiding to another, 'I don't know *what* she
can do now', she thought there must be *something* she could do:

> 'Live, Madam,' I thought, aware for the first time that
> Madam was quite old! 'Live, dear Madam, till I find that
> something.'

Meanwhile, through the good offices of the uncle of the girls at
Auchronie, Jessie went back to school. She enrolled on 4th
October 1933, a year after leaving Skene. Her address was still
St Katherine's Hostel, 24 The Spital, and her 'parent or guardian'

was the Hostel Matron, Helen MacCrimmon. She left school on 29th June, 1934, with no new qualifications. And now she was unemployed. But Miss Bella still had options for her. At a time of grave unemployment, the government had set up Junior Instruction Centres for Unemployed Juveniles. The Girls' Centre in Aberdeen was, not surprisingly, St Katherine's! In October 1934, now just 18, Jessie was enrolled in a Continuation Class, and completed 58 attendances out of a possible 78 – fairly typical of her peers, for once. A fee of 5/- was paid by her or on her behalf. She is described here as unemployed, and before she could finish this course, towards the end of February 1935, her life changed dramatically.

In another version of her 'Chronicle of Failure', Jessie used the same formulation as she used for her kind 'Madam' with regard to the Hostel Matron, to very different effect. An early telling off from Matron leaves the girl thinking:

> 'Don't you die', she had thought, as the Matron dismissed her. For the Matron seemed so old and wrinkled that imminent death became a disquieting possibility. 'Just don't you go and die till I prove to you that I *can* do something.'

When she is sacked from the store she meditates on Matron, and on her own problems of fitting in with the girls. Matron's stern view of Christian teaching was heavy on the idea that 'What is bred in the bone will not come out of the flesh'. Because her access to Jessie's record meant she knew Jessie's mother had been a prostitute, she calmly and fairly openly anticipated a similar fate for Jessie.

> The Matron of the Hostel would not take kindly to such a failure. Small and withered by the suns of Nyasaland, where she had been a Missionary for years, the Matron and Janie had not 'started on the wrong foot'. It was just that they had found no common ground on which to *put* their feet!
> She had not yet lost her enthusiasm for 'souls to save'. But Janie's 'Soul' had eluded her. Janie was *not* on probation. She

didn't break the Hostel Rules. Her years in the Orphanage
had so conditioned her . . . To swear. To smoke. To use
make-up were considered sins of such magnitude in the
Orphanage, that they were never even 'tried out'. Current
teenage jargon had never penetrated its granite walls. A
severe handicap that Janie herself had tried to rectify. Lock-
ing herself in the Lavatory, to sound out both the swears and
the jargon.

Yet another barrier to overcome: 'when I went to Aberdeen the
teenage girls of my own age couldn't understand what I was
saying; all it evoked in them was a fit of the giggles'. Faced with
yet another wholly new situation, with entirely new people, Jessie
desperately wanted to fit in with the other girls, use their
swearwords, learn their accents, not to show herself up as
different:

> As she had unwittingly done on her arrival at the Hostel.
> Yes, she *could* dance, she assured the girls, under an intense
> cross-examination of her potential abilities. As indeed she
> *could* . . . The Petronella. The Flowers of Edinburgh. And
> The Dashing White Sergeant. Dances that had sounded so
> outlandish to the girls that a Demonstration was urgently
> requested, and willingly enough given, to send the onlookers
> bordering on the verge of hysteria. She had never danced
> since. And must, she knew, have seemed so priggish to both
> the Matron and the girls.

More than anything, she wanted to fit in, to do as the others did,
'to be part of their singing subculture'. One account of the next
scene is in scrawled Biro on the back of a typed dramatised version
of *The White Bird*. But, even uncorrected and edited, it makes its
point unmistakably. Ginny, one of the leaders among the girls,
decides to teach Jessie *real* dancing:

> 'You just follow, that's all you've got to do – I'll lead,' Ginny
> encouraged; 'because I'm the fella.' Pushing me one way, and

pulling me another, in time and out of time, to the accompanying chorus of interested but hugely critical observers:

> Come on along and listen to
> The lullaby of Broadway . . .

'What's all this noise then?' The sitting-room door was flung open. Matron stood on the threshold, taking in the scene quietly as she always did, so that Ginny's explanation was really superfluous.

'We're just learning Jessie to dance!'

Wordless still, Matron went out, closing the door behind her.

The more Jessie wants to be like the others, the more she senses Matron's dislike and disapproval. She can't understand that Matron is not pleased at her joining the group. She is ultra-conscious that Matron will have her case history on file. In fact, daughter Avril said Jessie told her that Matron specifically compared her to, and denigrated, her mother Liz. The scrawled draft is less specific about what happened next, when Ginny continues to try to 'rehabilitate' her.

'You know, hen', she concluded one night, after a critical but embarrassing scrutiny of myself, 'you wouldn't be too bad-looking, if you'd make up your face a bit. Sure she wouldn't?' Ginny appealed to the others for confirmation. 'Sure Jessie wouldn't be bad-looking if she put on a bit of make-up?' . . .

With a will, and everything in her handbag that promised anything, Ginny set to work on me. What she didn't have herself, the others provided her with. Lustrous lips. Matt Finish Complexion. Doe-eyed look. And 'a wee touch of colour' . . . She worked with all the enthusiasm of a painter. Standing back to observe each stroke, adjusting it with the calm objectivity of the dedicated architect . . . I hardly recognised myself when Ginny had freed me and finished with me.

I don't think Matron did either, lured to the sitting-room by the sounds of loud approval from the girls. We waited for hers, Ginny trying to urge it on: 'Doesn't Jessie look *different?* She looks a real wee smasher!'

'Yes', Matron agreed, turning to leave the sitting-room. 'Yes,' she confirmed, contemplating me before she reached the door: 'you *look* the Part!'

Matron died long ago. But if it hadn't been for the girls she would have died that night, beneath my own hands in the strength of my anger.

I had gone berserk, and attacked Matron. The girls had to admit that at the Committee Inquiry. For no apparent reason that *they* could see. They admitted to that too, and it was true. But only a kind of truth. A truth that lay between Matron and myself. One she would never have admitted to. One that I couldn't ever find words for.

In *Somewhere Beyond*, the sequel to *The Childhood* (2), the Narrator recalls:

This was the one time that the Matron was too slow to put the door between herself and the usual quiet, last-minute barbs from her tongue. For I reached the door first. I remember shaking her by the shoulders till all the coward she was appealed in fear out of her eyes. I remember thinking as I shook, 'Now, you really have got something to report me for this time.' And it didn't matter . . . I'm not sorry. Never sorry. Never sorry. Not even when it meant a transfer to a Home for Difficult Girls and finally admission to a Mental Hospital – the only solution my guardian could now find.

Chapter Four: Mental Hospital

Jessie spoke little about her 'lost year', spent as a patient at Aberdeen Royal Mental Hospital. She wrote little about it also, and published less. Colette Douglas-Home, whose *Scotsman* interview of 16th July 1990 was revelatory in many ways, quotes Jessie in an overview of her situation around this time:

> She returned to the Orphanage and day after day she climbed a local hill. 'If I looked down on one side I could see buses going to Elgin where my mother was. If I looked down on the other side I could see the Orphanage and the farm. I was torn between wondering where I should go and I took a nervous breakdown.'

When Douglas-Home pressed for more information, she replied: 'I wrote a story about it called "Good Friday". It is all in there. In those days there was a chance you wouldn't get out.'[1] 'Good Friday', in *Where the Apple Ripens*, is a fine and sensitive story which condenses the year in hospital almost to a day, much as events and emotions are compressed in *The White Bird Passes*. Every tiny detail is significant, and it is a wonderful story. But Jessie was wrong, even evasive, here. It was *not* 'all in there'. There was, humanly speaking, a great deal more to say and, in fact, she spent a long time writing about it, although most of her efforts did not satisfy her. The most successful were entrusted to the more fleeting medium of radio.

She wrote a very moving radio script, *And That Unrest*, which was produced by Elizabeth Adair in April 1950, with Jessie herself in a small part. This dealt with much the same material as the 'Good Friday' story, the nature of the timeless vacuous drift of things, her experience of the ward, the distinctive natures of other patients' illnesses, her desire to get out, and her fear of being permanently incarcerated, and consequently becoming permanently insane. Also her unprecedented outburst of tears on getting news of her imminent release. But the play has more information, more structure. It has other new details, and there are several separate unfinished prose drafts, in first, second and third person. There is also the sequel to *The Childhood* (2), *Somewhere Beyond*, which is printed in *Somewhere Beyond: A Jessie Kesson Companion*. At the risk of accepting some fictional details as fact, I will try to reconstruct as much of the story as possible, using Jessie's own words where available. They may not have satisfied Jessie, or made a coherent work of art with consistent mood or tone, but I find every word meaningful, and redolent of a truly traumatic experience.

Aberdeen's Royal Mental Hospital was a large and growing institution in 1935. A major Reconstruction Scheme was undertaken in 1933 and largely completed in summer 1935, when a new Block for female patients was opened. Not far from the city centre in the Cornhill area, it included some fine buildings and pleasant wooded grounds (which explained, said Jessie's informant Jean, why young female patients were never allowed the freedom of the grounds – too much danger from the gardeners' boys!). It was perpetually congested, and new buildings were being built or adapted on this and other sites, including one at Daviot, in particular to accommodate private patients, who paid more than the rate which various parish authorities paid for patients such as Jessie. Aberdeen Town Council was guarantor for Jessie, and the majority were also parish patients. For its time the hospital was modern and liberal, and proud of eschewing padded rooms and restraining devices. It boasted a Shop and Tearoom for trusted patients, and a small Occupational Therapy Department. Jessie benefited from none of these, and in all her accounts the only available Occupational Therapy is knitting endless pink socks. All the patients shared in the benefit of ward radio. The hospital housed an average of 800 patients of all kinds, most of them legally committed.

But in Scotland since the 19th century there had been the other possibility, of admission as a voluntary patient, and this is what happened to Jessie. She was one of 18 'voluntary' patients admitted in that year. But if, at least technically, this gave her any options of freedom, she was not aware of them: all her accounts make it clear that she thought the doctors had complete control, and could assign her permanently to a ward for incurables, keep her in the Sick Ward in which she was first placed, or let her out, with unchallengeable authority.

As we have seen, the Hostel Matron was the immediate provocation for Jessie's breakdown, but not the cause. That surely lay somewhere in the series of crises and new beginnings, repeated experiences of love and loss, her conditioning in conflicting cultures, the extraordinary lack of continuity in her life. One factor only, besides her own character and determination, was to work to her benefit, when in the Mental Hospital she met a character from earlier days, now in a position to guide, befriend, bear witness to her past, provide continuity. But not at first.

Jessie was young, ill, and credulous: some of her accounts make that clear in retrospect. There was a patient called Jean, who had been 'too long "inside" to ever want to go "outside"', completely institutionalised. Jean 'helped' with the ward duties, endlessly dusting and cleaning. Jessie suggested that every ward, essentially, had a Jean, something between a boon and a burden to the staff, but a burden to patients. She passed on a bleak vision for patients' futures. She announced authoritatively that she, Jean, would never be released, because she had no family, no one to 'sign for' her. She added that the same applied to Jessie. Jessie believed her. This is further dramatised in the radio play *And That Unrest*, when the girl fortuitously finds the death notice of the second, kindly Matron she had known at the Orphanage in a local paper:

Narrator   You sat there, remember, you looked all round you. Everyone in the ward seemed just the same. Some of the patients were knitting endless pink bed-stockings. One of the old women was having her usual, cheerful conversation with herself in a corner . . . another was laughing, as she'd laughed since she opened her eyes in the morning, and would continue to laugh till sleep closed her eyes again.

Another played the piano – Scottish dance tunes she played
– and fast and furious in rhythm with her own rising
exhilaration. But you sat there with a 'dead-pan' face, Mary.
What was going on behind that 'dead-pan' expression?
Mary   She's dead. The Orphanage Matron. I've got naebody
left noo. Naebody that maitters. I'll never get oot o' here. I'll
hae tae bide here forivir. Maybe I'll go mad through time
then I winna feel or ken onything. I'd be happier if I stoppit
feelin' or kennin' things. I canna even greet for her . . . the
tears winna come . . . It's like bein frozen hard inside. An' I
canna tell ony o' ye aboot it because yer minds are hurt.

No one told Jessie what was wrong with her. But, being Jessie, she
managed to glimpse the diagnosis on the Charge Nurse's monthly
report, 'acute neurasthenia'. Forever unknown to her, Jessie was
thus joined to a whole tradition of gifted women. This label had
been attached to many talented women writers, especially from
the 1890s onwards. Elaine Showalter gives a fascinating account
in *The Female Malady: Women, Madness and English Culture,*
1830–1980 of the debilitating effect of trying to be and express
oneself as a woman in a world made by and for men. This shows
one important link Kesson has with her 'sisters'.

The appearance of the New Woman, with her demands for
education, work, and personal freedom, presented Darwin-
ian psychiatry with a direct challenge to its social gospel. At
the same time that new opportunities for self-cultivation and
self-fulfilment in education and work were offered to women, doctors warned them that pursuit of such opportunities
would lead to sickness, sterility, and race suicide. They
explicitly linked the epidemic of nervous disorders – anor-
exia nervosa, hysteria and neurasthenia – which marked the
fin de siècle to women's ambition.[2]

Showalter quotes a description of the neurasthenic given in 1907
by a simplifying and condescending male doctor:

A woman, generally single, or in some way not in a condition for performing her reproductive function, having suffered from some real or imagined trouble, or having passed through a phase of hypochondriasis of sexual character, and often being of a highly nervous stock, becomes the interesting invalid.[3]

On the other hand, an American woman doctor, who herself suffered from neurasthenia, attributed female neurasthenia 'not simply to overwork but to women's ambitions for intellectual, social and financial success, ambitions that could not be accommodated within the structures of late nineteenth-century society'.

Showalter documents the passage of neurasthenia from America to Britain, where it was mainly associated with intelligent young women:

For many late Victorian female intellectuals, especially those in the first generation to attend college, nervous illness marked the transition from domestic to professional roles. Similar to the fears and depressions described by Nightingale, Brontë, and Craik in the 1850s, these protracted and vaguely understood illnesses were now subsumed under the label of 'neurasthenia'. From the pioneering doctor Sophia Jex-Blake to the social worker Beatrice Webb, New Women and nervous illness seemed to go together.[4]

Ironically, the illness was most frequent among intellectuals and the well-to-do: Virginia Woolf, one of Jessie's all-time favourite writers, is only the most famous, and famously suffered the most acutely. There was no suggestion that it could visit 'the labours of domestic servants, the harshness of rural existence'. Here, as elsewhere, Jessie was a striking and solitary exception. Jessie MacDonald, moving from Orphanage to service to Hostel to Mental Hospital, was, unawares, part of a much wider problem of women trying to adapt to new possibilities which suddenly seemed to become available to them, virtually within a generation.

But, as always, Jessie's situation was both more extreme and more challenging than most.

Certainly, she was ill. She knew that. Every new situation up to now had been a new challenge, to which she responded. Now, it was different. She developed a routine, like everyone else. Hers meant standing desperately at one side of a window, staring out at 'all of the Outside World she was allowed to see'. Being waved at by the white-turbaned women in the Co-op dairy opposite in Berryden Road, who would every so often stop to wave to 'the Watchers at the Ward Window. Urgently. Demanding response. The way they might wave to attract the notice of a child in its pram.' They were waving, in friendly fashion, at the 'Dafties', as Jessie herself had, less kindly, as a child. The other 'Watcher at the Ward Window' was Miss Erskine:

> But sometimes a great spasm of laughter would clutch at her on the way to the window. Causing her to fling her head back until it hung downwards on her shoulders. Her neck arched upwards, her chin pointed up in the air, so that Miss Erskine herself looked for all the world like a quacking duck.
>
> She never discovered what it was that made Miss Erskine laugh so sudden and so fierce. She never saw the thing. But she knew it was there. Her body told her that. Trembling in the wake of Miss Erskine's laughter. And nothing was outwith her acceptance. For nothing lasted long. Not even Miss Erskine's laughter.
>
> There was no laughter this morning. Miss Erskine had taken up her position at the other end of the window. The lines of demarcation became clearly defined. Sometimes, only sometimes, you crossed each other's line of vision. But that was merely accidental. Neither of you were ever guilty of deliberate intrusion.
>
> There was safety in that. Reassurance. She could never really settle down for the day until the other Walking Patients had got themselves rooted into their self-appointed positions.

The Young Girl – her own age – had already posted herself by the Main Door of the Ward for her day-long vigil. Ready to pounce on the first man who passed through it, clock-winder or Chief Medical Superintendent . . .

And Mrs Cheyne. Tiny, fragile, beautiful like the ladies on Willow Pattern plates. She was my 'partner' on our daily walk, the long crocodile that wound its way round the grounds, two nurses in front; two bringing up the rear.

I got used in time to that third invisible partner that always accompanied myself and Mrs Cheyne on our daily walk, that 'Bad, Bad Cheyne Man, nip nip nipping at my neck, my poor neck'. Visible only to herself. The pain brought on by 'Bad, Bad Cheyne Man' was also real enough to herself.

The day was punctuated with calls of 'Lavatory, ladies!' 'Coats and hats, ladies.' They shared a dismal and variously ridiculous wardrobe of outer garments, and obeyed, without spirit. 'Therapy' in the ward consisted of knitting and, to some, the long thick pink bed-stockings for patients in the gentlemen's wards became a raison d'être. Jessie was at a disadvantage here. Apart from a lack of interest and enthusiasm, her trouble was that she didn't know how to 'turn the heel' of her stocking, and it just grew, absurdly. The staff were too busy to help. 'In the course of a year "my" stocking could have wound the whole length of the Ward, and out into the North Corridor itself.'

And the Sunday evening services held in the Hospital Chapel which the quieter patients attended. They were just like ordinary Church services – only the border-line between a quiet patient and an unquiet one is so fine, so swiftly crossed – that a cry like that of a hurt animal would sometimes break through the hymn – then the horror would come over you again, Mary, a scuffle of nurses – a patient led away . . . and you'd go on singing as if nothing had happened.

Jessie was in the Sick Ward, because she had attempted to 'harm herself'. It was kept locked at all times. The hospital report for 1936 says that:

> All melancholic patients should be considered suicidal, either potentially or actively so, and, because of this symptom they should be put under treatment at the earliest opportunity in order to protect them from attempts at self-destruction. Too many had made such an attempt before they were sent into the Hospital.

Jessie was not suicidal now: she was fearful and timid: 'I'm slow an' bewildered, kin! Crowds frichten me and I feel lost in the middle o' a street.'

She was less ill than many, and more sensitive to suffering. Here is a snatch of night time from *And That Unrest*:

Narrator   Remember   the   draughts,   Mary?   Paralde-
hyde? ? ? . . . It filled the ward with a smell like old, stale biscuits. But there was never a draught for you.
Voice   You'd lie and watch the troubledness falling away from the patients who had – what you thought, was the good luck to get a draught.
Voice   You'd see the shadows of their wild hair flickering on the wall.
Voice   And the woman in the bed next to you quiet one minute – convulsed the next.
Voice   And their troubled cries echoing through the ward.
Voice   Then the shadow of the nurse passing with the draught   . . .   and   silence   falling   gradually   over   the ward.
Narrator   And no more shadows – except those that flickered in your own mind – no more sound, except the uncertainties thumping through your head.
Voice   You'll never get out, Mary, you'll cease being an individual. You'll become just 'a thing'.
Voice   But you'll get used to it by and by. You're beginning to

forget things already. When last did you laugh naturally as
you should laugh at seventeen?
Voice   You've forgotten, haven't you? And song? When last
did you sing just because you *wanted* to sing?
Voice   You've forgotten that too, haven't you?
Voice   And tears?
Narrator   It is long since, your tears, and that's what makes
living, Mary. Laughter, tears, song – and you're forgetting
how to live.
Mary   No! No! No!

The appallingly unchanging nature of existence on the ward was
punctured by a series of ordeals, again best illustrated from *And
That Unrest.*

Narrator   Remember at the end of every three months how
there was an air of bustle in the ward? Charts were collected.
Night and Day Reports were scrutinised by the Charge Nurse.
And it seemed as if some invisible dice was being cast to see
which patients would be transferred down to that 'Forever'
place, Ward Four, for those sent there were incurable.
Doctor   (undertone) And I'm transferring five patients from
this ward, Nurse. Any improvement in Mrs . . . (fade)
Charge Nurse   Not very much . . . she still has bouts of
melancholia.
Doctor   And how is . . . (fade)
Charge Nurse   . . . but still very apathetic and . . .
Doctor   We'll give her another month up here to see if . . .
And Mary? Any improvement in . . . (fade)
Narrator   And you always caught your own name, Mary. And
when the doctor's gaze came to rest long and searchingly on
your face, your heart pounded so hard that it was the only
sound in the ward. Fear . . . thumping against his slow
decision as to whether you were going to Ward Four. And
then his gaze left your face and . . .

[And he gave Nurse a list that did not include 'Mary'.]

Narrator   And so great was your relief, Mary, that the sweat
    came out all over you till your body was wet – and your legs
    shook under you in a weak, tremulous gratitude because
    another three months had passed and you'd escaped that
    Forever Place, Ward Four.

It is made explicit in *Somewhere Beyond* that the girl had believed,
even been encouraged to believe, falsely, that her stay would be
truly voluntary: 'Although I had signed myself in as a patient, I did
not know then that I couldn't sign myself out again.'
    Then there was that one visit from Ginny, who arrives in *And
That Unrest* arm in arm with her new 'china', Meg. She is
immediately recognisable as the Ginny from the Hostel. In the
published short story 'Good Friday' Jessie exploits the comic
potential, Ginny and Meg shrieking with admiring laughter at
the 'fella' at the gate - 'Mustard! A real sheik!' And Ginny
surveying Jessie with complete amazement: she doesn't *look* daft,
but her clothes – long grey flannel dress and thick pink knitted
stockings – are so weird, that she can't get over them. She urges
Jessie, 'Beat it! Make a run for it! Scarper!' Ginny promises to
return, and Jessie knows that she is momentarily sincere, but
knows that if she were to return it would be to have another look
at 'the fella at the gate'. But in a scrap of handwritten draft we find
a bit of information which is now, ironically, of very little
moment:

    The Matron had left the Hostel, Ginny said. Sacked, said
    Ginny. '*They* had found her out at last! The new Matron –
    'You would like *her*,' Ginny assured me: 'She's a smasher!'
    She was young; she often played the banjo in the Sitting
    Room, and – best of all in Ginny's eyes, 'She likes a smoke
    herself!'

But how did Jessie recover? She herself on different occasions
gives three main answers to this, all of which no doubt have some
bearing on it. In the radio play, 'you became divided into two
different people'. One of these went on with routine as before.

The other 'newly rediscovered bit' stood away, watched, and spoke
to her. The first time, she was staring out the window as usual
when she heard:

> You will get oot, Mary! See the buses that are passin?
> Inverness – Moor of Dinnet – Glencoe – Stonehaven. Ye
> maun get oot tae see a' that places again!

This voice urges her to write to someone – her school teacher,
perhaps. It urges her to comfort and console others:

> Go on, Mary! Comfort her. Ye're nae really feart at *her*
> hersel' or any o' the women themsels. It's the thing that's
> happened till them that ye're feart at. Ye ken fine there's nae
> beetles on her bedspread bit she *thinks* there is. It'll ease her
> mind a bit if ye pretend tae kill them. Go on!

The second account is given much more as a matter of willpower.
After the awful suspense of the three-monthly selection, she
decides to suppress any and all symptoms. The doctor had pointed
out she was wringing her hands. She stopped. Doctors and nurses
were on the lookout for 'hilarious' or 'hysterical' laughter: she
resolved there would be no more.

> I *had* escaped transfer to a Forever Place for another three
> months.
>   It was then that I made up my mind that no matter what
> inflexible rule might keep me there, it would not be through
> Adverse Reports, which had assumed some ominous, mys-
> tical powers in my mind. Normal behaviour 'outside' was
> another thing from normal behaviour 'inside'. By *nature* I
> was easily amused and quick to laugh; now I laughed less,
> lest I should be reported as 'hilarious'. By nature I was a
> private person, seldom alone in my own company. Now I
> kept well within the perimeter of the other 'ladies', lest I
> should be described as Depressed. Swift to anger, I kept my
> mood under control, even when the pages torn from my

library book fluttered through the ward. Trying to go
'against' my nature was the thing I found hardest of all.
But it had results.

The third account features a near-miraculous reappearance, the
factual truth of which is supported elsewhere:

> If this was a novel, belief might well be suspended. That
> 'truth is stranger than fiction' has become a cliché, simply
> because of its truth.
>   'What are *You* doing here?' Somewhere far back in my
> memory I recalled the voice. It took me longer to recognise the
> face under its white nurse's cap, with the longer streamers that
> proclaimed their owner as a Charge Nurse. Margaret Fowler,
> who had been maid at the Orphanage when I first went there,
> when I was eight. I couldn't answer. Because I didn't know
> myself why I was there. In a Mental Hospital. Surprise at
> finding Nurse Fowler by my bed, my first feeling was of relief.
> Here was someone who *really* knew me, who had known me
> for a long time. In the days when I 'was going to be a teacher',
> and who had never laughed at the idea. *She* would *know*. She
> *must* know! The first relief gave way to tears. Tears for failure.
> Tears for shame. Everybody 'at home' would know now I was
> in a Mental Hospital. Tears for the Dominie. Most of all I
> think, tears for the Dominie. He'd know now. He had always
> had such faith in me.

In *Somewhere Beyond* the girl greets the Charge Nurse wonder-
ingly:

> You was the maid at the Orphanage when I first came
> there . . . You sat on the dresser and mended the sheets and
> you baked the scones, and made the peasebrose and bathed
> me on Sundays.

Nurse Fowler's appearance was crucially important, and helped to
convince Jessie of the continuation of her own personality. She

became an unobtrusive and dependable support, lessening and distracting Jessie's loneliness and gradually granting her encouraging privileges.

Mary: It was with the passing of the days that I realised that my relationship with Charge Nurse Fowler was both bond and barrier. For the country which had contained the Orphanage and reared us both had also conditioned our natures into a reserve which was rarely broken. Yet I was always conscious of her presence in the ward, and immediately aware of her absence.

It turned out to be of little importance whether people 'outside' knew of what she thought of as her disgrace: only two visits from outside are recorded, and clearly the world of the Hospital enveloped the patients and occupied a huge proportion of their attention. It was of great importance that a familiar figure from years past recognised and supported her – not by giving special favours, but by the recognition, and by treating her as a real person, with continuity in her life, who can deal with stern realities and ought to be allowed to understand them. One torn and half-burnt scrap of paper survives, sketching a kind of Temptation scene, in which Jessie was being sweetly deceived. Here is what can be made out: Jessie is ushered into a small office by a woman in some authority:

She had, she said, a suggestion to make. She was sure it would appeal to me. There was a place called Larbert. Did I know Larbert? I didn't? Well, anyhow, it was in Stirlingshire. A beautiful place. I liked walking, didn't I? And books? Exactly. How would I like to go to Larbert. I'd have all the books in the world; plenty of freedom to walk around in. But, apart from all that, I was an *Intelligent* girl. I could learn to file, to assist in the office of a Doctor there. I wouldn't get much of a wage, but I *would* get pocket money for my work. Think it over. If it appealed to me, and *she* certainly thought it would, she'd be back to hear my decision in a day or two.

I wanted to give her my answer there and then. There *was* no decision. Freedom, books, work, pocket money . . .

Nurse Fowler was in the Sluicing Room when the Junior Nurse brought me back to the ward. I couldn't get the wonderful thing that was going to happen out fast enough. The silence of her reaction didn't puzzle me. She never *did* like the Sluicing much, when she was short of staff.

It was only when she straightened up from the sink, dried her hands on the towel, turned and locked the Sluice Room door, that I knew there must be *something*.

Did I know what Larbert *was*? she asked. I did. It was in Stirlingshire.

'Do you know *what* it is?' I didn't. 'It's the biggest Mental Hospital in Scotland. You may not' – she said, as calmly as if she was informing a Junior Nurse that Mary wouldn't need senna tonight – 'ever get out of here. That I can't tell. But what I *do* know is, here at least you know where you *are*. And the people you are with.'

I owe few people as much as I owe to Charge Nurse Fowler. And even fewer who found it so hard to accept gratitude.

Not that I felt gratitude at the time. I only felt the numb desolation of a hope gone. But even in my numbness, I knew that Charge Nurse Fowler had told me the truth.

It went so silently, like a betrayer.

'You *may* never get out of here,' Charge Nurse Fowler had said. The curious thing was that once I had got over the truth, I felt better in my own [illegible] than I had done in over a year in the Hospital. A feeling of freed relaxation. I had nothing now to lose. But I had to gain, a kind of way of life for myself. My every move and natural instinct was no longer conditioned by fear of 'Reports'. My sense of the ridiculous flourished again, giving amusement to both myself and the staff – and the patients who could share it. I could bring the past out of hidden places and talk about it again. Ginny, Cissie. Especially Ginny. So vivid. So much larger than life. A species as alien to the young nurses in from the country as she had been to myself when I first knew her. I could show them Ginny. Let them 'hear' Ginny, till sometimes in agony they would beg, 'O, don't make me laugh – I can't laugh any more!' Or I would stand quiet with and by myself, no longer anxious about 'Unsocial Conduct'.

So she began to get better, although hardly aware of it, and encouraged by little privileges and special jobs. She was allowed to set out the bed patients' trays, 'knowing now, and keeping in mind, which ones were not to have knives or forks'. I have no way of dating the array of tattered paper Jessie left in her polythene 'black baggies', but find here an apt, if ironic, echo of that momentous scene where Ginny led the girls to Jessie's transformation:

Allowed for the first time to go to the Patients' monthly dance, where Patients danced only with the Male Attendants, and Nurses with the Male Patients. Dressed in my own clothes. The Junior Nurse who helped to get me ready, as enthusiastic as if she herself was going to *her* first Dance. My shoes were the only problem. They were too tight.

'Only natural,' the Junior Nurse said: 'Your feet must have grown a bit in a year.'

'There's no need to be so down about your feet,' said the Junior, patting my shoulder. 'I've got a pair might well fit you – you're about my size.'

'You can keep those shoes if you like,' the Junior Nurse offered when they were found to fit. 'They'll be handy for you when you get out.'

'Out.' It was the first time that anybody had ever voiced even the suggestion that I might get 'Out'.

True, she was a very Junior Nurse. Maybe didn't yet realise the edicts that surrounded the Act of Discharge. But at least, in her eyes, it was not only a possibility: she had sounded casual as a certainty.

The 'Patients' Dance' was my first ever dance, and the happiest dance in my memory. The Band played many

different tunes. But to me, the lyrics had all the same words:
'Out . . . Out.'

Next, she was moved out of the big ward, and into 'a wee bedroom
by yourself'.

Away from the world at night. Undistracted by disturbed-
ness around me, that not even paraldehyde could quite
subdue. The waste of life would catch at me. And hurry
clutch at me like a panic.

The radio play follows the details:

Narrator   Remember it, Mary? So quiet, so comforting, with
neither sound nor shadow. Only the Night Matron ever
entered it. How you looked forward to her nightly visit.
Young and gracious, sitting on your bed for a few minutes
speaking to you as one human being to another, easily,
naturally, about things which interested a young girl . . .
frocks, your hair, your teeth . . .
Third Nurse   Mary! You'll be in charge of all the ward flowers
night and morning. Just ask for the key to the sluicing-room
door.
Voice   That was another cool, quiet, private half hour that
strengthened you to face a day in the ward.
Voice   Remember how thrilled you were to be able to lock and
unlock a door for yourself?

In a draft of a prose version, she uses the first person:

It was Spring again. I don't know whether Charge Nurse
Fowler had remembered that one of my special jobs at the
Orphanage, one I'd always had pleasure in, had been the
garden. Weeding it. Planting out the daffodils when their
blossoming time was over. At any rate she put me in charge
of the ward's flowers. I could now be allowed into the Sluice-
Room all by myself. A privilege which I lost no time in

conveying to Jean. Her sour observation that it would be a long time before I'd be allowed down to the *laundry* in no way diminished my enthusiasm, since I had never had any aspirations in the direction of the laundry anyway.

But O the pain of all the Daffodils. They were the first things that had met my eyes on my arrival at the Orphanage. The first things I'd ever had anything to do with there. I thought *then*, 'I'll never smell a daffodil in all my life again, without minding how I came to the Orphanage.' And the thought had come true. Smell. That sense – which holds the reservoir of all experience behind it, has the power to open the flood-gates.

Given the freedom of the small staff kitchen, allowed to make the nurses' toast all by myself, a promotion about which not even Jean could sneer away. 'I haven't got time to bother with toast!' she said. 'I've got to iron Charge Nurse Fowler's *caps*!' Another job I never ever envied Jean – left to me, Nurse Fowler's caps would have ended up singed . . .

In the draft where she writes about becoming two people, one supporting and challenging the other, the former tells the latter not just to sit there, but to read, not just to read, but to write to someone – a teacher perhaps. As soon as she wrote, Miss Stewart from Aberdeen Central School arrived.

In Mental Hospital, my Teacher came once to see me. A great joy. Both sitting on my bed in my small room.

We recited that poem – sounds like by *Whitman*, but I don't think so – I love Whitman's work.

All men are Pioneers within their hearts.
And in their hearts they are forever cutting clover
They are forever drawing water from a well
They are observing over and over
The grounds they would clear
The forests they would fell
Knowing they will not leave the town at all
As like as not.

Then, in that small room in the Hospital, Matthew Arnold.
I think we went over – without a book – 'Sohrab and
Rustum'

Sohrab the mighty Rustum's son lies there
Whom his great father did in ignorance kill . . .

Do you know, in spite of all the years since knowing that
poem, those lines still prick my eyes with tears.
But that day in Hospital *was* a day of grace.

The other day of grace, which came soon after, was the Friday on
which she was suddenly instructed to have a bath – 'Saturday was
bath night!' When they are alone, the Charge Nurse breaks the
news:

'You're getting out!' They're waiting for you round by the
front. I didn't want you to know until the last minute! You
would have got overexcited. And that would have been that!'
    You couldn't be getting out. No place to go. No one to go
to.
    'You're going to your domicile,' Charge Nurse said. 'To
the Highlands. The place where you were born. To work on
a croft in the hills. It will do more for you than this has done.
Besides,' she insisted, 'I never want to see your face here
again!'

In *Somewhere Beyond*, she is more specific about destination and
duration:

Your Domicile, the parish of your birth, is taking you out . . .
For the next three months you're going to stay with an old
woman in a croft up in the Highlands. If you stick that out
for three months you'll never be back here again.

The sight of her own outside clothes folded on a chair by the bath
is too much for Jessie: in story, radio play and TV adaptation, she

bursts into tears. 'It's my claes, my ain claes. I canna believe it. I thought I'd never get out. I'd naebody to tak' me out.'

So the lost year ends, happily for the patient, but with a few disquieting omens for her future. In her words above, Charge Nurse Fowler shows she is aware the girl is at least very volatile still, and that she is not sure how much the hospital has done for her. The fact that there is no suggestion at any point of aftercare, or any check on her progress suggests that she will have to resume sole charge for her future, with little likelihood of proper care and understanding.

Chapter Five: New Life

Charge Nurse had said to Jessie, 'You're going to your domicile. To the Highlands. The place where you were born.' Some legal whim had decreed that, as Jessie was born in Inverness, she should be boarded out near there. Although she had been born there, she had never lived there and had no personal connections. There was no suggestion of returning her to her mother. Within a few months Liz would be taken into Craigmoray Institution, which had formerly been the Poorhouse, where Jessie had been taken into care before she went into the Orphanage. The new Institution had 24 beds for the chronic sick. Liz was now very sick indeed. She remained there for the rest of her life, dying in 1949, aged 64.

'Boarding out' was not a uniquely Scottish phenomenon, but it was employed much more thoroughly than in England for the upbringing of children in some way rendered homeless. Foster parents were paid to look after the children, and their motivation was sometimes questionable, occasionally simply economic or exploitative. Too little care, Jessie would argue, went into the approval of suitable foster parents. She also believed that far more should be done to help the mothers of such children, before the authorities resorted to removing the children. As John Murphy comments, 'The history of boarding out in Scotland is a fascinating story still insufficiently explored and documented.'[1] Lynn Abrams points back to the 1860s, when many parishes, especially urban ones, adopted boarding out as the primary means of finding homes for orphaned, deserted or separated children dependent on poor relief. Indeed she points to a precedent, the 1857 Lunacy Act, 'a way of reducing numbers in asylums'.[2] By Jessie's time it could be applied also to some non-dangerous mental patients –

'discharged unrecovered'. This was what landed Jessie in the remote village of Abriachan. Only a few years earlier this practice was taken for granted, as witness the matter-of-fact way it occurs in Lewis Grassic Gibbon's *Sunset Song* (1932). It will be remembered Mistress Munro had two 'dafties' boarded out with her from a hospital in Dundee. Andy, the 'daftest', seems just a match for Mistress Munro, until he is overtaken by a sex drive that threatens every female he encounters, and he is early removed by force back to the hospital. Tony, the other, with his secret mastery of shorthand, is clearly not as daft as he pretends. Gibbon seems to take their situation for granted, unsentimentally, and to have no desire to question the system. By the time Jessie reached Abriachan in 1935, it was already less common, and the arrival of 'the Patient' caused a certain excitement.

But the boarding-out of homeless children was unexceptional. 'In 1945 almost 90% of the 7000 or so in local authority care were being cared for in this way'.[3] Twin items of faith favoured crofting society, where children would benefit both from 'a natural, healthy environment' and 'the strict presbyterianism of the Free Church'.[4] Distance from home could be regarded as an advantage: the Secretary of the Local Government Board for Scotland recommended it in 1896, so that 'dissolute relatives do not discover the child and visit it'.[5] As a result of all this:

> At least until 1945 a Scottish child left homeless was far more likely than a similar child in England to be boarded out in a rural environment far away from his or her cultural roots or placed in a remote institution which sought to separate the child permanently from family ties.[6]

This situation was reflected in fiction, as well as in the concerns of those involved in child care. Intent moralist Robin Jenkins dealt very fully with the ethics of boarding out children and of adoption, mainly from the point of view of the would-be foster mother or adoptive mother, in *A Love of Innocence* (1963). Naomi Mitchison, who had herself been a member of the Clyde Committee (1945–46), the post-war investigation into the care of homeless children, had personally visited foster homes as far apart as Islay and Inverness-shire, and was deeply suspicious of possible abuses of the system. She was opposed to the remoteness of some foster homes and the amount children had to work: 'All the children on these crofts were working . . . These remote crofts depend almost entirely on primitive labour and the children will not learn anything which will be useful to them as modern agricultural workers'.[7] Clyde was generally 'sharply critical of the placing of city children in remote areas, especially Highland crofts where "the practice of taking in children is regarded as an industry, and the labour obtained therefrom often enables the guardians to maintain their crofts"'.[8] Mitchison raised issues of quite widespread and hidden exploitation of children in her novel *Lobsters on the Agenda* (1952), where she also highlights the unwillingness of good foster parents to inform on the bad.[9] Clyde made some sensible recommendations, but one weakness was that 'no child witnesses were called' – there was no attempt 'to look at the system from the child's point of view'.[10] This was something Jessie could redress. Personal experience and empathy gave Jessie a unique insight into the boarding-out of children from dysfunctional families, a practice which did not die out until well into the '50s.

Jessie may be said to have had some part in bringing about its disuse, although she wanted primarily to reform the system rather than campaign against it. Her radio play *The Childhood*, first broadcast in 1949 and repeated many times, caused a great public furore, and led to public discussion and a Scottish Home Department investigation, to which she gave evidence. We will come to that in due course, but one reason why her play is so effective is that it is based on her own experience, somewhat transposed. As she later wrote a quite different play also called *The Childhood*, I shall refer to this one as *The Childhood* (1), and to the other as *The Childhood* (2).

The Childhood (1) is printed in *Somewhere Beyond: A Jessie Kesson Companion*. It centres on a boy of ten (the age Jessie was when she was sent to the orphanage), forcibly separated, as Jessie was, from a mother with a serious drinking problem, and brought to an alien country hamlet from the streets of Glasgow, haunted perpetually by fears for the unfortunate mother, now without protection. He fears that his inebriated mother will slip and fall on the ice, for example, as Liz had done, spending weeks in hospital.[11] This central character is Danny, but we are occasionally reminded that his full name is Danny Kernon: even more private acknowledgement of the link with the author is given in a scene where other boys mock him, with repeated cries of 'Kernon is a Jessy!' The play is set in Abriachan, nine miles from Inverness, where Jessie herself was boarded out as a 'dafty' when she was 19. The high valley was undergoing the later stages of depopulation, and most inhabitants were old, with the exception of the boarded-out children. The play also mirrors one of the mercurial Jessie's main responses to Abriachan, as it forcefully presents Danny's initial fear of the high valley and towering rocks, followed by an ecstatic appreciation of nature.

Johnnie Kesson, who was 11 years Jessie's senior, had been boarded out in Abriachan with all his siblings many years before, because his mother in Glasgow had a serious alcohol problem. He had been one of the fortunate ones, who was settled with a kindly and affectionate foster mother. He came to regard Abriachan as his home, and returned there after spells in the army, when he was posted to Germany and Pakistan.

But as Jessie's play would point out, too many of the foster mothers entrusted with already emotionally fragile children were ill chosen and, at the least, deficient in imagination and sympathy. In letters to the BBC's Gordon Gildard, Head of Scottish Programmes, during the public furore created by the play, she railed against poor choice of foster mothers, lack of imagination, and, especially in the case of Glasgow children like Johnnie, the distance from home and the total contrast of environment.

Boarded-out bairns should not be massly congregated in remote, rural areas – because, however grim it sounds, the fact remains that the area takes on an 'in the Trade' aspect. And, on principle, even a good F Mother will not report an indifferent one. My man's FM, sweet and good herself,

sorrowed often over the heartlessness of FMs around her –
but never reported them.

Glasgow, Jessie wrote, was:

> the one city most guilty of sending its children away far – to
> areas like Skye, Islay, Arran, Black Isle, Glen Urquhart. The
> street-child takes a long time to adjust itself emotionally to
> such an extreme change of environment.

Her own experience taught Jessie this, and enabled her acute
insight into such a character as Luigi in *Another Time, Another
Place*.

ABRIACHAN

Jessie's first pondered and polished pieces about Abriachan were
published in *The Scots Magazine* in 1946. They are a passage in the
April section of 'Country Dweller's Year' by 'Ness Macdonald',[12] a
poem, 'Abriachan Summer', and a prose evocation, 'I to the Hills',
all three of which she would later feed into a radio play that meant
a great deal to her, *The Wise Lived Yesterday*. She used the short
poem to structure the play.

In the 'Country Dweller's Year' passage, it is the physical
impact of the place that she renders:

> A high hill-slope nine miles west of Inverness. It is curious –
> up there where one is surrounded by crags, deep gullies and
> all the sterner stuff that goes to make a hill – to find Spring
> so profuse, and green, and gentle.
>
> It would be hard to find one bit of brown earth on that
> hillside in April, for bracken, rightly called 'lovely curse' by
> Highland folk, spreads like a vast, young, strong plantain,
> and all through the bracken, in countless multitudes, cluster
> primroses that are thick and yellow and smelling like spice.
>
> The hill is composed of red rock, and in clear, Spring
> sunlight the rocks glow like fires.

It is so high up that you feel as if any moment you might
topple into Loch Ness below. They say the loch is bottom-
less and treacherous, yet, on calm days, it is, as Coleridge
writes 'a painted ocean'.

Spring in the hills would confront the greatest artist with
too vast a panorama. I doubt if he could ever capture it. For
Spring there is more than colour; it is music and scent. The
burns literally hum down the hillside, the trees have rhythm
in their shaking. The smell of Spring in the hills is a
blending of peaty thickness, bracken-mould, flowers' spicy-
ness, and clean, quick purge of the wind. Down in the
hollows anemones, bereft of smell, gleam in pale patches.[13]

The poem centres on the apparently ageless wisdom of these old
people whom time forgot.

Abriachan Summer

Summer drifts there slow
But it has its dwelling long.
It filters through the women's gossip,
Sheds its glow over the men's philosophies,
And time is not ticked off in seconds.
A summer day is all too brief
To hold Ian Dubh's reminiscences.
Nothing is lost to those among the hills;
They've seen the gullies brown in spate
These sixty springs;
But still they pause to contemplate
Common-place things;
Calum Mor's ewe silhouetted on the crag,
The white wake of 'St Ula' on the Ness,
The flails, dust grey in Domhnull's barn
Whose usefulness they resurrect
With tales of harvests long since threshed.
They never say 'The day is fine',
But tell you why;
And that the wind will change tomorrow,

And how, in four days' time, a storm will come.
They are a race lost and involved
In all the years.

*   *   *   *   *

Yesterday we savoured to the full;
And, while we scythe the hay today,
We'll talk of vivid summers
Sixty years away.[14]

'I To The Hills' combines the different elements of the place and
some aspects of Jessie's personal experience with extraordinary
economy. I want to quote a fair deal of it, therefore. Here the
Jessie figure is called Chris, and Abriachan is thinly disguised as
Brialach:

> It was the February after what Chris always referred to as *the
> lost year*. A year, spent between the four walls of a hospital
> sick-ward, *is* a lost year.
>
> In that February people had said to Chris, in the vague,
> kindly way people who see illness without having to undergo
> it themselves, can say: 'But a few months up above the hills
> of Brialach will do you good. It's nice up there.'
>
> *It's nice up there.* How inadequately people explained
> themselves! Or perhaps, thought Chris, Brialach had
> seemed only *nice* to them, because they hadn't lost a year
> of their lives.
>
> No adjective could ever qualify Brialach in that spring. To
> Chris, whose senses were acute to receive after her impri-
> sonment, Brialach was so high up that it seemed the
> scattered townships would topple any moment far down
> into the depths of Loch Ness waiting shimmeringly below.
> . . . The folk of Brialach had no place in the twentieth
> century.
>
> No place – beside Loch Lache stood the grey building
> where the Gaelic Sunday evening services were held. 'Life,'
> thought the few young people who lived there, 'must be
> more than just singing the lines of psalms after Alasdair Di,'

and so, each Friday night they danced where their forebears had worshipped.

'Had worshipped.' No longer did Kenny MacDonald, Jock an Mor, Maggie Achabuie, or any of the older Frasers and MacDonalds, who composed the population of Brialach, climb to the grey building. They still climbed the hills, but passed the building with the same fixed, unseeing look with which one passes by a friendship that once was, but now is broken beyond repair. To Caipla Moor beside Loch Lache they made their way. There, outside in the spring dusk they clustered, a small but dominant group. There Alasdair Di sang the first lines of the psalms, and the voices of the other worshippers rose at the second line . . .

But the building on the hill was for the Gaelic services. Five miles southwards by the shores of Loch Ness stood the real kirk. Five miles in any other airt would have been a journey. Chris never found it such in Brialach in spring. To walk again in a world without pain, without limits of walls; to talk with those of her own age, and to laugh with them; laugh that is – only if Uncle Kenny and Maggie Achabuie were far enough behind not to hear the laughter; for in Brialach humour was a commodity for weekdays only. And to plunge downwards through rough, hairy brackens, their roughness scarring her legs, and whiles to stumble into gullies, for bracken on the hillside laid traps for the unwary.

Syne lochwards for three miles, regretting that the Sabbath day demanded walking on the highroad instead of scushing through the soft, white sand by the lochside.

But losing all regret when inside the small, sunny kirk with Alasdair Di singing in a tongue Chris knew:

When Zion's bondage God turned back
As men that dreamed were we.

Then Chris was so joyous to be in a serene world again, that she thought Alasdair Di sang that psalm just to herself, since her happiness was like that in a dream . . .

The kirk and their crofts, these were the symbols of life to the hill-dwellers . . . The hillside was the barrier that shut

Brialach away from the momentousness and triviality of the
outside world. A visit to Inverness, nine short miles away,
took on the aspect of a great journey.

Time had no meaning on the hillside. Ten o'clock in the
morning saw the first wisps of smoke curling upwards from
the chimneys . . . Time had no hours; it had only seasons.
How serene and wise were these hill folk! Chris thought
they were like miniature kings, each with his croft as his
miniature kingdom . . .

The week was broken by the advent of the grocer's van.
Brialach's height defied the entry of motor transport into its
domain. Once a week the young folk descended the hill to
meet the van that was their grocer, butcher, draper combined.

The descent was slow, for the eggs, to be handed over to
the grocer in exchange for the week's messages, were precious. But once safely arrived at the foot of the hill,
responsibility ended. Allan, the grocer, was seldom up to
time, and removed from the heavy wisdom of their elders,
the young folk found that great clusters of birches, thick
growth of bracken, and spring dusk made exploration in
pairs a sweet thing . . .

[Sundays] You were permitted to go out on to the hillside
on condition that you went there to read 'The Book'.

Chris never forgot to carry 'the pretext' with her, but it lay
unopened beside her. For, high up in the shadow of the Red
Rock, she would lie, knowing that never in a lifetime could
she absorb the changing moods and varying beauty of the
vista unfolded below her.

She knew, too, that if she were taken blindfolded some
spring fifty years hence to this spot, she would 'smell' that it
was Brialach; for the peat loam, the spiciness of primroses,
the 'foggy' stink of bracken, the dusty smell of rock, was a
combination that could only belong to Brialach.[15]

This was a strange place to spend the run-up to the Second World
War: a radio talk indicates some of the ironies.

Thine are we, Christ. And on thy side, Thou son of God.
Against that man Mussolini, as far as we could make out . . .
But, I must admit, even more important to us personally was
the new Road and Bridge construction beginning in the Isle
of Skye. Work for years to come, and good money.

Jessie wrote still more about Abriachan, whether or not for the
projected autobiography it is not clear. It did not reach type, but is
scrawled in ballpoint, unusually not always readable, very much a
'first draft', and the only clue to its date is that she wrote it after
1961. This is clear, because she wrote it on one of her more bizarre
batches of writing paper – the insides of a pile of coloured dust
jackets she mysteriously acquired for one book, *Tiger Tennis in
One Season*, by Dr H. A. Murray, which was published by Elliott
Right Way Books in 1961. This time she writes in the first
person, and openly about Abriachan, and about Johnnie. Each of
these versions seems to construct one truth, one angle, and build
to a cohesive account of this phase of her life.

She describes the situation of the croft of Achbuie, which
means 'the yellow field where the broom is plentiful'. It is on 'the
highest bit of cultivated land in Scotland', and the difficulty of
finding the road if you don't know it is considerable.

Its occupants turned out to be as arresting as the hill itself.
Old crofters who spoke 'the English' only when necessary.
And even then in Gaelic, when they could find no word for
'the English'. Thin, shrill-voiced city children 'fostered out'
by local Councils. And here and there a simple old man and
woman, also 'fostered out'. They were described as 'Patients'- 'daft, but harmless enough'. And now I had come to
join the remote community. I was 'the *new* Patient', arousing
more curiosity than the others had done, because I was the
youngest 'Patient' they'd hitherto contained.

I was to be Christac's 'Patient'. She was the oldest woman
I had ever set eyes on, bent almost in two, with a 'withered
arm' that curved up and round, cleaving to her breast, as if to
protect it from some always imminent frontal assault.

She needed 'help', and I was pleased enough to be able to give it to her. Once, that is, I got used to my newly regained freedom. It took me a day or two to get over the fact that a door would open when I simply turned the knob. I was forever running in and out in reaffirmation of my freedom.

'M'eudail, M'eudail' – 'My dear, my dear' – the old woman would protest, bedizzied and bewildered by the tornado that whirled into her life, 'is there no settle in you?'

Jessie was aware of her own excitement, her need to be making up for lost time. Clearly, there was going to be little communication between herself and old Christac:

I didn't exactly count the days till my 'six months' trial' was up. Specific haste had lost much of its pressure. But I was aware that they were passing. 'East to the well' I went for water. 'West to the barn' I carried the straw for the byre . . . *Facts* I *could* gather. She had never in all her long life been beyond Inverness. But I didn't know if she ever had *wanted* to go beyond Inverness. She had never married. But I didn't know if she had ever had the chance . . .

The big bible, 'the Book' as she always called it, was the only thing she read, the only book she had in the house. On cold days, in her rocking chair in the stone-flagged kitchen, more than ever poring over 'the Book' on her knees, we could almost touch each other, for I knew the Bible . . . I loved the words of it and remembered them.

There were no fine-sounding words in my Catalogue. None that were worth remembering. But it gave me far more pleasure than the Bible. I'd sit choosing the dresses I would have, if I had money. Putting my different 'outfits' together, 'accessories' and all. The old woman never seemed to be aware that the girl who sat in her kitchen was beautifully attired in 'A Must for Spring' . . .

With considerable frankness, Jessie relates her early sexual brush with Niall the Trapper, in which she was only saved by the curiosity of the younger girls who followed her everywhere, respecting her supposed 'experience'.

He was a young man, not a 'lad', and a goodlooking one, beginning to tease the younger ones, with the familiarity of an older brother, tugging their hair, lunging to capture them. But it was *me* he held on to, when he caught me, struggling together, laughing at his attempts to set me off my feet, pinned beneath him. The laughter easing, taking on a different quality, an urgency. 'Could I not get rid of these damned bairns?' he urged, his face rough and hard against my own.

I would have done anything in the world to have 'got rid of the damned bairns'. I knew it was impossible. Most of all *now*, for they were aware the 'play' had ended. Rooted in the heather, they stood watching silently, as rooted as the boulders behind them that neither time nor man had been able to move. Urgency still within me, I raced down the hill, the younger girls after me, shouting in triumph:

Jessie loves Niall the Trapper

Jessie loves . . .

She did? She didn't? She didn't *know*! She never set eyes on Niall the Trapper again. But she now had someone who crept into her dreams.

COURTSHIP AND MARRIAGE

Jessie admitted in several interviews in later years that she had often found it hard being married to Johnnie Kesson, because there were so many areas of her life he could not share. He was no intellectual. She wrote him little poems when they were courting, which he could not appreciate. He was proud of her work, immensely so, but never really understood it. He was slight, and short, never strong, and latterly plagued with ill health and deafness, through which she nursed him with devotion and exhaustion combined. A mismatch, then? On one level, certainly, but I do not think so, in the last resort. The marriage, which Jessie once said she had given a few months, lasted 58 years, and was based on a trust, affection and comradeship that he uniquely gave her. He was as solid as a rock, and his being older provided her with something of a father's protection – at last!

Inevitably, perhaps, the union lacked something in romance and excitement. In a drama review in 1952 for *Woman's Hour* Jessie revealed this in passing:

> Though most women want their husband to be a good man, it must be exhilarating to even once have been loved by a reckless man! – so think it after sixteen years of happy but unexciting plodding along.

Their inability to communicate in some areas may well have been inadvertently an extra spur to her writing. She had to write, with the 20th-century woman's need to construct her own female story. She had to write, too, because she was necessarily her own psychotherapist: she had to explore and try to hold together different aspects and phases of her extraordinary life, to construct a fairly reliable sense of self. If she could have told Johnnie all this, she might not have had such a great need to write and rewrite her life. And although the story of Niall the Trapper above shows that Jessie was more than ready for sexual experience, Johnnie respected her, and courted her, and they genuinely fell in love, perhaps transiently on her side. Like Janie at the end of *The White Bird Passes*, after her year in hospital, Jessie was surely 'ready for the knife': she could have done a lot worse than Johnnie. She wrote to Peter Calvocoressi in 1957:

> Janie at eighteen[!] married for two reasons, 'safety' and kindliness, and in doing so entered a No Man's Land, the only place she ever really fitted into. Because it was vast and free of accident. And not sad in the true sense, except for loneliness sometimes.

She offered her fullest account of their courtship in her much-corrected scrawl:

He was going to a dance that Saturday night, and had come down the Hill to the van for razor blades. He quarried the red sand rock, on the other side of the Hill, so that I had never set eyes on him, not till a voice behind me asked if I 'would like a sweetie?'

Forgotten things, sweeties. I couldn't remember when I had tasted one. The old crofters with whom we lived knew to a farthing how much of the flour, sugar and tea we carried up in our pillowcases could be purchased by the eggs and butter we carried down to the van. Money was an invisible commodity, another of the 'forgotten things'.

That was how I first met Johnnie. The first man or boy, apart from the brief encounter with Niall, who looked at me, and spoke to me as if I was an ordinary young girl, and not just 'old Christac's Patient'.

We met often after that on Saturday nights at the grocer's van. We walked together – followed always by the children – the five mile walk along the lochside to the kirk. The ten miles walk was never long enough for all we had to say to each other . . . The old Precentor would 'twang' his precenting fork against his ear to find the true note for himself. And, having found it, would start off himself, our voices following behind him to catch up.

> I joyed when to the House of God
> Go up they said to me
> Jerusalem, within thy gates . . .

He always got to 'Jerusalem' before us, and having arrived safely within its gates lost his urge for speed, allowing us to observe *with* him that

> Jerusalem as a city is
> Compactly built together
> And to that place the tribes go up
> The tribes of God go thither.

And Johnnie had a fine tenor voice, very sweet and true. We didn't sing to God in the kirk, we sang to each other.

It was when we started meeting by the Red Rock on Sunday afternoons that the old woman took to murmuring to herself in Gaelic that sounded disapproving. But walks were allowed on the Sabbath, provided I took 'the Book' with me, and could tell her on my return what I had read from it. O, Orphanage Sundays! How much I owe you!

'The Book' served me simply as a pillow as we lay side by side, sheltered from the sun, in the cool shadow of the red rock. No precious time was ever wasted on verses that were heart-known. No fault to be found by the old woman on my return to the house in my recollection of Isaiah:

The wilderness and the solitary place shall be glad for them; and the desert shall rejoice, and blossom as the rose. It shall blossom abundantly.[16]

But the old woman brought nastiness into the desert-turned-garden:

I couldn't understand why the old woman had begun to mark days on the Calendar that the van man gave her at Christmas. Special days? And why special? Nor did she seem willing to enlighten me.

It was one of my thirteen-year-old 'followers' who gave me the answer: 'She's marking off the dates of your periods. To make sure they come.' Distaste for the old woman began only from that instant. Irrational, I know, she was probably doing no more than one of her duties as my Guardian. But it was the *idea* that repelled me. She was too old and withered to be involved in such a private thing. Something I felt sure had been outside her own experience. I never afterward found her eyes rest on me, without wondering if *she* was . . . wondering.

But, according to Jessie, there was no need to wonder. She always said, and in a draft actually wrote, that she had no real sexual experience before marriage, and for a clear and specific reason – fear. With her background and experience, this is particularly understandable. Here is how she imagined answering another woman who was 'wondering', her landlady, on her wedding day:

> 'That's what it was, fear of pregnancy. Having neither kith
> nor kin, I would have ended up in the Workhouse. That's
> where parentless girls end up to give birth to their bastard
> bairns. I just didn't fancy the Workhouse.'

I could have added to that – but could never find the right
words in which to explain my *other* reason for my celibacy,
stronger, perhaps, than the Workhouse: 'All through my
childhood, spent between Kirk and Orphanage, I was conditioned to look on Sex as Shameful, Sinful. When I was
free of both Kirk and Orphanage, the conditioning stayed
with me.'

So, in spite of experiencing desire, as she vividly described in the
encounter with Niall the Trapper, and often in her novels, she
typically longed in anticipation for what she seemed to imply
turned out to be less wonderful than she had believed. When she
was writing her radio play *The Wise Lived Yesterday*, about that
strangely special time in Abriachan, after the traumatic year in
Mental Hospital, she wrote at length about it to Archie P. Lee,
who was to direct it, enclosing a further passage of the young girl's
reverie:

> O, Archiest, I used to stand on that hill, at seventeen, just
> profoundly in love with love. I loved it hot, I loved it cold, I
> loved it forever and forever – and there was little to it when I
> was confronted with it – or maybe it was my dream of it that
> was so much bigger than reality. I have portrayed a little of
> that in the reverie, but only a little.

She told him a story, too, in the same letter, which she presents as
'truth', but for which I can find no other evidence:

> Enclosed is the hill-side scene. I didn't make it too place-
> descriptive; that would have been padding. I confined it to
> her thoughts. They are indeed authentic.

Truth being ever stranger than fiction, our original, hill-side girl became so overwhelmed by the oldness, vastness, far-offness of that hill, that she ran away from it one very rainy day. She ran just as she was when the mood to run took her, barefooted, hatless, coatless, and with her aunt's old apron on! She was half way to Inverness when she met a fellow who must have had pity on her rain-sodden appearance. He offered to pay her bus-fare. Our girl refused, partly out of stubbornness – but mostly because she wanted 'to walk' that vast hill and its old, out-of-the-world people out of her system. She got a job – and didn't return to Brialach till her honeymoon, a year later. She married the fellow who offered her her fare on that rainy day. His name was Kesson. The honeymoon there was very lovely – only wasn't it ironic that I had to go back to 'Brialach', to the hill, to discover all the things that in my hot-blooded, restless teens I thought I was missing because of the far-offness of the hill? Yes, my old aunt was wise. I was young enough to pity her for being 'out of things'; the truth was she'd savoured them all, and knew how little they were worth.

This story doesn't specify when she ran away, but all her writing about Abriachan is about spring and summer. If the 'six months' trial' was important, or she thought it was, she may have run away in September, when it was finished. She began working in Woolworth's in Inverness. She and Johnnie married on 9th April 1937, but if Jessie only went back to Abriachan once, for a honeymoon, and if Avril was conceived, as Jessie claimed, at the Red Rock, then it must have been a delayed honeymoon, perhaps in July. This odd little story is the fullest she ever told anyone about leaving Abriachan and getting married to Johnnie. Apart from that, she often told how when she was in Inverness to get married the pair went to the address in Edinburgh Road, to the 'big house' Matron had told her she was born in, and discovered it was the Workhouse. Although she kept quiet about this for many years, she told us that when she found it out, it no longer bothered her.[17] They were each in digs in Inverness at the

time of the wedding, Johnnie with people he had known in
Abriachan, who acted as witnesses. On the marriage certificate
Johnnie is described as a 'general labourer' and Jessie as a 'shop
assistant'. She was working in Woolworth's, and she too was in
digs with a woman she had got to know in Abriachan, who was
not encouraging: in an unfinished, hastily scrawled piece called
'Sweeter Than All The Roses', Jessie wrote:

> My landlady hovered in the doorway of my bedroom, the
> bearing of a cup of tea in her hands. It was the first time she
> had given me a cup of tea in bed. It was the first time I'd *ever*
> had a cup of tea in bed. Yet the gesture seemed appropriate
> on my wedding morning.
>   'You can.' she suggested, as she drew the curtains aside to
> let in the grey light of a grey March morning, 'change your
> mind. You've still got time to change your mind.'
>   Her suggestion horrified me. I'd always known that she
> didn't care much for my husband to be: that didn't influence
> me. He hadn't asked *her* to marry him.

Another draft concerning the same occasion suggests reasons for
the landlady's anxiety, which are not necessarily a slight on
Johnnie:

> 'It's beyond me' – my landlady, reflecting to herself, turned
> aside from the window. And beyond me, I realised, as we
> looked at each other across a chasm of silence . . .
>   She could have been fifty. But she was younger, I ken that,
> with two small sons, the elder was nine . . . Widow?
> Divorcee? Forsaken Common-Law wife? I never knew.
> Any would have accounted for her resentment against my
> wedding. The tight down-drawn lines of her mouth, her
> 'working' black skirt, black cardigan, black stockings. Her
> swollen ankles over-lapping her shoes. Clad ready to set out
> for her various morning charring jobs. My small enough
> contribution and her charring jobs the sole income which
> kept her roof over *both* our heads; surely a common denom-

inating factor which *ought* to have led to shared
confidence . . .

I couldn't find *one* tongue with which to set my landlady's
mind at ease; to explain what to her seemed a foredoomed
misalliance.

And the landlady was not the only one lukewarm about the
match. Jessie told her family that the minister also warned her
about Johnnie, intimating too great an interest in alcohol, and
suggesting a whiff somewhere of shoplifting.

There was no money for a big wedding – and there were no
guests, no relations. Jessie told Dr Donaldson on the telephone
that they found a wonderful freedom in the lack of family, and
responsibility: 'no ties, no loyalties – free of the suffocating
expectations of close others – nobody really to get embarrassed'.

But perhaps it was also a little lonely, a little sparse. 'No white
wedding dress. No Church wedding. Just a quiet ceremony by the
Minister, in his own Manse. Furtive and hurried it must have all
seemed to my landlady'.

An outfit from a clothing club, who sent an unbecoming bright
red hat with the blue outfit, because the blue one was sold out.
One wedding present only, a tea-set from the girls at work in
Woolworth's. The Minister was the Reverend James Morton of
St Mark's West Church, Inverness, and the Manse at 49 Fairfield
Road. And family legend as well as the account to Archie P. Lee
records the honeymoon near Abriachan, at Loch Lache, and goes
on that it was spent in a tent by the loch, and that the tent was
stolen! After that, a minor detail, that she bartered her wedding
ring some time in the '30s, for a loaf of bread. She told her
interviewer they could have replaced it many times, but reckoned
it just didn't matter. And that's all.

But a long time later she gave someone else a splendid
account of the original post-wedding honeymoon, and chose a
fine writer who keeps a journal. This is Alastair Scott, travel
writer and photographer, who accompanied Jessie and Joy
Hendry on their stressful journey in search of the haunts of
Jessie's early life, and who took the photographs for the article

Above left: A Badentinnon
family group – left to right:
Archie, Peg, Minnie,
Grandmother, John, *c*1918
(courtesy of Mina Skea)

Above: Liz McDonald's
sisters, Jane, Minnie and
Jessie at Badentinnon, with
Jessie's half-sister,
Peg *c*1918 (courtesy of
Mina Skea)

Left: Grandmother with the
unforgiving Grandfather at
Badentinnon, *c*1918
(courtesy of Mina Skea)

Elgin's Ladyhill Lane (demolished 1974), with John Foster's home, Ladyhill House, in the background, *c*1909 (courtesy of Alistair Campbell and Moray Libraries and Information Services)

A school photo from Skene Central, *c*1928. Jessie is in the centre of the photograph (preserved in Jessie's papers)

Jessie revisits Archbuie croft, Abriachan (courtesy of Alistair Scott)

Jessie revisits Proctors Orphan Training Home (courtesy of Alistair Scott)

Jessie at the cottar house in Udale, where *Another Time, Another Place* was filmed (courtesy of Alistair Scott)

Jessie with her producer, Elizabeth Adair, at the BBC in Aberdeen in 1950 (courtesy of Elizabeth Adair)

Above: Peter
Calvocoressi,
publisher and friend,
in the 1950s (courtesy
Peter Calvocoressi)

Right: Michael
Radford, film director
and friend, 1985
(courtesy of Camera
Press Ltd)

Left: Country people in London: the Kessons at home in 1983
(courtesy of Roger Perry/*The Sunday Times*)

Above: Dr Jessie Kesson in her 'Scarlet Goon', University of Aberdeen,
1987 (courtesy of John Macintosh/University of Aberdeen)

Portrait of Jessie Kesson, Edinburgh Book Festival, 1985
(courtesy of Gunnie Moberg)

which appeared in *The Scots Magazine* in October 1989. He
wrote an account in his journal of the impact she made on him,
which I don't think has been bettered, and which reminds me
of the impact she made on me when I first met her at the
Edinburgh Book Festival in 1985:

> Jessie Kesson has so much fun in her she is a one-woman
> riot. I've met only two or three people who regularly laugh
> so much tears stream down their cheeks, but none who do
> so as regularly nor as copiously as Jessie Kesson. But then
> she leans over and puts her hand on my arm, and quotes,
> 'But I laugh that I weep not'. Her memory is awesome. She
> talks endlessly, never-never stops, a hoarse, rough voice, a
> groan above a whisper but excited as if she fears time may
> not allow her to finish. She is nervous and covers it with
> verbosity and enthusiasm – verbose she may be but she is a
> spell binder. Out tumbles history, stories, experiences. She
> always fits a joke in and laughs herself speechless fre-
> quently, nudging up her glasses with the act of dabbing
> a Kleenex at her eyes . . .
> . . . She takes small steps, always loses her way, heads off
> in an instant for the wrong door, chain-smokes all day,
> dribbles ash all over herself and clothes – and just makes you
> want to take care of her. Her company seems so precious.

Scott's account of her describing her honeymoon in bawdy vein:

> Said she believed sex could hold together a bad marriage for
> two years, but not after that. 'Ah mind my first week o'
> marriage, me and Johnnie were nay oot a bed for a week –
> except, that is, for a pee. It would hae been better hid we had
> ane o' they chanties un'er the bed. Oh aye, a week it wis – we
> hid half a pun o' balony an' a packet of ginger snaps. Mind,
> we hid oor teeth then. Nane o' this dookin' 'em in the tea.'
> (She told this story in the breakfast room.)

YOUNG MOTHERHOOD

After the wedding, the pair enjoyed a brief period of anonymity. They went to live in Aberdeen, at more than one address, and had their first child, Avril. Then Johnnie, who had become unemployed, got a job on Skye, and left Jessie and Avril with her half-sister Peg and Archie when he set off. But Jessie was unhappy there, and soon joined him on Skye. She left very little account of these years, but if even half of this quasi-autobiographical 'fiction' is true, life was not too quiet. There is just one published story about the time in Aberdeen, a story of innocents abroad, in which she pokes quiet fun at the young couple in the aptly named 'Green Memory'.[18] Again Jessie (now Cassie) is 18, and now five months pregnant, and she and Chae are desperate to find a room. Cassie ingratiates herself with her prospective landlady in the Spital, near the Hostel where she'd stayed as a teenager: 'No, we hinna ony bairns yet, only I'm five months on the wye. But I'm sure it wull be a quaet bairn because Chae and me are baith quaet.' They get the room, but before long are visited by 'two gentlemen', who demand to see their marriage lines, and are told: 'You're the only legally-married couple in this house. The sooner you get somewhere respectable to stay, the better.'

They find an attic on Cairncry Road, ironically close to Cornhill where Jessie had spent that lost year. 'Messrs Wimpey had laid their last cable and Chae's wage envelope had been replaced by twenty-five shillings from the dole.' They stretch this for two 'luxuries': each week Cassie buys 'one napkin and one ounce of wool' for the baby's pramsuit, and Chae very seriously invests sixpence on the Football Pools. Their much-anticipated first Christmas, with Cassie 'feeling some of the feelings Mary must have felt on that very first Christmas', is an anticlimax: the rabbit, as much as they can afford, is rotten, and they have to return to 'the commonplace contents of the tattie-pot'. In March, as her pains begin, the two walk to the Maternity Hospital, two miles away, where Chae leaves her with a problem:

The Sister, withered and old, her voice parchment like her appearance, asked Cassie's address. The silent seconds lengthened into centuries of contemplation, for Cassie had never before needed an address. The world contained millions of shadows called people, but only two of the shadows had being – Chae and herself. No one needed their address. There was only Chae and he knew where to find the attic on the Cairncry Road.

'Fan Chae comes the nicht,' Cassie explained to the waiting Sister, 'I'll tell him to get oor richt address fae the landlady. We bide in an attic in Cairncry Road'.

So the two innocents became three. Habitually, and possibly sensibly, Jessie avoided writing about her pregnancies, the births and the children, but once, in 1960, she gave a talk on *Woman's Hour* about having her first baby, and moved many listeners to write to her about the secret need to count the baby's toes.

I carried my first child through what seems to me now to have been nine months of inviolable innocence, and wonder. There was a feeling of wonder within me all the time. And a kind of self-sufficient power within me too! I had never knitted anything before. Nor have I knitted since! Yet I managed to knit *all* my *first* child's clothes. Knitting patterns simply seemed to unfold their intricacies to me at that time. Though they have remained closed mysteries since! I remember *feeling* for Christmas for the first time. We lived, then, in a tiny furnished attic with a sloping roof and a skylight window. Any star and every star that hovered within that window's compass brought to my mind an old childhood verse, which time should have erased:

> The Christ Child sat on Mary's knee.
> His hair was like a crown.
> And all the flowers looked up at them.
> And all the stars looked down.

. . . I was so strong and well. And beds were so badly needed, that the Doctor decided to send me home three days after my baby was born. In those days, mothers were kept in the Hospital for ten days. The first thing I did on getting home was to undress my baby, so that I could see her *whole* and *complete*. I couldn't get her clothes on properly again. And I must have been weaker than I realised. I suddenly felt terrified of the small naked creature who *belonged* to *me*! Terrified that I would hurt or break her. Terrified because I didn't know how to put her clothes on! She started to cry. I found myself crying too. When my Landlady came in to see what it was all about, all I could say to her was, 'My baby has got *all* its toes!'

Her experience touched a chord with a large number of listeners. Avril Walker Kesson was born in the Maternity Hospital, Aberdeen, on 18th March 1938. Her parents' usual address is given as Quarry Lodge, Cairncry Road, Aberdeen.

Johnnie was never going to be overemployed. So when he got the chance of going to Skye to work on the roads for William Tawse of Aberdeen, the new father decided to go. He felt he must go: we are now talking of 1938, when jobs were hard to come by. Leslie Robertson of Old Meldrum worked there with Johnnie until mid-summer 1939. When Jessie followed in hot pursuit, there was nowhere to stay – the story is the three spent the first night on Skye under a bridge. But then there was a house at Black Park, Broadford. One of Jessie's very first radio pieces was about Skye. Jessie herself performed *Over the Sea to Skye: an Aberdonian remembers an Island*, somewhere between a story and a monologue.[19] Given the variety of ways Jessie felt at different times about each phase of her life, the characteristic mood swings illustrated in her writing, it is important not to overestimate her attitudes in this one piece, but the programme makes Skye sound like an island-Abriachan; calm, traditional, Gaelic-speaking, slow. (But the fact remains that when she went to Skye she neither smoked nor drank, and when she returned to the mainland

she was an avid smoker, and had developed a taste for whisky.)
A radio talk from 1954 fills it out somewhat:

> I think of those years as years of contrast; a woman cleaning
> her small byre with her bare hands; gleaming, modern brakes
> flashing past her. An excavator looming giant-like on the
> road, and beyond it, far out at sea, Murochie the Postman,
> rowing the mail over to the Isle of Pabay.

By this time the reader will not be surprised to learn that Jessie
'wasn't quite eighteen' when she went there. She was excited in
anticipation, and rejoiced in the reality. The older Jessie smiled
indulgently at what she claimed was the first poem she ever wrote:

> Way to the west, 'mid seas and crooning islands
> Lies Tir Nan Og – Land of the Ever Young.
> There, when the gloaming steals across the Highlands,
> The sweetest songs that earth hath heard are sung.

She described approaching Kyleakin on a lovely June day, with a
lone piper playing. The people she describes are timeless, one
obsessed by living in the house her great grandfather had built,
another having gratefully returned to a bare, hard-working existence on 'the sullen soil of the Black Moor' from 'the wealth of
his fertile Australian orange-groves'. But Armageddon was approaching. 'Wars mean destruction not construction': no one
would be building roads on Skye for a while. It was time to
return to the mainland. She said Johnnie was 'restive to join up
with his old regiment'. As for herself, she was

> feeling personally and selfishly angry about having to leave
> my house. I knew that never again while I lived would I get a
> tall house on a moor, furnished down to a teaspoon, for five
> shillings a week.

Leslie Robertson said she wanted to make for Inverness, but there
was not much work to be had there. 'She found her mother about

Elgin,' he said. Jessie also told Colette Douglas-Home that one of
the first visits she and Johnnie paid as man and wife was to Liz,
now very ill in Craigmoray:

> We went to see her. She couldnae walk and was crawling
> along on all fours. She had a growth and was too old to
> operate on. Her speech was affected, and her walking and
> her sight, but she was perfectly conscious.

Douglas-Home continues:

> Johnnie got a job as an unskilled cowman. 'The only bit of
> the job description he was qualified for was the unskilled
> bit,' she wheezed with laughter at the memory. They moved
> into their farm cottage with Jessie chiding the lorry driver to
> go slowly so that darkness would disguise the fact that their
> furniture consisted of a bed, a table and two chairs.[20]

So a new chapter begins, and Jessie becomes a cottar wife.

Chapter Six: Cottar Wife and Writer

Johnnie and Jessie were fortunate in their first fee – the 'unskilled cowman' began to work for Maitland Mackie at Westertown Farm, Rothienorman, Aberdeenshire, in 1939. The Mackies were interested and approachable, and Mrs Isobel Mackie, in particular, encouraged Jessie's writing ambitions, as other employers would do later. His running of the farm is respectfully mirrored in *Glitter of Mica*, where the farmer, Darklands, is based on Maitland Mackie. Although the mood of that novel is sombre, and conditions for farm workers generally are exposed and criticised, and the selection of such North East name as Darklands and Cauldwell underlines this, the farmer plays a minor role with dignity and humanity: there is no hint of personal criticism.

Jessie had a gift for friendship which is attested to everywhere, and Mackie is a good example. He was four years her senior, and the son of a successful farmer. His father eventually succeeded in his ambition of giving each of his six children their own farm. The background was solid, and the family strong: nothing could be further from Jessie's life experience. But young Maitland was not spoiled, and he worked his way through the system: he entitled his autobiography *A Lucky Chap: Orra Loon to Lord Lieutenant* (1992). He was a Liberal, and stood for Westminster in 1951 and 1958, but his main contributions to public life were local: he was Chairman of Education for Aberdeen County Council, and Convener of the Council, and in due course he became Lord Lieutenant of the County and much more. He invited Jessie to visit in 1957, impressed with the work she was doing with teenagers at Cowley, and wanted her to talk to local youth leaders. When she sent him a copy of *The White Bird Passes* on its publication in 1958, he was delighted as well as impressed. He was very proud of his literary former cottar wife, and turned up at Aberdeen University in 1987 to give a big hug to the new Doctor of Letters. And when Jessie revisited her early haunts with Joy Hendry and Alastair Scott for *The Scots Magazine* in 1989, she was thrilled that he travelled 40 miles specially to be photographed with her at her first cottar home.

Jessie's friendships were catholic. When we met in 1985, she was full of stories about some very old friends, former cottar neighbours, who had been down staying with her in London recently – and that night she was bound for the estate of Smeaton in East Lothian, to spend the night and 'have a news' with George and Anne Gray. This was her custom most times she came to Scotland, for readings, talks or filming. She first met the Grays through Maitland Mackie, and had a long friendship with them, including the period after Johnnie's retiral in the early '70s when the Kessons rented a beautiful cottage on the estate.

But as the cottaring life wore on, we hear less and less of farmers like Maitland Mackie, or of farmers at all. More and more, as they moved on, sometimes as often as every year, the humiliation of the system provoked Jessie to anger. Farm workers had very few rights, and she encountered all too much snobbery, as well as hard, hard work. Cottar wives were also especially underpaid. David Kerr Cameron estimates: 'A cottar wife at a North-East dairy toun in the 1930s, milking morning and night in the dairy byre, seven days a week, might be adding as little as 5s 3d (26p) a week to her ploughman husband's wage.' And John R. Allan wrote in *Farmer's Boy*: 'If I were a woman, only the direst necessity would make me take service at a farm'.[1]

Jessie explained the job situation to contemporary young people on student television after her Aberdeen graduation. She could still detail all the 'perks' of the job – no rent to pay, two gallons of milk a day free, about ten sacks of potatoes, bags of meal. But the perks could not begin to cancel out the insecurity, or the way the workers were treated. She prided herself, rightly, that she had made an important record in *Glitter of Mica*:

the nearly uncivilised way we lived in those days. I mean, you never got the sack. If you weren't asked to bide on by late March or the beginning of April, you jist went doon the road. The farmer either asked you to bide on or he didna say a word! I mean it was absolutely amazing. The term days were the only days you had off – because you see the cows had to be milked Saturday, Sunday, Monday, Tuesday, we'd no days off or nothing. Our first fee, Johnnie's and mine, we worked at this farm, Westertown of Rothienorman, was £72 a year. And I worked in the byres as well, and that was the first fee. And the apprehension, as we come along the cottars' row when the late Spring wis comin' in – his the fairmer seekit ye? Oh dear. I mean this was absolutely primitive! It's worth recording; these are the kind of things that are forgotten, you know.[2]

Again David Kerr Cameron fills out the picture, in a chapter of *The Ballad and the Plough* which he entitles 'Nomads in Farm Carts':

The cottar folk of the farmtouns travelled light. Each year, usually at the Whitsunday Term but sometimes the Martinmas one as well, they threw their pitifully few possessions into a farm cart and took the road to a new toun, like pilgrims to a promised land. Few, in fact, travelled hopefully, for the years had taught them better, but in time the May 'flitting' became an addiction, a rooted custom of a rootless society. It may even have been a kind of protest against the tied-cottage tyranny of that time that made a married farm servant – a skilled grieve, ploughman, bailie or orra man – give his wife and children as hostages to fortune . . . Charitable though it may seem, it was an iniquitous system that blemished the name of many a good farmtoun and gave the unscrupulous farmer an unbeatable advantage . . . His special commitments made the cottar's lot the least enviable . . . It was not lack of intelligence that snared him forever in the fields of some cottar-toun, it was the pinching poverty. It

made sure that he had no room for manoeuvre. Often it
robbed him of all dignity.[3]

When Jessie made up her mind to escape, the odds were hardly in
her favour.

When she had been a cottar wife for many years, in 1949, she
gave a talk on *Farm Forum* in the Scottish Home Service.

What struck me most when I first became a cottar wife, was
that my neighbours' gardens bloomed fully and gaily with all
kinds of annuals and bi-annuals, but never with apple trees!
That was significant. In those days we hadn't enough
security to plant apple trees . . .

Round about the middle of March we became restive;
we'd hover about the doors in small groups, and the hoary
joke that we shouted to each other over our gates had more
apprehension than laughter in it: 'Are ye workin' for bidin'?'
we'd cry to each other. For, by the end of March, a farm
worker – and his wife! – knew their future fate. Either the
farmer would speir at us: 'If we war thinkin' o' bidin' on for
anither year?' or he would be ominously silent on the subject.
His silence meant that at the middle of May we'd start
'packing', and at the end of May we'd hoist our bits of
furniture on the top of a lorry, move off to some other farm,
settle down; secure till next March came round; we'd 'plant
oot oor yairds', but never with apple trees. They need time,
and time was the one thing the cottar wife was never sure of!

One of the most important things in the cottar wife's life
is her *house*. In twelve years I have had *one* decent, up-to-
date house. Most of the others I've occupied defy description; in that you probably wouldn't believe me if I did
attempt to describe them. It's enough to say that in one
of them I knew my own rats; beautiful, fat, glossy creatures.
They were so plentiful, and became so tame that they
lunched with my hens; hens and rats shared the same
feeding trough: maybe the hens thought they were some
sort of domesticated animals! In another house half the

ceiling collapsed during a white-washing operation, and most of the houses I've occupied have had this in common: they were dank and old, they had no modern conveniences, and they took the heart out of one to try and clean them . . .

David Kerr Cameron, himself raised in a series of cottar houses, conjures up 'a world of bare stone floors and the chill of the linoleum square', and comments:

It was a *Grapes of Wrath* existence that, in the North especially, never really got unionized and it was always cheaper for the farmer to change the cottar than to repair the leaky roof of his dwelling.[4]

Jessie's *Farm Forum* talk also indicates the possible degree of isolation for wives, relegated to small distant clumps of houses:

So very often groups of two or three cottar houses stand together in remote places. We women have to depend so often solely on each other's company. Ask any cottar wife what she considers her greatest blessing, and she'll tell you, 'a good neighbour'. Ask her the greatest curse, and she'll tell you, 'a bad one!' And this is a *fact*, where there are three cottar houses together, one of the three wives is always – to use a telling doric phrase, an ootlin.

This is, of course, the situation so convincingly evoked in *Another Time, Another Place*. And a cottar wife who aspired to be a writer was already an ootlin, sharing all the hardships, the monotony, the limitations with her fellows, but knowing not even one person who understood her quite different preoccupations. It was un-heard of for a farm worker to be a writer. Ironically there was another, John Reid, who went on to use the pen name David Toulmin. It is an indication of their lack of time off, and communication, that Toulmin reckoned Jessie had at one time been cottared about three miles away from his family, but they never met until I was able to introduce them, in 1987, at Jessie's

Honorary Graduation in Aberdeen. Toulmin only knew of her existence because they shared a doctor, who was amazed to have encountered two nascent writers in cottar houses.[5]

Although the system disgusted her and the farms began to blur, Jessie's lively companionship made her well known and well remembered wherever she went. As late as 1980, when *The White Bird Passes* was on television, she got letters from people who had shared bus journeys with her, or, like Betty Wilson of Huntly, who worked in a shop at Lossiemouth, had endured her wiles for 'something under the counter' to help eke out wartime rations. When I wrote to all the local papers in the north of Scotland asking for memories, dates, addresses, letters, I was inundated with calls and letters, which admirably fleshed out these years, except that people were mostly vague about dates, so that I cannot be sure of the sequence. During the war and the later '40s, the Kessons lived at a variety of farms, including Johnstone Cottages, Leslie, where they were working for Mr Insch of Johnstone Farm. Another employer was Mr Spence of Farness Farm, Peddieston, near Cromarty on the Black Isle. Mrs Elizabeth Matheson is the widow of Murdo Matheson, who was Headmaster of the two-teacher School at Peddieston where Avril Kesson first went to school. Jessie told the couple about her writing, and brought them several articles to read. 'My husband advised her to get in touch with Neil Gunn, Brae Farm House, Strathpeffer. She sent him articles and he encouraged her to send them to *The Scots Magazine*, where they were later published.' They also stayed at Udale Cottages, Poyntzfield at Jemimaville on the Black Isle, where Jessie encountered the Italian prisoners-of-war, and where later *Another Time, Another Place* was filmed. It was here that she re-encountered Betty Cameron, whom she had known at Aberdeen Central School. They also went south: October 1946 found them at Hill of Fiddes Cottages, Udny Station, Aberdeenshire, and they worked at Talbothill near Aberdeen, and Cults.

It was at Poyntzfield that they met the Italian prisoners-of-war so important to myth, story, radio play and novel/film, in *Another Time, Another Place*. She wrote unselfconsciously at the time about

looking after them in the *North-East Review*, and much later to
Peter Calvocoressi:

> During the war I looked after three Italian prisoners . . .
> Toni, a barrow boy from Naples. Paulo, a carpenter from the
> hills near Rome. And Marianno, studious and in love. We
> worked together in the fields . . . We were gay often, but
> often in the times when no letters came from home for
> them, it was not so good . . . I learned a lot of Italian, and
> they picked up Scots! . . . And dear, how much 'Macaron' I
> consumed in these years! We cooked and made toffee when
> depression was with them. And I loved when they sang
> Italian songs.

She mentions Toni's aversion to work, and attraction to women,
but says she ruled herself out from the first day: 'No posseeble!'
Michael Radford got a different impression, as he told me,
when Jessie and he were writing the novel and film together, but
he could not speak for the facts. When he and Jessie were writing,
'Johnnie was sitting in an armchair reading his cowboy novels
about four feet away'. Radford sensed Jessie was uncomfortable as
they approached the scene where the young woman and Luigi
made love. (Certainly, she seemed later anxious to play it down,
pointing out that there was virtually no explicit sex in the novel:
'Half the sex wis in her heid!') A row blew up, with Jessie
screaming at Radford that he didn't understand at all. At last
he left, hoping it would blow over. Two or three weeks later, he
records, he got a drunken phone call from Jessie, from a pub. She
said, 'Johnnie's got something to tell you.' As drunk as she was,
Johnnie said, 'While she was doing it with the Italians, I was
doing it with the farm servant,' and he put the phone down.
Johnnie had apparently told her he knew about the Italian
connection, but she had not known about his goings-on. No
one can vouch now for the truth of any of this, but it adds to our
image of the patient Johnnie, and to that of Jessie, who, as
Radford pointed out, talked a lot about sex, but probably experienced very little.

Always Elgin seemed to act like a magnet for Jessie, whether for itself or because it housed Liz, now desperately sick, whom Jessie visited on the two days off each year until the end. So the spring of 1947 found them at Coulardbank Cottages, Lossiemouth, and eventually they stayed at Linksfield, Elgin, for four years. It was from a local farm at Wester Calcots that Jessie was to set out for London in 1951, but there had been no talk about London until the year after Liz's death.

The range of memories that Jessie's name provoked was not always flattering. Several women commented that she neglected to brush her teeth, and no one could say much in favour of her housekeeping. It was widely noticed that she was so absorbed in her writing that she neglected both Avril and Johnnie, who were left to fend for themselves, and that the house they were living in was always 'a tip'. The shortage of furniture and household goods was legendary, as were a number of co-operative community ventures to supply the deficiencies when Nan Shepherd or 'the BBC' arrived, and had to be offered tea, preferably out of matching cups! An anonymous correspondent wrote:

> I myself was abroad around 1943, but my parents got very friendly with Jessie Kesson. She lived at Johnstone Cottages, Leslie. Her husband worked at Johnstone Farm. I believe she was active holding plays, concerts and dances at Leslie School for the war effort.

A splendid vignette from the perspective of an eight-year-old was supplied by Rita Davidson, whose father was grieve at Talbothill. She said the Kessons lived in a but 'n' ben beside the cottar houses. They lived in just one room, with a bed recess. The other room was left empty, with no carpet – just a row of shoes. Among these was a beautiful pair of high-heeled black suede, and little Rita used to take great delight in dancing and clattering round in them on the sounding wooden floor. She remembers Jessie at the table, smoking endlessly, writing. Johnnie would come home to a black pot on the stove, take the top off, ladle out soup and eat.

Hugh Fraser of Poyntzfield remembers 'flitting' the Kessons into

Aberdeenshire in his haulage bus 'Any Ware to Any Where!' Jessie, he said, was very well known around Elgin in her younger days, if 'never very tidy'. The furniture was so meagre – bed, two chairs, small table and three tea-chests – 'you could put it in a wheelbarrow'. And Bunny Little of Elgin phoned to tell about Jessie's friendship with his grandmother, the late Meggie Little, who was a cottar neighbour of the Kessons at Linksfield. Meggie was a drinking crony of Jessie's, along with Chrissie Hubbard, who entertained me thoroughly in her Elgin home with stories about her long friendship with Jessie, begun when she was at Linksfield.

These glimpses of Jessie in the '40s are occasionally unsympathetic: people blamed Jessie for leaving Avril with the contents of a syrup tin, and short of clothes, for example. But Avril herself, retrospectively, has more understanding of that time. Jessie had only left hospital in spring of 1936: she had no aftercare, no follow-up, and her life since had been another series of dramatic changes. Avril remembers being afraid of her mother's quick temper and difficult moods, much as Jessie remembered Liz. And she remembers black days, such as one when Jessie cut up Johnnie's only suit in a tantrum. Whether her writing was indeed her most effective therapy, or whether she was just naturally and gradually recovering, she did become easier to live with, and when Kenny was young, seven years behind Avril, he did not have the same frightening experiences.

WRITING

It was the writing that was to flourish from now on, alongside and often at the expense of other things. She began to get published. Her first poem was the one I quoted from *Over the Sea to Skye* in the previous chapter. After this, publications come too thickly to notice every one, but it is perhaps worth quoting this first poem in full, as it shows Jessie as nowhere else, in thrall to William Sharp ('Fiona Macleod'). Jessie continued to admire Sharp, as witness her choice of title for *The White Bird Passes*, but as she found her own voice she refrained from echoing his, as here:

Tir Nan Og

Way to the west, 'mid seas and crooning islands,
Lies Tir Nan Og – Land of the Ever Young.
There, when the gloaming steals across the Highlands,
The sweetest songs that earth hath heard are sung.

And still their echo steals to me down Lowland way,
And I can see the peat reek curling slow;
And still bog-myrtle wafts its fragrance down to me
From the land of singing hearts and souls that know.

So sure am I that I shall never, never die,
As long as Tir Nan Og lies to the west,
For there, asleep, 'mid bracken on the hillside, lies
All that is young in me, all that is best.

Then some far day, when limbs grow tired, and heart
   throbs slow,
I shall return, and waken from its sleep
My youthful heart I buried there so long ago,
And gave to Tir Nan Og, fair Tir Nan Og, to keep.

Uniquely, the poem is signed 'Jessie Grant MacDonald', and it
appeared in one of Scotland's most popular story magazines, *The
People's Friend*, on 14th December 1940.

But *The People's Friend* was not the right place for Jessie –
although it would do her a good turn before long. The 1940s
were to introduce her to a succession of new people and writing
opportunities, widening her horizons and creating more inherent
contradictions with the cottar life. In fairly quick succession, she
became part of the *North-East Review* group, had her crucial
meeting with Nan Shepherd, met J. B. Salmond and was encouraged to write regularly for *The Scots Magazine*, and had her
greatest thrill, encouragement and a memorable meeting with her
literary idol, Neil Gunn.

In 1940 a group of enthusiastic young men in Aberdeen got together to found a new magazine, *North-East Review*, to offer the area a different and more demanding kind of fare from that on offer from the D. C. Thomson perennials, such as *The Weekly News*, *The People's Friend* and *The People's Journal*. Hunter Diack, later teacher and autobiographer, co-founded *North-East Review* in February 1940 with R. F. Mackenzie, later a progressive educationist and author. When these two went off to the RAF in 1941, there were a number of joint and/or successive editors, including actor Vincent Park, an older man John Foster (no relation to Jessie's ever-absent father), librarian W. Lindsay Simpson and the poet Alexander Scott, who returned from a spell in the forces in 1942–44 to complete his English degree at Aberdeen and edit the *Review*. They were young, energetic and enthusiastic, and although Jessie could not share their company regularly when she was in the Elgin area, or indeed nearer but without time and transport, they did provide her for the first time with a sense of intellectual compeers and discriminating taste. She did occasionally meet some of them, although this is something we only learn of in asides. Dr Donaldson kept notes of a telephone conversation in 1986 when Jessie mentioned drinking with Alex Scott in Aberdeen, and said she slept in the bath. Also, she and Scott were at Biggar on Hugh MacDiarmid's birthday (year unknown). Alex Scott and his wife Cath remained good friends, who visited her in London, as did Derick Thomson, the Gaelic poet, who had been on the fringe of the *North-East Review* group, and his wife, Carol Galbraith, the Gaelic singer, whose voice Jessie especially admired. Vincent Park frequently took part in Jessie's early broadcast plays from Aberdeen in the late '40s.

Lindsay Simpson she only met once, but they conducted a kind of epistolary romance by post. He was a brilliant scholar who could not find a job appropriate to his talents in Depression Aberdeen, and he was a librarian at the Rowett Scientific Research Institute there. Jessie kept none of his letters, nor his writings, although she clearly remembered them, and was proud that what she considered the best of his writing, 'Balm of Hurt Minds', was prompted by their one meeting. Their correspondence was extensive. Her first

written account of their relationship was to Peter Calvocoressi in
1957:

> We all started together on a small war-time review, so
> there's little we don't know about each other! It was a
> *gallant* little review: Hunter Diack was its first editor, then
> John Foster, then Alexander Scott – good Aberdonians!
> There was one very sweet editor, a scholar, a recluse and
> eccentric; also a good religious man. I always remember one
> week when we were terribly hard up – I was nearly taking to
> the by-ways in search of fag ends. It was Easter, and the
> postman brought a little parcel. Inside was a St Christopher
> and ten shillings in threepenny bits, and a little unsigned
> note, sic: 'A small token of regard for your good self and your
> work published in *Scots Magazine* and *North-East Review*'.
> It was one of the most pleasant surprises I ever had. I didn't
> know who sent it. Long after, I found out it was the editor of
> *NER*. We became, and remain, very good friends, with one
> *minor* ruction, which I also never forgot. A controversy on
> regional writing and dialects was going on, this particular
> writer running down 'the Doric' – at least it *is* living and
> spoken, while Lallans is manufactured – no Scotsman dead
> or alive *ever* spoke it! I was real wild, and wrote in a reply,
> not knowing the significance of the word, 'But this is Balls!!!'
> Lindsay, the dear scholarly recluse, was genuinely shattered.
> I got a *terrific* written lecture on that word! 'Do *not* use it
> again. Not even as Brandy Balls, Linseed Balls – *any* kind of
> balls whatever!' And I never did, till now, but this is
> different, since it's only being related.
>
> Lindsay's poem 'Chinese Mistress' was the finest thing I
> ever read. But he retired away to his library and never wrote
> again. We only actually met *once*. Such a peculiar day it was –
> with everything exquisite. I could *never* describe it, but he
> wrote of it in 'Balm of Hurt Minds', and it was as clear and
> vivid as the *day* itself. We went to the Orphanage, my
> Orphanage, it was the first time I had seen it since I left. It
> was unchanged, even to the picture in the dormitory,

'Maidenhood', 'a world of wonder in her eyes', Tennyson?
We went to a variety show at night. A fat policeman was
always saying, '*Years* have rolled on,' and we laughed so
much at *nothing*. Just happiness.

He it was too, who helped Alexander Scott the poet so
much, published an appreciation of his early poems at his
own expense. But all these things and that kind of person
seem dreamlike, now. It's such a *rush* here.

Lindsay's usual writing name was W. Lindsay Simpson. It was
under this name that he published articles on fifth columns, the
unfairness of rationing for the poor, the Baltic States, Latin,
Lambeth and hunger in India. But during his own editorship he
signed his contributions William Innes, a new selection of his own
name, which was William Lindsay Innes Simpson. 'A Chinese
Mistress', the poem Jessie so admired, was signed 'William Innes',
and preceded by a longer introduction in story mode, where the
first-person narrator hears his father's sad and tender story of
loving and losing his Chinese mistress. But the prose piece he
wrote for Jessie, 'Balm of Hurt Minds', was more carefully
disguised: it was signed 'George Stewart'.

It is a touching little memoir of a single meeting, set not at the
Orphanage and the music hall, but on a visit to a cottar home at
Udny Station. Were there perhaps two meetings, not just one? It
is very varied in tone, from the prosaic to the celebratory to the
comic, but it definitely conveys the feeling of a very happy
occasion, 'a day of great personal happiness long looked forward
to and sincerely enjoyed'. After getting lost, the narrator arrives
'by the side of a fir widdie, at a cottar house with a porch and a
corrugated shed with a door swinging in the wind':

> Yes, they were expecting a visitor. And this was him. I
> wonder how he appeared to the waiting friends of whom he
> had heard a great deal one way or another but had never
> actually met. Being solemnly introduced to people you feel
> you have always known, with whom you have corresponded
> with cordiality and intimacy, of whom you have conjured up

brain pictures and imagined shapes – how strange it is to see the visible form and how moving to hear them speak.

He paints an idyllic if poverty-stricken 'cottar's Sunday afterneen' with cats, a five-year-old girl and a wife who 'had both comeliness and skill and stood well in the esteem of her man'. There follows a comic description of his trying, the previous day, to find goodies to bring from rationed Aberdeen; apples, two tins of soup, 'a daud of jellied beetroot and a haggis' and so on, and 'ninepence spent in the Joke Factory secured the most ridiculous false face I have seen for many a Halloween'. Back to the Sunday, and 'three or four hours of quiet happiness, pleased to hear each other's news and views and future schemes'. The ending describes the household by quoting the 45th psalm: 'housel of myrrh, aloes and cassia'.[6]

The relationship was probably fading by the time Jessie was in Devon, in the early '50s, but Jessie told Dr Donaldson that she was 'shattered' when she heard, in 1959, of Lindsay's suicide. The verdict was an open one, but no one seems to have doubted that this reclusive solitary man had taken his own life, after wrestling at length with problems of religious vocation, and a series of entirely chaste love affairs with women. Jessie wrote to Dr Donaldson in 1987, rather awkwardly, uncertain in tone, whether because of her residual feeling for him, or because of embarrassment at his sexual ambiguity and her past naiveté. (Mina Skea had a story of an occasion when Jessie had to share a bed with a woman rumoured to be lesbian: Jessie sat up all night in a chair.) She was remembering Alex Scott:

> I've known him a long time. In fact we started our writing lives at the *same* time. Both young then. Indeed, we shared more than an ordinary friendship with an Editor/writer of potential (never fulfilled: he committed suicide, on the banks o' the Dee). He gave great encouragement to Alex and self. In his way he was in love with us *both*. I didn't realise at the time, naive was I, believe it or not!! Not even when he sent me photos of naked boys and wrote to me about Lesbos, explaining it.

Yet he sweetened life for me. The kindest of men. His
gifts, rare; cherries for my dress, aconites at Easter -
    'These wild aconites are candles
    Lighting us . . .'
We only once met. A meeting which produced one of his
finest writings, 'Balm of Hurt Minds'.

He had a spirit of mischief too! I got used to it, but
embarrassed at first, the country Post Woman handing me
postcards, her mouth drawn in disapproval – 'How are we set
for a bit of Adultery tonight?' (We lived 800 miles apart.)
But the Post Woman didn't know that! I bet the village was
Agog! You maybe understand now why I am wary of
inquisitive thesis writers. Imagine if they met above Post
Woman . . . How on earth could I convince anybody of a
simple truth, a man with an impish, slightly diabolical sense
of humour?

I learned *much* from the books he always sent. I was to him
'the Highland Mary Webb'.

These relationships were new and important for Jessie in many,
many ways. And the *Review* and its various editors offered new
opportunities to the novice writer. In 1941 she had poems
printed in at least seven numbers, including two in Scots.
(Two other 'possibles' in Scots are unsigned.) In October and
November she produced 'Railway Journey', the short two-part
unsigned prose account of her childhood, the first published
attempt at capturing that extraordinary childhood, which was
never either finished nor completely laid aside until 1958, with
the eventual publication of *The White Bird Passes*. She went on
writing for *North-East Review* until it folded for lack of paying
customers in October 1946. By that time she had gained in
confidence and in skill, although I would argue that already in
1941 she was a fine writer.

And it was in 1941 that she had her momentous meeting with
Nan Shepherd. Here, as so often, Jessie's grand myth of her life
simplifies or omits the literal facts of the case. In later years she
used always to 'blame' novelist Nan Shepherd for her starting to

write, although they met on 4th April 1941, when, as we see, she had already begun in a small but promising way on her own account, and the competition Shepherd encouraged her to enter for was not until the autumn of 1941. She told the story many times, with the force of legend, here in an article on Nan Shepherd for the *Aberdeen University Review* in 1990. She had been cycling to the train for her six-monthly visit to Liz, and she remembered the date for a special reason

> On 4 April 1941 to be precise. Precise, because as I was getting ready to go on a train journey 'the wireless' as it was then known announced the death of Charles Murray.
>
> 'Hamewith', I remembered, as I cycled along the eight miles from my cottar house to Inverurie Station. 'Hamewith' . . . 'The road that's never weary' . . . was how our Dominie introduced us to Charles Murray's poems. And as Hamewith – never Charles Murray – he remained to the Dominie and to me . . .
>
> It was in this reflective frame of mind that I cycled my way to Inverurie, arriving at the station just as the guard was about to raise his green flag. I scrambled into a carriage, stumbling across the feet of its only occupant. Gathering myself to my feet, dusting myself down, I surveyed the occupant on the seat opposite me. 'A Lady', I decided. In those days in my mind women were divided into two species, Ladies and Wifies. Farm workers' wives were Wifies in this category . . . I really resented that. I didn't feel old enough to be a Wifie . . .
>
> 'Hamewith's dead,' I said to the lady across from me, the event still much on my mind. I knew by the look on her face that she hadn't heard the wireless that morning. 'This morning,' I assured her. 'I heard it on the wireless.' Little did I know then of her long friendship with, and deep appreciation of Charles Murray's work . . . We 'tired the sun with talking' . . . Murray's poems. Doric words . . . She got off the train at Rothiemurchus. Before leaving she took from her knapsack a strawberry-coloured silk headsquare. 'A small

memento of a lovely journey', she said, handing me the headsquare.[7]

A letter out of the blue from Nan Shepherd later that summer began, 'Do you remember a lovely train journey in April?' It told of a Short Story Competition, 'Sangschaw for Makars', which was being run by the Aberdeen Scottish Literature and Song Association. Jessie entered and won first prize, and a friend and mentor for life. But, incidentally, Shepherd was somewhat embarrassed by Jessie's myth-making: in her last letter to Jessie in 1982 she was still protesting that 'the Lady in the Train – has her role quite exaggerated'. She added, 'What the lady in the train relished so much about that journey was just the sense of life gushing out in all sorts of ways – it was a life-enhancing journey.' Shepherd remained a friend and correspondent, and a critic, who reviewed *The White Bird* enthusiastically, and whose opinion Jessie greatly valued.[8]

The early '40s were to hold two other momentous meetings. When Jessie tried *The People's Friend* again with stories in 1942, the percipient editor printed one, 'This Wasted Day', in February, but sent another direct to J. B. Salmond, the editor of D. C. Thomson's prestige publication, *The Scots Magazine,* from 1927 to 1948. This was a good move, as Jessie's face would never fit the *Friend*, then dominated by such skilled popular novelists as Annie S. Swan, Anne Hepple, Winifred Duke and D. K. Broster, and a prolonged effort to conform could have harmed her individual gift. Salmond's 'discoveries', he claimed, included Joe Corrie, Eric Linklater, Neil Gunn and Lewis Grassic Gibbon, and he befriended James Bridie, A. S. Neill, Edwin and Willa Muir – and Jessie Kesson. (His role in Scottish letters during his editorship looks like a rich field for research.) Jessie wrote about him to Silvie Taylor, who contributed a centenary profile of Salmond to *The Scots Magazine* in 1991:

How I revered *The Scots Magazine.* I'd been writing short stories for *The People's Friend* when their editor sent one direct to J. B. Salmond who from then on nursed me in my writing.

He encouraged young writers, but also used the work of established writers – Marion Angus, Violet Jacob, Flora Garry – a grand stable for a young filly like myself, one which increased my confidence and sharpened my aspiration.

His friendship for Jessie included giving her 'the first and best holiday she ever had, with the Salmonds at Newport, where her seven-year-old daughter looked in wonder at her fish knife and told them, "We dinna hae knives like this at hame." "It was true," said Jessie, "but the lack of them didn't in the least embarrass us in that gracious household" '.[9] Silvie Taylor wrote to Jessie that she was well remembered by his secretary of those days, Agnes Brownlee, who remembered taking her to a party.

She contributed to five issues of *The Scots Magazine* in 1942. She was still devoted to the idea of writing poetry, and experimenting with it. Much of it was preoccupied with deaths in the war, where many of her contemporaries were lost. These include English poems like 'Escape', 'Again They Die', and 'Missing', and a better one in Scots, 'Oor Sight's Sae Dim', with the explanation, 'For Wattie, posthumously awarded DFM'. This is a lively memory of sitting together in school, her helping him with essays and dates, and he her with her bugbear, arithmetic.

> He wisna unco clever, an aye he lippen't me
> Tae help him wi' his essays, an' dates o' history.
> But fan it cam' tae coontin', I'd a heid as thick's a tree.
> An Wattie he wad wirk the sums in the twinkling o' an e'e.
> Syne roon the corner o' his airm I keekit cannilee.
>
> An' mony ploys an' dools we shared thegither,
> An streeve, an' 'greed, an' phraised wi' ane anither,
> As bairns wull . . .

Her poetry is very varied and, as Neil Gunn was to point out, when it worked it could be very good indeed, but she undervalued her prose, and the condensed 'poetic' texture it gained, trapping life experience into myth. The prose in *The Scots Magazine* that year included 'The Years Between', a story in which a girl, Elsa, returns years later to 'Murdoch's Wynd', to find it changed, and that her male friend Streak has died in the war, and 'Triumphant Day', a first writing of the episode in *The White Bird Passes* where the child Ness is humiliated because she has nits – but her mother tells her the story of Elgin Cathedral, and she wins the essay prize. Jessie continued to write for *The Scots Magazine* until 1950, but her contributions became scarcer as Dr Salmond moved towards retirement in 1948, and she was concentrating on the more lucrative and very satisfying field of radio.

But one of her proudest moments came in May 1945, when a fine Scots poem 'Fir Wud' elicited an admiring and encouraging postcard from her literary idol, Neil Gunn.

Fir Wud

Happit frae daylicht's cauld clarity.
Hidden the road.
An', here for lang
a yalla-yitie quietens the warld's steer,
an' mortal thochts,
wi' the lift o's sang.
Like velvet atween ma hot bare taes
the fir loam shifts.
Birstlin; things stick till ma claes
an' the foosty guff o' an ancient wud drifts
owre and bye.
If, foriver in this wud I jist could lie
an' tine ma thochts,
an' smell the resin, loam-filled air,
an' watch the queer wud dirt gaither
tae battle on ma hair!
Sharpenin' draughts nip owre ma face.
Nivir sae wide awak', I shut ma een;
Syne, like a lustful quine,
gie a' masel tae the wud's embrace.

Gunn's postcard, Jessie later remembered, said, 'I have just read
"Fir Wud" in *Scots Magazine*. A first class poem judged by highest
standards. If you would continue to write poetry of that quality
you would do more for Scottish literature than by any amount of
prose.'

Added to this, an invitation to cross the Firth and visit him
at his home. I was young then. Yet I set out on that visit to
the man whom in my own opinion is one of Scotland's finest
writers, without apprehension. I knew from his work that he
had an instinctive understanding of women. Almost a
tenderness . . .
    There was a nip in the autumn air the day I visited Neil
Gunn. A fire of logs from an old apple-tree burned in his
hearth. He didn't stand on ceremony. He didn't even sit on
ceremony. A tall man, he lengthened himself out on the
floor, leaning his back against an arm chair. Taking my cue
from him, I also took to the floor beside him. He had the
young eyes of his boy Ken in *Highland River*. [Jessie would
name her own son after that Kenn] . . .
    We talked through a long afternoon into evening. Re-
plenished and re-fuelled by his wife. Gracious in letting us
have space and privacy to hold our hour and have another, as
the Irish say. Strange, we didn't discuss writing, but the
differences between the rural way of my Aberdeenshire and
Neil's Highlands. Of crofters now lost in the shadow of
farms which have become factories. Of the relationship
between farmer and farmworker. The Highland farmer
and his worker had a much more democratic relationship.
Perhaps derived from the old clan system when Chief and
man shared the same name and were part of the same family.
Our farmer at the time. A gentleman farmer. Always kilted
and buckled, often invited my husband, his *cattleman*, to go
duck-shooting or to share a dram together. *That* could never
have happened between master and man in Aberdeenshire.
    Perhaps as a result of that talk I got a letter from Dr J. B.
Salmond, then editor of *The Scots Magazine*, that Neil was

giving up the series 'Country Dweller's Year', and suggesting that I might take his place. THAT was when I thought to myself, 'I'm a *real* writer now.'

She wrote the 'Country Dweller's Year' throughout 1946, which was a triumphant year in publishing for her. Besides these twelve articles on subjects very near to her heart, she contributed three poems, including 'Abriachan Summer', to *The Scots Magazine*, and five major prose pieces which have already been quoted, including 'The Near Kingdom', 'I to the Hills' and 'The Shadow'. During the same hard-working months, she had eight major prose pieces in *North-East Review*. These included 'I Must not Dream', the tale of a little girl punished at school for hearing and responding to poetry being taught in the other class, 'Judgment', where the children steal the hens' stale biscuits, and 'Makar in Miniature', the finest rendering so far of what was to become *The White Bird Passes*. But she was already looking towards fresh – and more remunerative – fields to conquer. She had been trying to write 'the book' all the time, having a version typed for her in 1944, and in 1945, after an unsought audition at the BBC in Aberdeen, she wrote and read her poem 'A Scarlet Goon' on Vincent Park's programme, *Aberdeen Awa': Town and Gown*, which was produced by Elizabeth Adair, the beginning of a long and fruitful partnership with the latter. She began to lay siege then to the BBC, with plays and poems and monologues. Two were produced in 1946, and six in 1947. The writer had a new medium to conquer.

Chapter Seven: The BBC

Broadcasting in Scotland started with local radio stations, Glasgow in March 1923, and Aberdeen six months later, on 10th October at 15 Belmont Street. Edinburgh and Dundee were also in operation by late 1924. Of these, according to John Gray, 'For largely technical reasons, Aberdeen remained largely autonomous and outside the regional scheme' [of the 1930s]. He also points to Moultrie Kelsall as an 'outstanding creative broadcaster'. 'As a result its actual output was large, varied and original.' Gray's 'golden age of Scottish radio' was between 1947 and 1955. He praises producers such as Robert Kemp and Archie P. Lee, and James Crampsey, and later Stewart Conn and Gordon Emslie, all of whom would have dealings with Jessie in due course.[1]

But the most important figure in Jessie's early radio career was none of these: it was Elizabeth Adair.

After an audition I joined the Corporation in the summer of 1940 as the first woman announcer in Scotland. Stationed initially in Glasgow, my three months' trial period extended to twenty-one years. After one year Andrew Stewart, then Controller of the Scottish BBC, invited me to return to Aberdeen (my home town) to open up broadcasting again. There had been a lull in production during the first two years of the war.[2]

In 1938 the Corporation had moved to a more permanent home. During the war years, she recalled,

the staff at the BBC took it in turn, two at a time, to do fire watching in the black-out on the roof of Beechgrove House. We climbed up through a trap-door to a corner of the roof where we sat on chairs looking for enemy aircraft! Periodic-

ally the engineers on duty brought us cups of tea to warm us
up.

Moultrie Kelsall was Aberdeen station director for seven years,
and Elizabeth Adair much admired him:

> In my opinion Moultrie was brilliant – tall, dark-haired,
> attractive, with a lightning brain. He set a high standard in
> production and acting and woe betide any artist who failed
> to come up to this standard.

Adair flourished under his regime, pioneering experiments in
Outside Broadcasting all over the North East. Jessie was to make
part of this:

> I had the idea to broadcast a rural play actually amid the
> stooks in a field (instead of in the studio, depending on
> mechanical or recorded effects) so we 'borrowed' a farm from
> a friend near Stonehaven and the cast ran across the pastures,
> leapt the tinkling burn, slapped the cows in the byre and
> made their exit in the rumbling farm-cart. This was one of
> Jessie Kesson's first plays especially written for radio and was
> called *Ultimate Landscape* [*Over Lendrum*, 1957].[3]

Miss Adair remembers Jessie taking full part in the above: 'She
liked to be intimately connected with her radio plays, taking small
parts or voices in the background.'

The partnership that she and Jessie created together was close,
inventive, imaginative and sensitive. Jessie said, 'I've aye been very,
very lucky in my producers; they did it very, very brilliantly you
know,' and she was right: James Crampsey, Archie P. Lee,
Stewart Conn, Marilyn Imrie were all sympathetic and understanding and ready for discussion, but the relationship with
Elizabeth Adair was formative, and very happy, and they remained friends, communicating occasionally by letter or Jessie's
habitual monologic late-night phone calls after she went to
London in 1951, until she died.[4]

Nan Shepherd, who had suggested that Jessie attempt the short story prize in 1941, had meantime become a friend of Jessie's. One day, out of the blue, she arrived at the farm where Jessie was living, creating consternation among the cottar wives, who all had relatively little means and struggled to make ends meet. Jessie wrote about it in 1990:

> I well remember our second meeting. As unusual in its way as our first meeting. I was working in the byre with my husband, milking the cows of the residue of their milk after the milking machines were taken off, when my next-door neighbour hurried into the byre to tell me that 'A Lady' was 'gaun aboot looking for you'. I could think only of Nan Shepherd. Hospitable by nature, I felt a rising panic – how to entertain her to tea in the manner to which she surely was accustomed. My table furnishings were by no means fully implemented. Odd cups. Odd plates. 'And nae *proper* butter or jam dish,' I confided to my neighbour. A problem which she understood. Pondered. And provided a solution. 'Dinna worry, wifie. I'll get haud o her an tak her up to the byre. Jist you keep her here as lang's ye can. An we'll see fat's to be dune' . . . Dear Mistress Watt. Good neighbour, best of friends.
>
> Thus it was that Nan Shepherd found herself captive in the byre while I, in an effort to detain her as 'lang's I could' continued to 'strip' cows which already had been 'stripped'. Bemused beasts because they had thought their ordeal was over.
>
> When I got to the house with my guest I found that 'My table' had indeed been 'furnished'. Not by the *Lord* but by the combined offerings of my cottar neighbours. In recognition and recollection of such a gesture, 'My cup' *still* 'overflows'.[5]

The chronology is uncertain but, although they probably met seldom, they were good friends by October 1945, as can be seen from a poem, 'To Nan Shepherd', in the *North-East Review*:

Two hoors did haud oor years o' kennin' each the
	t'ither's sel',
While words poored forth, swift burns in spate, syne
	tint themsel's in the myrrh's thick smell.
We twa grew quate tae listen till oor thochts
	gang loupin' through the wuds, and owre the distant hills.
Jist aince we cried them back, and changed them wi'
	each other, like tokens,
Sayin', 'Keep mind o' that still river faur trees glower
	lang an' deep at their reflections.'
Nor could the jostlin' fowk and noisy street touch for
	a meenit oor communion.
Tho' I held oot a hand in pairtin',
I wisna aince my lane on the homeward track,
For, through myrrh's smell, past wud's tremendous green,
My frien' jist followed me, the hale way back.

An intense love of nature was something both women shared,
although in conventional class terms they were as distant as Jessie
was from Elizabeth Adair. The class differences never mattered
much, but Jessie was much more aware of them than were the others.

According to Jessie's myth again, it was Nan Shepherd who
suggested her name to the BBC. Elizabeth Adair again:

> I had invited her to attend drama auditions at the Aberdeen
> Beechgrove Studios where at that time, about 1944 [1945], I
> was Programme Producer. She very nearly didn't come at
> all! . . .
>
> She tells me now that the envelope was opened with
> trepidation because typing meant officialdom! Most un-
> willing to spend the bus-fare from Elgin to Aberdeen on
> what might come to nothing, she was persuaded by Johnnie
> – for once throwing caution to the winds – who said, 'You
> just never know.'
>
> So she set off on foot along the railway line that ran past
> the cottage towards the station, pondering whether to spend
> the money on the bus-fare or her cigarettes for the next day

or two. The cigarettes won. She retraced her steps homeward along the railway track to confront a disappointed
husband. 'There's still time,' he urged, 'The auditions go on
all day. Catch the next bus. You just never know.'

At the Studios Moultrie Kelsall, as Senior Producer, was
conducting the auditions. Jessie sat nervously awaiting her
turn. Her description of him – 'The handsome Moultrie was
of a species I had never encountered before. The end of a
hard and maybe fruitless day glittered wearily in his eyes.
His dark hair high and aloft, himself trying to bring it down
with sharp staccato hands. No, I couldn't play the part of a
grandmother or an old tipsy wife. So I read Violet Jacob's
poem "Tam in the Kirk", one of my favourites. He thanked
me and walked me to the front door.' When Jessie got home
she told an expectant husband Johnnie, 'A waste of time. A
waste of money. The mannie just said Thank you.'

But within a week she received a telegram from us asking
her to write and read a poem in my radio production of
Vincent Park's *Town and Gown*. She wrote a lovely poem 'A
Scarlet Goon' and that spelled the beginning of a long
collaboration – she writing, I producing, at least thirty
features and plays on radio from Aberdeen.[6]

But here it seems to me that Elizabeth Adair is unconsciously co-
operating with Jessie in creating the broad myth. Again, the
timing does not exactly fit. 'A Scarlet Goon' was read by Jessie on
13th October 1945. But the Glasgow files contain a letter from
Moultrie Kelsall to Elizabeth Adair, apparently continuing an
ongoing discussion of poems and stories submitted to the BBC by
Jessie before 31st August 1945. He thinks her material 'mixed',
but, 'There's not the slightest doubt, however, that much of the
material is worth using.' He goes on to imply that perhaps the
BBC is in danger of dragging its feet in this regard:

> The great thing, I feel, is that this woman has unusual talent
> and should not be discouraged by being left for a year before
> anything of hers is used.

Jessie, it seems, must have submitted her material well before the famous audition Indeed, her dialect poems may have occasioned an invitation to an audition without any intervention from Nan Shepherd: Adair points out that Kelsall was fascinated by the dialect of the North-East of Scotland.

Throughout her career, the various BBC files on Jessie make fascinating reading. Her offerings are discussed at length between staff, and many times she is asked to rewrite, or even dismissed with fairly brutal frankness. The early Kesson is bursting with naive enthusiasm. She sent in six poems, of which three had been previously published. Elizabeth Adair sends them to Moultrie Kelsall (Glasgow), who suggests passing them on to Robert Kemp (Edinburgh) if Adair cannot find a placing for them. Just after Jessie's first broadcast, Kemp writes to both the others: 'Have either of you got this girl's poems? I thought of putting some in Chapbook, but they don't seem to be with me.'

Early evidence of Jessie attempting the story of her childhood is seen in a letter Jessie wrote Moultrie Kelsall in October 1946, sending a script and demanding detailed advice:

I read your article on radio plays in BBC booklet with great interest, which explains why I've submitted the enclosed effort. It isn't really a play, it's a 'dramatised portrait'. That sounds very la de da, but what I've tried to do is to give a Scots character life.

It's rather an unusual portrait, but you see I'm dealing with what was an unusual person – quite the most fascinating person I ever knew. What's more, I know she would not have minded me writing her epitaph because we were like one person.

I know so little about the mechanics of writing for radio, so I hope you will take that into consideration when you're passing judgment on it. And I'd be very pleased if you'd tell me its faults. If it isn't good and I've wasted your time reading it, I'm sorry. And will you please write your verdict direct to myself? Thank you very much for that.

This letter also typically gives entertaining glimpses of her life's hassles:

> I am very tired. Our house was falling about our ears – it was condemned sixteen years ago! And so we flitted to the above address. I've been working – creating mentally. I'm expecting an addition to my family – creating physically – so between flitting and a' thing else I'm fair scunnered!

Kelsall replied obediently on 5th November, and sent back the script with helpful comments, treating her as an equal, and not pulling any punches. He asks for simplification of technique, shorter speeches, some expansion and development, and less pompous language:

> Why should Dave on P 5 talk about 'probin' the ethics o' happiness'? In recent things of yours I've read in the *North-East Review*, for example a recent story about the girl going to the Maternity, your dialogue was much less high falutin'. You of all people, I would have thought, would have realised that simplicity is one of the primary virtues.

Clearly, he is already entertained by her epistolary character. He goes on, 'I'm sorry to hear that you are so trauchled with houses and bairns. I hope you're oot o' the bit by now as far as the former is concerned.'

An entertaining postscript to this particular correspondence comes seven months later. Moultrie Kelsall is leaving the BBC, and Jessie writes regretting this and admiring his recent production of Neil Gunn's *Sun and Moon*. As if in an afterthought she asks, 'Could I have "Lisa" back before some quite impersonal person finds her? Thank you very much.' And further down, 'mind to return "Lisa" – no, dinna fash yersel', cremate her! It's just that I wadna like abody's een glowerin' intae the secret places o' life.' Connoisseurs of Jessie's mood swings may detect a little definite sharpness here: why has he taken so much time to comment on her creative baby, while she has had to spend hers taking care of the physical one? (Kenneth Kesson was born at home at Coulardbank, Lossiemouth, on 29th December 1946, which no doubt explains why she forgot and subsequently mislaid Kelsall's helpful letter.) His answer begins, 'Lassie, lassie, I sent you back "Lisa" on the 5th of November last year with a registered letter full of good advice all laid out in lettered paragraphs.' No indication of irritation as he goes on to ask about the progress of the novel, and whether she wants him to show it to John Keir Cross.

In her cottaring days and long after, Jessie used to have to travel very light. She did not keep copies of *The Scots Magazine* or *North-East Review*, nor of her radio scripts. With the best of help from producers and archives, I have not been able to track down all of them, let alone the pieces that were rejected. And there was little correspondence between Jessie and Miss Adair when they worked together. So what I have to show for their years of co-operation from 1946 until 1952, and then at intervals between other producers until 1957, is a pile of mainly short scripts. The missing scripts concerned subjects from Burns (*Till A' the Seas Gang Dry*, 1947), and the Orphanage (*Bless This House*, 1947), to Lodging Houses and vagrants (*No Fixed Abode*, 1948) and the Lane (*The Street*, 1949). It is not possible to establish exactly how many scripts are actually missing, as Jessie had a habit of changing titles, which is bad enough. Worse, as we shall see later, she was capable of giving exactly the same title, be it *The Childhood* or *Friday* or *This Wasted Day* to two completely different scripts! Jessie was as prolific with radio scripts, once she got started, as she had been with articles and stories for periodicals. So in 1946, with Miss Adair producing, she herself narrated *Over the Sea to Skye*, a 20-minute memory; and *Apples Be Ripe*, subtitled 'An Aberdeenshire Autumn', which deals with the different faces of autumn in country and city. She had a story to tell about that, which she wrote to Ian Parsons of Chatto in 1957:

Once wrote an Autumn script for Scotland. I called it
'Apples Be Ripe', from a very old English folksong. Producer liked the title, asked its source. She's very sweet, very
lovely, but shy and reserved. I never forgot the expression
on her face when I told her the verse from which the title
was taken:

> Apples be ripe
> And nuts be brown.
> Petticoats up
> And trowzers down!

We used it none the less! I think only me and the producer
in all braid Scotland knew where the title came from, and we
kept *that* secret to ourselves, not wanting to upset the
susceptibilities of the 'Wee Frees'!

Jessie's life, her pattern of different work, her very different co-
workers, grew more and more bizarre, more full of contradictions.
She still had bad times: Avril remembers her burning Johnnie's
only suit in a rage. Other reports suggest that she ran away at least
once, leaving Johnnie to cope with Avril, and Johnnie had to
search for her through the Salvation Army. Young Kenny would
play happily with tinkers, while Jessie was invited to speak at the
prestigious private school, Gordonstoun. On what was possibly a
snobbish or defensive whim, Jessie insisted on sending Avril to a
fee-paying primary school which she could not afford. This again
led to contradictions: Jessie held a birthday party for her daughter
at a local hotel, because she did not want to shame Avril by
inviting her friends to their unsatisfactory cottar house. She also
found herself having to write what she called 'shite' for *The
People's Journal* to help pay the school fees. One brief example
will show that she was right, and that these articles need not be
preserved for her complete oeuvre: these were the only things she
ever wrote simply for the money, and it shows: from a typical piece
headed 'She Wears the Breeks':

The woman who blatantly 'wears the breeks' uses the wrong method – she puts her man's back up! 'Whether you like it or no' I'm gaun awa' tae oor Maggie's for the weekend – you can please yersel.'

By all means 'wear the breeks' – but wear them prettily – well camouflaged under your 'rings and things, and buttons and bows'.

More, a 1947 letter survives on a page torn from a jotter, a letter from Jessie to Avril's headmaster, who had clearly sent the child home with an open letter complaining about her having fleas, and a very ragged vest. Jessie begins with what she calls 'the *facts* about complaints regarding Avril'. She acknowledges 'we are subject to fleas':

The wood of old houses are a veritable breeding place for fleas . . . There is always the few who escape. If hard work and willingness would send fleas to their eternal doom, there wouldn't be one in my house I can assure you.

This account is backed up once more by Betsy Whyte, in *The Yellow on the Broom*: she tells how much the travellers hated moving into an old house in Brechin for the winter:

Mother had a constant fight with the fleas in it and – as her only weapons were paraffin, carbolic soap and water – it was a losing battle. Our skin used to come up in large blotches with their bites, for we were all very fair-skinned. (15)

In her letter to the headmaster, Jessie acknowledges the vest problem, blaming it largely on the lack of clothing coupons, but quite soon she moves onto the attack, turning the tables and assuming the moral high ground:

What does vex me is that in this almost Civil Service world where postage seems such a cheap commodity, that such communications are not posted *privately* to the parent.

Avril, like the majority of children, is sensitive; how sensitive
children are few educationalists seem to realise. I thought I'd
done much to destroy this bogey of blind officialdom. It
seems it still exists. Education and children are the subjects
closest to my heart . . . My book . . . Perhaps it will result in
letters being sent direct − and by post − to parents . . .

Avril does not want to go back to school, but I have
impressed on her that she doesn't need to feel ashamed of
either herself or me. I am pretty sure few mothers of
Springfield children work harder than I do . . . If you want
Avril withdrawn from Springfield immediately let me know.
I'd much rather take her away than have anything adverse
reflected on her.

And more in the same vein, referring to her own recent achievements, and her own deprived childhood.

Jessie and Elizabeth Adair lived in very different worlds. Adair
recalls that, 'Contrary to what one might expect in a "country
lass", she was always smartly dressed, well-tailored suits in dark
colours.' But little did she know the 'making-do' Chrissie Hubbard remembers, when Jessie went out with a dress on back to
front, because the front was stained, or where Jessie's almost
always second-hand clothes came from, in the days before charity
shops. Jessie herself made two wonderful stories of her life's
contradictions for Peter Calvocoressi in a lively letter in 1957:

Elizabeth Adair, who has produced nearly all of my Scottish
Radio Features, always comes to me to have her tea when
doing BBC programmes or auditions in the town of 'the
Lane'. On one memorable occasion we were just in the
middle of our tea, when the door opened and in walked a
Tinker I had known since crawling days. This wasn't
unusual. She always dropped in to do a bit of 'business'
with me, and have her cuppa − but she had never before
arrived at the same time as BBC! However she didn't seem
in the least concerned, and went on as usual. Conversation
like this.

'My God, Ness, but you've got bonnie bairns!' – aware of BBC producer, peering closely at the same.

'What a bonnie woman! Is this one of your Mother's folk?'

At this point I had to introduce them. First time, I'm sure, that a BBC producer ever met a Tinker *socially*!

So my old Tinker just set down as usual and had tea with us. 'Business' proceeded as usual, afterwards. She unearthed from her pack a pair of boots.

'They'll just fit your man. A couple bob to you. Dirt cheap. Seein' it's you.' (I was shattered at BBC discovering the source of my wardrobe!) Particularly Elizabeth Adair. She is *exquisitely* beautiful. Extremely shy and reserved. So much so, that she is called 'The Frozen Angel', which *infuriates* me. I personally have never found her so. We've worked so closely and long together. It's just that the gay Lotharios of the studios have no effect on her. They can't believe it. And it hurts their vanity. She's *anything* but cold. She's a shy darling. I taught her a lot of things unconsciously; she isn't nearly so shy and easily shocked now. She gave my Tinker a lift in her taxi, and never *forgot* her tea with the Tinker!

But the funniest thing of the lot happened once in the High Street of 'the Lane'. I was queuing up for a bus to take me to Aberdeen to do a broadcast. I was dressed in my first and only *new* fur cape. I hoped that everybody behind me was observing fur cape and were duly impressed by same! I also carried my script in big envelope with BBC lettering and crest – hoped everybody observed this too! Then I heard my name shouted from other side of the street. I could not mistake the owner of the voice, and felt myself shrinking at least an inch! The voice belonged to the town's most often jailed Tinker. We had been children in 'the Lane' together, same class at school as well, and once we were both so dirty that the teacher sent us out of the class to clean ourselves up. It was a lovely day, so we thought we would go and catch tiddlers in the River Lossie instead. This Tinker boy was the best tiddler catcher I ever knew!

We ken a place where the trout leaps great,
   Me and Davie!
But Davie's dead.
   And the half o' my hert's in the mools beside him.
   We got a real strapping next day at school. But both felt it had been worth it! Anyhow, an experience like that, shared, cannot be dismissed. And we had always remained friends. So I looked across High Street to owner of voice: black as coal, swathed in rabbit skins! Bus queue stared, amused, at this notorious character too. He brought himself over and proceeded to do 'Business' with me. We often had little wardrobe deals, but never publicly before. It went like this:

   'I've got a frock. Not a *mark* on it! Out of a *Big* House. You'll get first chance of it. Two and a Bender! You're getting it for nothing! At two and a Bender!'

   I felt that listening bus queue decided that *new* fur cape had come from same source! It didn't hang so proudly on me after Tinker had departed (with my promise to purchase frock 'if it fitted' at Two and a Bender – 2/6).

In 1947, with a daughter at a fee-paying primary school and a baby son to tend, Jessie still found time to write six plays for the new medium of between 20 and 30 minutes, *Highland Spring*, *Sleeping Tinker*, *The Last Journey*, *This Wasted Day*, *Anybody's Alley* and *The Child's Christmas*. Subjects ranged from a dramatisation of the prize-winning short story 'Sleepin Tinker', of which a late version can be found in short story form in *Where the Apple Ripens*, to an old woman dwelling in memory, or another facing eviction, to a radio version of 'Anybody's Alley', which is quoted at length in Chapter 1.

   But her ambitions were also to produce other kinds of programmes. She wanted to initiate a popular Scottish comedy show, somewhere between *The McFlannels* and *Much Binding*. She tried this kind of thing fruitlessly for Howard M. Lockhart, as she would later with Gale Pedrick in London. This 'sit-com', *Awa' tae the Cleaners*, was to centre on the doings of two BBC cleaners, and their encounters with the stars. She writes to Lockhart wistfully:

The strange thing is, I usually write sensitive, serious scripts, but when we have a break at rehearsals, I have the rest of the cast in tears with laughing: sometimes they're hoarse when we go to start again, and I've found that it's the sort of 'impossible' things that make folk laugh – so that's what I've done in the enclosed script.

The script does not survive, but Lockhart's answer does. He doesn't think it quite comes off, and continues:

In any case, as you have built up such a fine reputation as a writer of sensitive, serious radio programmes, do you think it is altogether wise to descend from the sublime to the ridiculous?

She sent a hopeful letter to James Crampsey in April 1950 about another projected comic series, set in a country-town hotel, and he pulled no punches in reply:

I return herewith your script *Lounge for Non-Residents* which has now completed its circuit of our Reading Panel. We could not possibly put on this string of gags, greetings and apophthegms, not to mention adverts, held apart rather than together by a Frenchman's observations on the unspeakable Scot. Sorry, Jessie, but no.

Other projects which never came to fruition included applying for a job on *Children's Hour* in 1950, a series on the life of a lady almoner, an offer to adapt S. R. Crockett's *Some Uncommon Men* for radio, and yet another series, this time based on a country family. What many of these have in common is the series idea: a regular income would have made life so much easier, but at this stage it was not to be.

Meantime she was writing versions of *The Wise Lived Yesterday*, the Abriachan play, for Archie P. Lee, and suggested another covering her hospital days (eventually *And That Unrest* in 1951, leading to *Somewhere Beyond* in 1962). Lee reacted guardedly,

understandably given the BBC's Reithian sense of responsibility
for its audience: 'Any programme about mental trouble is a very
ticklish one. There are so many people who can be wounded by
what you depict. However, it is a very arresting theme and I
believe a very important one.' Internal letters which she would not
see were much franker. Here are three summative comments on
They Told Me You Were Dead, of which I have traced no script, and
which Jessie herself thought a disaster when it was on air:

RFD   This is good engulfing Kesson. On page 5 you come
      up for the third time, on page 6 you go down for good
      and like it. With a bit of merciful cutting there should
      be few dry eyes even beyond the North East. Oh dear –
      Yes.
JC   There's little doubt that this autobiographical piece
      with its implicit cry for charity and love and under-
      standing between man and man and specially between
      woman and woman will make effective radio. As RFD
      suggests, merciful cutting here and there, particularly
      among the purple patches, would make its impact all
      the stronger. YES.
GG   Yes. EA should produce. The number of 'bitches'
      must be reduced. The perspectives will need careful
      watching.

Jessie also considered adaptations, sometimes with insufficient
knowledge. She attempted Daudet's short story, 'Le Petit Chose',
betraying enormous ignorance of different traditions when she
tried to render a French Roman Catholic priest as a Scottish
minister. She suggested adapting Sholokhov's *Virgin Soil Upturned*:

Have you ever read *Virgin Soil Upturned* by Sholokhov who
wrote *And Quiet Flows the Don*? It's full of humour, drama,
pathos, and above all humanity. It describes how a small area
was turned into a Communal Farm, how something in us
loves our *own* possessions, the horse we helped to give birth

to, the corn we sowed, and how reluctantly we give them
over. It's got fun too! . . . the nun who was Anti-Soviet and
had all the peasant women over sixty worked into a panic,
against the Communal Farm, by telling them that Soviet
Agents were making wooden boxes for the old women to sit
on and hatch out the eggs! It would make such good radio,
it's so full of action.

Crampsey said Sholokhov was not for the Home Service: Adair
liked the idea, as a change from Jessie's autobiographical obses-
sions. Eventually it *did* come to pass, rewritten as a 'historical' play
set in Scotland in 1316, without taking history too seriously.
Robert Kemp, himself an accomplished playwright, and Features
Producer, Edinburgh, wrote complaining of 'modern turns of
phrase', and anachronisms, but concluding: 'She is a wonderfully
good writer, humorous and vivid, and I am in favour of this script.'
Forty Acres Fallow was produced by Adair for the Scottish Home
Service in November 1951, when Jessie had left Scotland.

Jessie began to plan to go to London after her mother's death in
1949. She had continued to visit Liz when possible, and once took
Avril. But her mother was difficult, and unpleasant to the little
girl, who was not taken again. Jessie went alone. Liz had said to
Jessie, 'When I die, you will be free.' Jessie's greatest, deepest,
longest fear had been that her mother would die. Now she was
indeed empowered. She had been shunted from institution to
institution, from one oppressive cottaring job to another. Now she
would take some control of her life. For the first time she could
make a big decision, choose a new life, and her choice was daring
and hazardous.

When Liz died, Jessie asked her friend Chrissie Hubbard to go
up to the hospital with her. Chrissie saw Liz for the only time in
her coffin, and this was the only occasion she ever saw Jessie cry.
But Jessie resolved to bury her mother with dignity from their
cottar house at Linksfield, and in the presence of Liz's family, who
had rejected her so long ago. She demanded attendance. Mina
Skea's mother, the most hostile, at first refused, on the grounds
that her sister had been dead to her for 40 years. When she did go,

she made no pretence of grief, something which rather impressed Jessie. Jessie rarely spoke of this time, with the exception of her frank interview with Colette Douglas-Home in 1990.

> She wanted to be buried with her family and would I see to that. Would I get her remaining brothers and sisters to come to her funeral.
>
> She was sad about going. I remember her crawling along and still she would say 'Life is sweet'.
>
> I did get in touch with her family. I knew they wouldn't let her be buried with them, but I asked them to attend. It was the only thing I ever asked of them. They said they didn't get her flowers when she was living so it would be hypocritical now she was dead. I bought two or three bunches and put different names on them.
>
> Women didn't go to funerals in those days. I went and that was when I lost my religious faith. My uncles wouldn't take the cord to lower her, so me and the undertakers lowered my mum into the grave. I said "Bye, Mum' and I knew it was over. Do you know, I wept. But I tell you a strange thing, I wept like a fountain and after that I was cleansed. The greatest fear of my life had always been that she would die. When she did die that fear was removed and for the first time I lived my own life.

When Jessie went to London, she did not simply shift from Scottish producers to English ones. Although her work was as likely to appear on the prestigious and recently established Third Programme as on the Scottish Home Service, she usually continued with Scottish producers, and enjoyed visiting Scotland for the productions. Name changes, as hinted earlier, make it very difficult to follow every play. *The Childhood* (1) was also called *The Hill*, and a version was offered to Chatto under that name. A later, longer version, intended to make its point even more firmly – for Jessie felt quite missionary about the business of 'boarding out' – was called *The Mourners*. But it lacked the impact of *The Childhood* (1). Similarly, *The Childhood* (2), the *White Bird* story, began in English as *The Voice*, and in Scots as 'Makar in Miniature', before it became a classic that overshadowed *The Childhood* (1) for younger listeners, even such experts as Stewart Conn.

I will look briefly at the achievement – and appropriate roots – of both *The Childhood* (1) and *The Childhood* (2). The former is now available in *Somewhere Beyond: A Jessie Kesson Companion*. As was shown in Chapter 5, the play partly mirrors Jessie's actual situation as an ex-Mental Patient boarded out at Abriachan, but it centres on the plight of a ten-year-old Glasgow boy boarded out there, who desperately misses his mother, whom he is accustomed to protect, especially when she is drunk. So it mirrors Jessie's own feelings at the Orphanage, as well as creating a wider canvas, which effectively speaks for the inarticulate Johnnie and all his like, who were boarded out and had no voices to express themselves. There are few characters, chiefly Daniel as boy and man, his fellow boarder Kate and the Old Woman. Danny's first experience at his new school is the strap for mispronouncing 'butter', Glasgow-fashion. Many of the children have tried to run away homewards, unsuccessfully, and all have been belted. The Old Woman perpetually questions, accuses and threatens. She eats better meals than the children, and grudges peats for the fire. She is supremely uninterested in Danny as a person with feelings.

Jessie supported the cause of the boarded-out child with unique passion, which seems to be personal, and with reference to her mother, and the result of a passionate identification with the suffering child universally. She swore she could tell, meeting people in the street, whether they had lived in an Orphanage or been boarded out. She gave powerful evidence at Perth to the Boarding-out Committee of the Scottish Advisory Council on Child Care, which was at work from September 1948 to January 1950.

The boarded-out child had the scales weighted against him from the very start – otherwise he would not be removed from his home. Therefore extreme care was needed in selection of Foster Mother.

My suggestion was to do more for the mothers of these unhappy children: poverty, bad housing, being up against it can so often warp a woman who has the basics of a good mother . . . OR To have more places like my Orphanage, a small country house, meant to hold eight children. This prevents families being broken up, as sometimes does happen, when a F Mother can't take a whole family. To have it staffed, like the Orphanage, so that, though the children must learn to work, they have also time to play and be children. It's in Public Eye all the time; little can go wrong, since local Dominie and Minister are trustees, and always in close contact with children.

The Clyde Committee had tried to tighten up practice with regard to boarding out, but as Abrams points out: 'No child witnesses were called and thus the question of the child's perception of his or her status within a family and community was not addressed.'[7] But Jessie was a major figure at the Boarding-Out Committee: 'Mrs Jessie Kesson, who was able to speak about the boarding-out system from the point of view of one who had been herself a boarded-out child'. The Committee's Report very much endorsed her views, assuming that future children's officers would be specially trained, and insisting that 'only exceptionally can children develop naturally if they are in the care of old persons not related to them'.[8] It goes on:

The suggestion has been made to us that children who have been brought up in a town or city and have been taken into the care of a local authority find it particularly difficult to settle down to a country life. We were impressed with this view, which we think is particularly applicable where a child is over eight years of age on being taken into care.

. . . We do not think it is desirable that any area should become a colony of boarded-out children . . . A community without the normal age grouping of the population is an unnatural environment for a young child.

Through her friend the Elgin Welfare Officer, Jessie quietly continued to organise some things behind the scenes:

> I have seen to it that B O girls in their teens who break the 'one coat per year' rule simply by means of growing fast, get another coat when they need it. That another B O girl, who was very *tall* and very dull in school was *not* kept back and embarrassed by small girls overtaking her. I went to the very wise rector of the school, explained
> 1. that girl would never pass her exams.
> 2. that learning was not the aim for her; she was going into service. But being so tall and being kept among small girls was not good for her mind . . .
> And always I've been doing the small bit I could personally do for those children.

These quotations are from a series of long letters to Gordon Gildard at the BBC, who was handling the flak from the publicity. One final letter ends:

> At this moment I have my eye fixed on a most unsuitable Foster mother. The neighbours speak about her in whispers, but are afraid to do anything. Isn't that so cowardly? I'm going to have a talk with her, and if there's no improvement I'll raise the town. It's the publicity that I hate, but there *will* be an improvement – I'll frighten her to death!

It is the narrator, Daniel as adult, who tells us of Danny's initial terror of the hill, and his perpetual fear that his mother will die, like Janie's fear in *The White Bird Passes* (Liz *did* die two months before the play was first broadcast). Danny is soon consciously torn, as Jessie was at Skene:

> For all that my heart cried out to be back in the small street off the Garscube Road with my mother, my mind knew that this was the last year – the last chance – it would have to store up the things I'd never see or learn again. All I did, all I

saw in that last year, took on a terrific, hurting significance. Even now it comes leaping out of my mind . . . I looked on each day, event, place, in that year – as if I were looking on it for the last time – and I was never out of trouble for not seeing and doing the ordinary things that I should have seen and done.

He falls desperately in love with both poetry and natural beauty, and eventually achieves some wholeness:

After that I was happy; I lost need of any personal affection at all from the aunt; her coldness skimmed over me – and it didn't hurt me any more. I even lost need of the near memory of my mother. I belonged so fully to my own mind, to the brave words I learned in school, to the things my eyes saw, to the music my ears heard.

When his mother fails to make contact on his birthday, however, Danny is desperate, and the Old Woman quite unsympathetic. He wishes her dead, and she dies soon after. The old folk cannot understand why none of her many previous boarded-out children come to the funeral. But Daniel the narrator can see and speak for them:

But *I* knew that it was neither forgetfulness nor ingratitude. I saw the children, reflections of Kate and myself, small shadows going east to the well for water, west to the barn for straw . . . seldom playing, laughing in whispers, sitting in dark corners learning the Bible. Never knowing active unkindness, and never once knowing what it was to be able to put their heads on the 'aunt's' knee and sob out the bewildering hurts of childhood. I saw them all, and I knew it was not forgetfulness that had kept them from the burial, but remembrance.

After the funeral, Danny is returned, too late, to Glasgow. His mother has suffered a stroke and is lying in hospital, insentient.

Manhood beckons. This is a beautifully crafted and very moving short play, which had an astonishing impact nationally, and to no small extent led to the Boarding-Out Committee and its report.

As an early but mature version of *The White Bird Passes*, *The Childhood* (2) is also very different from the novel. The first part of the play is dominated by the voices of quarrelling women in the Lane. The narrator's mother, in contrast, is quiet and hardly prominent. There is no suggestion of prostitution; she works in a market garden for low wages, and has to pawn blankets when in need of cash. The play concentrates on Mary, again as child and adult narrator. Memorable happenings in the Lane include the women's fights, Mary and her young friend experimentally getting 'saved', a scene with the tinker Beulah boasting, and a man who hangs himself.

> The manner of Bert's death, and my mother's white, still-faced attitude to it frightened me. If Bert could die . . . my mother could die. So people *had* power over their own lives! They could die if they *wanted* to die. What if I ran up to the attic one day and found my Mother looking like Bert, all black and . . . She often said she wished she were dead when the rent was due and the money was gone. What if one day . . . that fear took hold of me and haunted me in all the days to come. I was afraid to leave my Mother alone for a moment. I stayed with her in the attic.

Part 2 of *The Childhood* (2) covers the Orphanage years. The child misses the Lane, and her Mother, and when Mother visits, mysteriously ill, the girl is ashamed of her – and then ashamed of being ashamed. She has the one chance of reconnecting that Danny was denied, but makes little of it, unknowing:

> My mother swore to Mrs Thane. And I hated her for doing so, hated her so coldly and fiercely that it shocked me. I would never have believed that I could have hated my mother so. In that moment I wanted to die, or to run away to some dark hole and hide myself. The fir tree in front of

the window began to swim in front of my eyes, a great blur of green. And if my eyes dared to look at the dark, quiet figure that was Mrs Thane, the agony in them would have said to her, 'I'm sorry she swore at you. O I'm sorry.' But when we went up to the Ducks' Wood together, my hate left me, and there was nothing in me but pity for my mother. I had looked so forward to meeting her again. Everything that I learned in the Orphanage I stored safely away in my mind, thinking, 'This is to take home, I must never forget this.' And now, I couldn't tell her *one* of the things I'd saved for her.

Mary passes her exams, and is ambitious to 'teach English'. But we know what the Trustees will have to say about that. The play ends with Mary setting off for her farm job, the younger children envious, the Matron trying to support her in a life that is 'often unfair': 'Keep looking forward, Mary, you never know what the years will bring to you yet . . .'

And this chapter ends with another new start for Jessie. She talked about leaving Elgin in 1950, the year after her mother's death, but postponed it. In 1950, it seems, her scripts found less favour with the Scottish Home Service. Elizabeth Adair wrote to Glasgow in April 1951 to say Jessie had been for farewells: 'She seems to have recovered from her resentment over the non-acceptance of her scripts during the past year.' Jessie's unpredictable resentment or sunny acceptance of adverse factors was to continue to threaten her relationships for life. In this case Adair wrote to her in October and made clear that *Forty Acres Fallow* had been allocated to the end of November by a meeting early in July. Sadly, this gives the lie to one of Jessie's favourite myths, that the week she went to London she got a job, found a room and wrote *Forty Acres Fallow!*

The Legend of the Journey

I wis a cottar wife. I'd aye been wantin' to leave the cottars and that, always, and I think this is maybe the bravest thing I ever did; I think, I'm nae sure but I think it wis. The Elgin Townswomen's Guild were daen a pageant, and they asked me if I'd dae Marie Curie – well anything, but my favourite was Marie Curie and I did that, and I got £20. I thought it was a big sum of money. And I thocht right – I'm off to London, so I'm off and I said to Johnnie, if I get on, I'll get ye a' doon. If I dinna get on, I'll be back. So off I go in the bus with my £20. I winna tell you a' the details o' that, and remember I'm from a cottar house, and I didna' know a living soul, I widna dae't now. Anyhow, I am sitting and my money's jist aboot gone and I thocht oh, I'll hae to go hame, I've enough. I'd enough for the train and I hidna got onything you see, an' it was a spring day, it wis April or March, because it was the night o' the Welsh International comin' doon to play and it was awfa funny in a wey. I think it was Waterloo Station . . .

Anyhow, before the train comes in, this woman wi' a black scarf roun' her heid, nae stockings on, I aye remember, ye ken the wifie that might have had pee-marks doon her legs; ye know what I mean. A homely wifie; she hidna, I'm sure, but she could have been. So she sat doon, and we were speakin' . . . Well you ken how ye start chattin'. I said well I come fae Scotland and I was looking for somewey to bide, and I couldna' get naewey to bide so I'm gaen off back.

She invited me hame to Muswell Hill tae her place. I got a job within a week. I sat doon and I wrote a play. Also I got a job cleaning the Nurses' Home in the Colney Hatch, you've heard of it, the great Mental Hospital (*Scottish Writers Talking*, 68–69)

Chapter Eight: London: The Fifties

Nan Shepherd wrote that what had impressed 'the Lady in the train' was 'the sense of life gushing out in all sorts of ways'. This remains typical of Jessie and her approach to life almost to the end. As she gets to London, her life becomes even more complex, more difficult to contain between the covers of one book. I will treat it from now on in approximate decades, and in each chapter will try to outline it under very general headings, such as Life, BBC and Publishing. But Jessie's 1950s in particular seem to defy structure: they accommodate a brief adventure to Devon and a bizarre epistolary love affair: I can only ask the reader's indulgence.

LIFE

Our interview with Jessie in 1985, quoted above, is coloured with myth as well as history, like everything else, and she 'forgot' Avril was with her. So the family moved to London. From then on, apart from one excursion to the South West, Jessie and Johnnie lived there until 1971. Although they moved almost as often as they had when cottaring, all the moves were short-distance ones. Jessie came to feel at home in North London, in particular in the areas of Muswell Hill, Palmers Green, Crouch End and Highgate.

And for a while Jessie had very hard jobs at odd hours, to accommodate the children's school times. By this time Avril was 14, and Kenneth seven. One such job was cleaning the Queen's Cinema at Palmers Green. She savoured the myth as she told us of cleaning the outside steps and 'the men's dirty lavvies, and they *were* filthy!' One week, she related, she had a play on the Third Programme, but when the cinema manager told her, 'You know, you're the best scrubber I ever hid,' she thought that the greatest

compliment: 'Because the play was something I could dae and
rather enjoy daein', and this was something I hated daein' and yet
I still did it'.[1]

DETOUR TO DEVON

Considering that Jessie's one great ambition had been to move
south to London, where she would be able to write for radio and
television, and mix, she hoped, with writers and poets, it is odd to
find that within a year the family moved *out* of London. She had no
sooner, it seemed, become established there, with her own rented
flat, and her first bank-book, than she took a step in the dark, to
Devon, which she soon realised was a false step. She had heard of
John Keir Cross through Scottish BBC before she met him, and his
reputation must have made him a stimulating prospect.

John Keir Cross was an unusual and unconventional Scotsman.
Born in August 1914 in Carluke, Lanarkshire, he wrote *Aspect of
Life: An Autobiography of Youth* when he was 22, and published it
in 1937. It begins with a typically dramatic flourish: 'About two
years ago, overcome by the ennui that attacks young men of
twenty who smoke too much, read too much, and hold uncongenial jobs, I set out to commit suicide.' The drab routine of a
boring job in a small Scottish town was the main problem. Even as
a schoolboy he had been attracted by the 'wild, unhampered
freedom' of travelling people, and Bottle Jean, his equivalent of
Jessie's Beulah. As a young man, he threw up a monotonous job
and took to the road as a wandering ventriloquist, performing at
street corners and village greens around the Scottish Lowlands,
before adventuring all the way to London. The blurb on the dust
jacket describes him as 'iconoclast, itinerant ventriloquist, aspiring
playwright and composer of music': in London, he was interviewed on the BBC's *In Town Tonight*, as a result of which he
eventually landed a staff job with the BBC, until he gave it up to
do more writing. In *The Naked Civil Servant*, Quentin Crisp
described Keir Cross's life as 'a recipe for success': 'Never before
and seldom since had I witnessed such indefatigability and such
singleness of purpose.' He wrote adventure novels, and a large

number of children's stories under different names. He became at
last rather too attached to the whisky bottle, as a result of which
his considerable literary gifts were too often confined to skilful
adaptations of the classics for adult or child listeners, and his last
steady job was as one of the team scriptwriting for *The Archers*. He
died in 1967.

Kessons and Keir Crosses met in Muswell Hill in 1952, not
long after the Kessons moved south. Audrey Keir Cross had two
small children and another on the way. Born in the country, she
longed to return there. But the omens were unfavourable for the
following adventure, right from the start.

Jessie recommended an Irish nanny. But after she was appointed, Audrey came home one day to find the baby alone, and
when Nanny came back with the others, she was drunk. Nothing
daunted, John and Johnnie planned a farm in Devon for Audrey
to work, helped by Johnnie, while John and Jessie would each
pursue their writing in pastoral seclusion. An added bonus for
those working or hoping to work for the BBC, was that rail travel
was very convenient to Paddington in those days, with one coach
being detached to a branch line. Higher Hisley Farm, Lustleigh,
is on the edge of Dartmoor. It is a small farm of about 30 acres of
steep land with large granite boulders in the fields. It has a very
old listed farmhouse, typical of the many Devon longhouses to be
found on the Moor, as well as a roomy cottage for the Kessons.
Keir Cross stayed there until 1957, and wrote a children's book, *A
Sixpenny Year*, clearly set there. It reads in part like propaganda for
farming over city life, despite 'the great realisation of how much
more there was in farming than strolling contentedly round
haystacks on blue summer days'. Whole chapters are natural
description:

> The colours changed on the Moor. New strips of green
> appeared over the back of the swaling. The trees turned
> bright as the buds on them burst into tiny crushed leaves.
> The animals grew glossy and plump on their diet of fresh
> grass. The whole enormous panorama of the valley seemed
> transformed as the season's growth advanced.

But soon Jessie saw it differently, in spite of its beauty. It made her homesick.

> It was on that farm high amongst the cleavage rocks of Devon that I was assailed by a terrific homesickness for Scotland such as I have never experienced in London. Looking down from my high perch amongst the rocks to the picture-postcard village nestling far below, to the red, red soil, to small, green patches of fields enclosed with high, green hedges, I felt I was looking on a vividly coloured illustration in a child's story-book. It just wasn't my country-side.[2]

It did not last long. Publicly, Jessie repeated the public story:

> I was up in Scotland for a radio play. In my absence Johnnie, my husband, and a well-known writer and broadcaster got together and decided to take on a farm, both families sharing the venture. By the time I got back to London it was a fait accompli. I viewed the project with mixed feelings until the optimist in me took over and I thought to myself, 'Now there's a turn-up for the books – a fine step up from being a cottar to being the wife of half a farmer.'
>
> The project lasted a year. We discovered that two writers don't make one farmer.

Established facts are few. It certainly did not last a year – probably less than six months. Audrey Stock, Keir Cross's widow, told me she found Johnnie little help on the farm, and saw he was not happy. She said Jessie left the Cross children with wonderful memories of bread and dripping and 'jammy pieces'. But she said Johnnie neglected a new calf, which died, and she had to end his wage to pay another helper. Meanwhile Jessie was for the first time in a situation where there was always whisky available, and intellectual conversation late into the night. Audrey Stock opined she was happy, and said twice, 'She was having a rest,' but a few of Jessie's letters betray deep unhappiness. She was desolated when

James Crampsey said he could not afford to bring her north for a
new production of *Sunset Song*. Her letter is short on facts, but
clear on state of mind:

> Tho' I don't mind admitting to myself that I've been the
> biggest kind of fool in coming here, I should hate anyone
> outside to know of my folly. I think I only now realise what
> Milton meant when he wrote:
>> But, tho' his tongue dropped manna,
>> And could make the worse appear the better reason,
>> 'Tis always false and hollow.
>
> That was the lure; but no one would believe that; so one
> licks one's wounds, animal-like, in the dark. I am vexed,
> because I was getting on fine in London; had my own flat;
> my own bank-book – my first ever! And my work was liked;
> and there I went and gave it all up, *knowing, foreseeing,*
> exactly what was going to happen; and it did!
>   . . . I have been writing hard to save up for my 'escape' . . .

This letter is dated 17th September: the Kessons were at Higher
Hisley by 27th August 1952, and back in London by November.

   In Devon, Jessie had still had the odd droll, would-be adulter-
ous postcard from Lindsay Simpson. But another postal relationship had begun, more serious, and much more beguiling. To
introduce it, we have to start with the day Carol Galbraith met
Jessie. Carol Galbraith, Gaelic singer, married Derick Thomson,
Gaelic poet, who had been on the edge of the *North-East Review*
group. But as Carol was ten years younger than her husband, she
met Jessie first in London in summer 1952, and here gives her
impressions of their first meeting – and how she heard of the new
admirer. She was led upstairs:

> to a big room with a bare wooden floor and what seemed a
> few wooden benches in it. I was left at the open door on my
> own. On the far side of the room diagonally across from
> where I stood was a harmonium and a woman sitting at it,
> side on to me, playing basic chords up and down with a great

flourish. I wasn't sure what to do, so just waited there assuming she'd stop and come over to me. She didn't. She seemed to concentrate more and more on her playing, and with feet pumping and body swaying she gradually groped towards a hymn tune and began to intone 'Father of Peace and God of Love'. I felt like an intruder, but as I didn't know the house and I couldn't retreat, I just stood there, and after a verse or so I found my voice joining in. Then with neither Amen nor hiatus, musical or rhythmical, she began 'O Love that wilt not let me go'; then moved on to 'There were ninety and nine that safely lay'. With a similarly smooth transition 'Eternal Father strong to save' was lifted up. That fine ballast of a hymn was actually allowed to die away. A brief silence, then she jumped up with a laugh, came over to shake hands and then led me down for tea.

She 'talked and talked' to Carol Galbraith 'about various people, mostly unknown to me' and fired questions, hardly waiting for the answers. Many others, Elizabeth Adair included, have testified to her habit of talking like this on the telephone, sometimes late into the night. Carol Galbraith goes on:

Next she nearly ca'd the feet from me by becoming suddenly calm and very dignified-looking and saying she was '*really* in love with a *POET*', and rhapsodised about him. She spoke of him regularly during that summer too, but never referred to him in later years. Perhaps it was an idealised relationship. In spite of my interest in poetry I had not known any of his work, and anyway I felt she always showed a deep affection and strong sense of duty towards her husband and children.

Jessie also recorded her affection for the Thomsons and Alex and Cath Scott in letters to Dr William Donaldson, remembering:

a grand night we had, with other old friends. Derick Thomson and his dear wife Carol (Galbraith), the Gaelic singer, as sweet a singer as Derick is a poet. Many a fine

night Derick and Carol spent in my flat in my early years in
London. I had an old second-hand organ, and we'd give the
'psalms and the paraphrases' big licks round that old organ in
my wee flat. I hope you – even once – heard Carol sing.

SHAUN AND SHONA

In some ways, Jessie Grant MacDonald and Johnnie Kesson were
particularly well suited. Michael Radford went so far as to say to
me that no one could live for long in close proximity to Jessie
except Johnnie. She had no experience of a father or a father figure
(minor possible exceptions being her Dominie, and 'the Mannie').
She had had no real experience of stability when they met, after
Elgin, Skene, two bumpy experiences of early employment and a
year in the Mental Hospital. Johnnie had, at least, shared a
boarding-out experience; and was older and more experienced:
above all, he was not afraid to talk to her, as the younger men at
Abriachan were. Their marriage withstood everything thrown at
it, and although he tended to be seen, especially later, as the
weaker party, Jessie's need of him was just as great as his need for
her. She told Sheila Hamilton of the *Evening Express* in 1983: 'He
is my ballast. He is a very comforting person.'

But Johnnie was never Jessie's intellectual equal by any means,
and did not share her interests in reading, talking and communication. So with him almost as a safety belt against overinvolve-
ment, she went on to make close if largely epistolary friendships
with well-educated or artistically gifted men, including Lindsay
Simpson, Shaun Fitzsimon, Peter Calvocoressi, Stewart Conn
and Dr William Donaldson. From all accounts, there was a
romantic aspect to both of these first relationships with Lindsay
Simpson and Shaun Fitzsimon.

Many letters survive of the romantic friendship with Shaun
Fitzsimon, whose relationship with Jessie was at its height from
1952 until perhaps 1954 or '55. All these are addressed to Jessie,
except one from Shaun to his brother. The last letter so far traced
dates from 1962. Shaun Fitzsimon was an aspirant poet (although
he was never to have much published). But to be greeted as a

fellow poet must have meant a lot to Jessie. In the course of the correspondence he addresses her as Aurora, whether after the heroine of Elizabeth Barrett Browning's poem *Aurora Leigh*, the eponymous heroine of which was a poet, or the Greek Goddess of Dawn; and as Sappho, the greatest-ever woman poet. He also calls her Lalla Rookh, after Thomas Moore's princess who fell in love with a poet. Perhaps twice, he calls her Jessie. He settles into Shona: as Avril Wilbourne remembers, his name was pronouced as in 'shown', so this made Shaun and Shona into a most appropriate pair.

His letters are highly emotional. The first survivor dates from February 1952, when Jessie was 35, and Avril was 14 and Kenny seven. Jessie was already living in London, and apparently they did not meet for some time. Jessie had been published repeatedly in *The Scots Magazine* and *North-East Review*, and was quite celebrated on Scottish radio, but this kind of excited exalted recognition was clearly irresistible, especially if it was also safe:

> When you is [sic] deeply in love, deep, deep, in love, the great Inexhaustible springs[?] up in one. And when it's love between poet and poetess it's the end in delight, I think.

In the same month he wrote to his brother Matt in a characteristic state of excitement, but apparently meaning he is committed to celibacy:

> I will never forget the past ten or so days for a L – O – N – G time. I've never known such exaltation . . . Jess and I are in loviddy dove. Perhaps you guessed. But don't get ideas. Us and Jess are pre-natal – strictly. I'm wild about her, and very deep in. Just feeling this love. But what am I saying. Read my sonnets. They say it all.

Shaun lived in Glasgow, initially with his father, who was 70 in 1952. His later letters show him on his own, in apparently squalid conditions, which even Jessie, never one of Nature's housekeepers, took exception to. By 1952, Jessie was established in the South, but made frequent trips north to Glasgow or Edinburgh or Aberdeen in the course of her work for the BBC. These occasions were when they met, but clearly the relationship was mostly a matter of letters, and the meetings could be stormy. He is remembered without affection by one Glaswegian as 'the poet in the kitchen' at her party, and clearly Jessie was not always feeling friendly and patient: one letter apparently from early in the friendship includes a sonnet, and a 'p.s.': 'wondering if I'll hear from you today, tomorrow, and if you won't stay in a bad mood or not, tempestuous, unpredictable, dearest one.' But more characteristic of the early phase of the correspondence is: 'I always hate the first week after you've gone. I take it sore.' Jessie kept his letters, as she did not keep Lindsay Simpson's, but it is a sad process to read them, because Shaun emerges as so febrile, so full of fantasy, so impractical.

He is apparently unemployed on principle: he misses hearing one of her plays on the radio because he has to go to the [Labour] Exchange. He claims he does not want to create difficulties in her life, but he can write to his 'Lalla Rookh': 'Do I sound ro-man-tic. Then please excuse me. I'm in love, spiritually *and* fisically.' Tellingly, he goes on, 'All this a nonsense note. But I *like* writing it. And *love* having someone to post it to.' It is in a second 'p.s.' to this whimsical letter that he writes: 'If we discover "foreverness", Shona, will you marry me? If "YES" send me telegram on the day you get this since the suspense will be costing.' His handwriting changes with his mood, and his mood changes often: Jessie was too wise a woman not to recognise his instability, but the correspondence nevertheless presented her with an outlet, an intellectual forum, an undemanding wooing. Shaun writes a great deal about what he is writing, and his conviction of how good it is, but I have only so far traced two poems he had published, 'The Golden Macadam' in *Saltire Review* 1, April 1954, and 'The Journey's Finish' in *Lines Review* No 6, September 1954. They are wordy and obscure, reminiscent perhaps of the early MacCaig, of the two volumes of 'Apocalyptic' poems that MacCaig later tried so hard to suppress. But Shaun is also generous about *her* writing,

both her radio plays and her letters to him: 'Sappho, that bit about
your mother just about broke me. It made me love you with a wild
wildness. I felt ever so privileged that you should tell me.'

None of Jessie's letters to Shaun has to date been traced, but it is
clear that she was as committed to the correspondence, and to
weekly telephone calls, as he was, at least at first. But as early as the
summer of 1952 he was getting rather paranoid about her sending a
letter with the stamp upside down, and he wrote in July, 'When I got
that letter from you at the beginning of last month I felt, rightly,
that it was all up, that it was time to move away . . . that is, I didn't
survive the fact of your admission that we could never be together.
If, as you say, it was a trick, I fail to see what it was meant to do if not
to silence me forever.' He says it is 'deep red hell to hear you talk with
two voices'. But there is no indication at all that Jessie ever remotely
considered leaving husband and family for this volatile man who
discussed with some fascination why he was attractive to homo-
sexuals – and who was to suggest, years later, in the course of a
begging letter, 'Maybe we have an affair some time. What say? We
might meet in Paris after all accidentally . . .'

The relationship flourished in the early '50s, although from the
beginning it could be stormy. The romance was over by the mid-
'50s, but the correspondence continued fitfully until it tailed off in
1962. After a gap he would boast of his opportunities, including
that he had been offered a job as secretary to the wife of a
millionaire. For a year Shaun was in Hospital, with the same label
that had been affixed to Jessie, neurasthenia. Jessie wrote to her
old Elgin friend and drinking partner, Chrissie Hubbard, when
she was working at Cowley in the late '50s:

I occasionally hear from Shaun, when he's needing money.
Poor soul, he has been in a Mental Hospital for the past year.
But that's all over on my part long ago. Though I write to
him occasionally to cheer him up. I work so much with men
now, that I never bother about them. They get in my hair
sometimes, they resent, very naturally, a woman being in
charge of them. Just the same, the PT instructor is very good
looking! I can admire them, but that's all.

Shaun rarely dated his letters, so the sequence is hard to trace, but he did write in April 1956, clearly after a lengthy silence, 'I haven't seemed to be able to adjust myself kindly to Glasgow since I left Hospital a year ago.' As a result, Jessie sent some poems to John Lehmann through Peter Calvocoressi, which were rejected: 'nothing but poetic cliché and tinsel in his work'. In 1959, Jessie received a letter from a woman friend who had clearly also had a difficult time with Shaun. She writes:

> Lord Shaun? These days I am almost afraid to write about him, I feel so bloody biased. I think my charitable feelings for Shaun left me long, long ago. There is still so much of the child in Shaun that I think he needs one hell of an experience in his life. His life has been such a mental one, up in the clouds kind of thing, that he has no natural reactions left in him. I have the idea that he actually calculates how he will feel, respond or react to things, but then maybe I *am* just biased.

While he confides in Jessie that their friend had 'no firstness', he writes that he thought about her the previous night, and reports, rather bizarrely: 'I indulged in the thought of how it mite have been if the *three of us*, somehow, had chanced it together.' In a letter of the same time to Peter Calvocoressi, Jessie wrote half-jokingly that hassles at home half-made her want to accept a long-standing invitation and abscond with the 'Poet'. 'Sad about that. We are both growing old now. And let all our young years pass – intacto. Feel that was waste somehow.'

He was delighted for Jessie when she got her contract for the six-month job at the BBC, although back in Glasgow he was apparently working at the local Co-op. He writes triumphantly, '*New Poet* has accepted and paid for some poems . . . I feel happier now that I'm writing again.' When Jessie heard from Alex Scott that her previous correspondent Lindsay Simpson had committed suicide (this happened in October 1959), she wrote to Shaun, who wrote: 'Poor Lindsay Simpson. I mean to go like that. He must have been a real solitary. It must have been a great shock.' But this

letter quickly moves on to Shaun himself: 'You rightly intuited me
not well . . . a sick line these past months and not at all well. It's
mainly neurasthenia.' He must move: his flat is to be demolished,
but he has been sleeping in a bed recess with a built-in bed and has
no money for a second-hand bed or for removal expenses, 'My
present predicament, the blackest I've known . . . how much of an
outsider I am, really . . . disregarded and truly alone . . . without
hardly a friend I can turn to.'

Shaun wrote many poems for Jessie, including a long one
entitled 'The Great She', which survives only in fragments. Here
he is reconciled to her absence – 'The silence left by her who is
adored/ is silence like the sun upon my brow.' The correspondence
ends with a short poem dated 'Tuesday 5th June '62': He writes
that he likes it better than any he has ever sent her.

You Who Rocked Kingdoms In My Head

To savour once again the little bittersweet
disorder of your shoes flung off with what a smile
and easy as the flow of streams to stream to you
in heartache open as a wound, now that
reviving springs revive the land with light
and what was gone reports with words like guns
that shoot the shadows dead – less sentimental
than a drowned tear: you who rocked kingdoms in
      my head,
as likely as a breeze to carry spring smell,
as likely as a poem of hawthorn's song
from out the plentied order's inner rule.

Since spring is what the trees say with their leaves,
let us abide by whom we most adore
among ourselves, and who we are the most:
let reviving springs alarm the land with you
and what was gone report with what a poem
to blot this dark, in mental earthquake's time
      the laughing champions.

LIFE AND WORK IN LONDON

After Devon, other jobs Jessie undertook back in London in the
'50s included the stand-by, Woolworth's, waitressing at Lyons,
and a hard year as Night Charge at a Church of England Home
for polio and spastic girls: this she said was the hardest job of all.
There were 70 girls, aged from 11 to 16, and she worked 12-hour
shifts, and ten nights on, two nights off. This job inspired a radio
play, unusually taken from her recent experience. Produced by
Elizabeth Adair in Aberdeen in January 1954, *Green Glass, Goblin*
follows the Night Charge through an evening with extraordinary
sensitivity. Here she ponders the phenomenon of Christmas at
the school:

> Here, all around me, are the everyday reminders of the
> children's physical handicaps. Their body braces and hip
> braces lying beneath their beds; an essential part of
> themselves, inanimate only at night; their wheel-chairs
> serried along the corridors; forlorn in their emptiness.
> These symbols are sharp and clinical on the mind and
> eye. Christmas confused the symbols; and conflicted the
> emotions. Coloured balloons flying high, beyond reach
> of the wheel-chairs, contrasted starkly against iron
> braces, and prodded the onlooker in the regions of
> wasteful pity.

But from that came a surprising career change. She was head-
hunted to be Inspector in Charge of the Cowley Recreational
Institute in Brixton, working directly under the Principal, the
Hon. May Ammon, daughter of Fabian peer Lord Ammon.
These Recreational Institutes, according to Jessie's friend and
colleague Thelma Shuttleworth, 'were invented to catch children
coming back from evacuee homes to heaps of rubble'. Bertram and
Thelma Shuttleworth were involved in theatre and teaching,
respectively. They were sorry for Miss Ammon, who was a very
insecure person, who found it hard to smile or be light-hearted,
and was not very easy to work with. They later took Miss Ammon

to live with them. But Jessie's relationship with her was to prove uneven, to say the least. She was very proud of the appointment, thrilled by the working conditions – £14 for a 15-hour week – and initially happy with Miss Ammon. A touch of snobbery is apparent several times in Jessie's references in letters to working directly under a peer's daughter. In many ways, Cowley was St Katherine's Club writ large: no wonder Miss Bella, always somewhat snobbish herself, was thrilled at the new job! Five evenings a week, young people could play table tennis, join discussions (Jessie's particular métier), learn dressmaking or boot repairing, or play a range of sports. Jessie visited Cowley in July 1954, and started in August. She took the Discussion class, and was responsible for overseeing the work of a wide range of other teachers. She really loved the work, and the substantial difference it made to their finances:

> Though I sometimes grumble at the lovely time lost at my job, it is lovely to be able to buy a crab for tea, and Tweed perfume, and plants for my garden. I wanted a lilac bush and lily of the valley for *years*. Bought them this spring, and it was like the healing of an ache when at last I saw them mine and planted them.

She became involved in some of the basic problems of youth work, as she had been unofficially since she lived in Elgin. As early as October 1951, a letter from Auchterless School, Turriff, invites her to speak at the inaugural meeting of a youth club. She wrote to Peter Calvocoressi in August 1957:

> The whole pattern of Youth work, the whole need of it has changed so much since the war, that this must be the most difficult phase ever. Knowing How to give *What*?? We have 400 teenagers in the course of a night – no 'Angry Young Men' among them. Only apathetic ones, and sad little 'unknowing' ones . . . The results are so slow, and you could break your heart because of the 'unknowingness'.

This job experience clearly leads to Helen Riddel's disillusionment in *Glitter of Mica*, although Jessie was not as easily discouraged as Helen.

At first all went well: Miss Ammon included Jessie in theatre visits with distinguished people, and took her out to dinner à deux. Jessie referred to her with admiration in a *Woman's Hour* discussion:

> a person with whom I work, who's sacrificed her whole life to her parents . . . She's never felt it was a sacrifice – it's me has used that word – it's given her pleasure to do that. She chose to do it. She could have put her father or her mother – because they have plenty of money, they're quite well off – she could have put them to be cared for elsewhere. Instead she nursed them for years and she never regretted it.

But increasingly they were uneasy together, and nervous tension accumulated. According to Mrs Shuttleworth, the Hon. May had been neglected by her Fabian parents in favour of political causes, and was very insecure – more so than either Jessie or Thelma, who had both come from orphanages (although Thelma may well have underestimated Jessie's insecurity). It has been suggested that Miss Ammon envied Jessie's intuitive way of relating to the teenagers: if one brought a gun to the Institute, for example, she would just ask for it and would be given it. In Spring 1958 Jessie heard that the Principal was very ill and she would have to take over, and also that one of their boys had been killed by a car at the Easter Holiday camp. She dreaded taking on the administration at the Institute, and began to realise how many of her male colleagues, in particular, wanted to usurp her: 'I've discovered how many are *itching* to wear my shoes – mostly the men!' She particularly dreaded a necessary visit to the boy's parents. In the event, that visit went surprisingly well, with the parents helping Jessie to cope, although she was very sick, 'inside heaving', in a nearby Ladies' toilet soon after. In June Miss Ammon was back, and gave Jessie 'a diamond and onyx ring, the loveliest gift I've ever had' as a thank-you.

The exact circumstances of Jessie's leaving Cowley in 1960 were unknown to her for many years, because all the nervous tension that made her sick each time she arrived to work with Miss Ammon climaxed in a party where Jessie got very drunk and made a scene. Only when Jessie and Thelma re-established communications in 1988 did the story come out. Jessie had got very drunk at a party on a Thames boat, and in very unladylike language had expressed all her accumulated frustrations:

> I had no memory of ever being on a boat on the Thames. But a memory came back to me of a boat beside a pier, and myself being helped out of it.
>
> I regret that. I would neither willingly nor deliberately have hurt Miss Ammon, despite the hiatus between our temperaments . . . I was so aware of our lack of empathy that many a time and oft I would arrive at Cowley and make *straight* for the nearest lavatory to be sick . . . caused by apprehensive awareness . . . I always felt the staff were aware of it, which naturally diminished what authoritative confidence I did have.

The sage, religious Thelma, now distinguished in scholarly Oxford circles because of her long friendship with Charles Williams, wrote often to Jessie from January 1988 onwards about failing to be reconciled to her life. Jessie confided in a draft letter that she had had 'a real crush' on Thelma's husband, Bertram, who never forgave her for the denouement on the river, but there is no sign that she sent it.

The Kessons had at least four London addresses in the '50s, but they stayed longest at the only house they ever owned. Johnnie was working for a builder, who put an opportunity his way, to buy a nice house in Woodside Road, Wood Green, where they lived from January 1953 until June 1962. They got it relatively cheaply, because there was a sitting tenant in an upstairs room. Johnnie's wage was never high, but as long as he was earning and Jessie was at Cowley, there were no real problems. It was from Woodside Road that the beautiful Avril, by now a model, was first married, at the age of 16. She had insisted on leaving school, and went to work at the New Lindsay Theatre for 10/- a week. Her parents, understandably, wanted the pair to wait, but Avril needed to assert her independence. Jessie and Johnnie did not go to the wedding, but lent their house to the newly-weds. Avril never saw her mother cry, but her father told her Jessie did so on that first wedding day. Avril and her husband were often abroad, so they had no permanent home, and were often with the Kessons, sharing the house, rubbing along amicably on the whole, according to a talk Jessie gave on 'Mothers-in-Law' on *Woman's Hour* in 1959. In it she admitted being jealous of her son-in-law and his closeness to her daughter. Writing to her old friend Chrissie Hubbard in Elgin, Jessie put a good face on it all:

> Avie got married a fortnight ago! She's very young, just seventeen, but she was very much in love. Her husband is a diver for the navy, a very good job. He's an extremely nice fellow. He goes to Hong Kong in June, for two years. I wanted them to wait for two years till he returned, but Avie wanted to go with him. So I gave them both my blessing. The wedding was very quiet. She did very well in London as a model. She's really a beautiful girl, although she was quite plain as a child.

In June 1957 Sharon, Jessie's first grandchild, was born. She was going to have great joy in her grandchildren.

But a combination of misfortunes was to make it necessary to sell the house. After Jessie left Cowley, she was working again at her old stand-by, Woolworth's, earning dramatically less. And Johnnie began to suffer very poor health. In August 1960 he suffered a severe coronary thrombosis and was in the North Middlesex Hospital for six weeks. In April 1962 he had another heart attack, and another six weeks in hospital. His earning potential was now, at best, lower than ever. Jessie wrote to Joanna Scott-Moncrieff at the BBC in October 1960:

I will have to give up this house, I could never pay for it on Woolworth's £6 4/-! But I was thinking out at 'Patch' in the back today, that perhaps I'll never own two apple trees and a pear tree again.

Always a great lover of flowers, she lamented those too, at length.

THE BBC

It was perhaps all very well for Jessie to write to Gordon Gildard, head of the Scottish BBC, saying she was off to London because she wanted to write for television and so wanted to see it first. At least Gildard knew a lot, by this time, about her quality, and the impact her best work could have: witness the stramash about *The Childhood* (1). But her campaign to take BBC London by storm was extraordinary, in different ways naive, ambitious, unrelenting, un-self-critical. It began with a bizarre handwritten letter, dated within days of her arrival in London, and addressed to 'The Head Producer, Television':

I've had many sound scripts broadcast in Scotland but I'm very keen on television; it can show people with a small, distinct, living clarity – or *should*, for I've never seen television. That's why I came to London. I've been here about a fortnight. I haven't, alas, seen television yet. The folk I know round the doors here can't afford it.

I must live while editors 'give careful consideration', so I took the first job I could get – ward-maid in a big hospital. I'm kept at it from 6.30 am – 3.30 pm, and my heart's not in it. I have such a love for creative dramatic work. Have you any job in Alexandra Place [*sic*]? I'd like to learn producing. If I had a training I think I'd make the grade.

Indeed, I'd be pleased to get a start serving in your canteen, if you have one, so that I could learn something of the craft in my time off.

Unsurprisingly, the letter was filed stamped 'Rejected 22 May 1951'.

Undaunted, Jessie sent in a version of *The Childhood* (2) on 28th May, which was described in an in-house memo as 'completely hopeless'. She filled in a form applying for work to the Variety Booking Manager in June, wanting to do comedy parts. She sent a script called *No Fixed Abode* to Dorothy Baker, Features Script Editor, who was to become a good friend and admired critic. Soon, Jessie was writing to her:

> I met Moray McLaren last week: what fun we had! He was staying at Savoy Grill, I was staying in a shed, which laughter heightened the afternoon for us both!

Like others later, Dorothy Baker soon found herself wrestling with script and writer on a project called *The Teens*. She sent a long internal memo full of criticisms, ending:

> When one adds all these criticisms up, it may seem ridiculous that I should be bothering you with such long and detailed remarks on a script that seems to go wrong everywhere. At the same time, there is a freshness, vigour and strength about it which escapes analysis and makes me feel that here is the raw material for a very good script.

Jessie was lucky indeed that so many members of BBC personnel, both in Scotland and in London, glimpsed the inherent quality of her work, messy and badly typed as it usually was, and had the patience and insight to work with her until the final scripts attained excellence. Eventually many scripts were accepted, both for the Scottish Home Service and for the Third Programme.

But she also kept on with the daft ideas, prompted no doubt both by her conviction that she had a gift for comedy in writing, such as she undoubtedly had in person, and her long-standing wish to get a full-time job in broadcasting. She seemed to have no idea about time and planning: in April 1953 she wrote to the Producer of *Mrs Dale's Diary*:

I read in *John Bull* that Lesley Wilson has temporarily given up creating Mrs Dale, to create her own baby. Do you think you could give me a trial to fill her place till her return?

Then in spring 1954 she tried Gale Pedrick, Script Editor, Variety. She hoped to poach Molly Weir from *Life with the Lyons*, and create a new series round her as a cinema usherette. Within a month she had another suggestion for Pedrick because she had read that *Educating Archie* was 'going off to come back in a different shape'. Of course, she had a shape in mind. In the inevitable internal memo Pedrick wrote: 'I have told her (tactfully) that if she is going to write for the Variety Department, she must bring herself to listen to a few Variety programmes (!)' He adds, 'She is really rather a difficult person to help.' Jessie's indignation that her inability to hear programmes because of her working night shifts and her fury that she be blamed for admitting this, knew no bounds. Variety gave up. Jessie did not.

She went on writing for Scotland, with an occasional short contribution to *Woman's Hour* in London, and in October 1956 got in touch again with both Dorothy Baker and Joanna Scott-Moncrieff, who had just been appointed Head of *Woman's Hour*. She told Baker about the job at Cowley and sent a short story for the Third Programme, and wrote more straightforwardly to Scott-Moncrieff, asking for work, and using the Cowley job experience as a carrot: 'Have you got anything you'd like me to do? That sounds very blunt!' Describing the Cowley job, she claimed it had given her 'diplomacy, poise, and so many things I previously lacked':

I thought I might get a chance to work with you, even in a humble capacity, so that I can learn the techniques of radio . . . If I cannot work with you permanently, I wonder I wonder if I could get a series, interviewing 'Women in the News', or 'Women out of the News'.

She was finally given a chance to take a tape-recorder and make her own Outside Broadcast on the well-known territory of Cowley in May 1960, and yearned to do only one per month, so that she might give up the 'day-job' and concentrate on writing.

Woman's Hour slowly began to prove a source of work. She gave talks on *Town and Country* and the impossibility of returning to the past, *We Can't Go Back* in 1957. Although she missed 'the community of country folk' and scenery, the basic reason is that she has found a place for herself in London. 'I can't go back, because a farm worker's wife had little part in the life of the community . . . I just longed to be the performer.' She said it was lovely to be better off, and buying their own house, and most of all, 'I have had the opportunity to use what talents I have.' This talk was chosen for a *Woman's Hour* anthology, to her great delight. She was appearing on *Woman's Hour* more often by 1959. She would achieve a grand ambition in 1960, when she was hired to work on *Woman's Hour* for six months, and had the time of her life, doing a second six months thereafter. Meanwhile Dorothy Baker's efforts on her behalf were aided by David Thomson, another North-East Scot based in BBC London. The two spent a long time trying to reduce the script of *The Mourners* to a workable state. This was Jessie's final contribution to the 'boarding-out' theme of *The Childhood* (1), and centred on the reactions of the different people, adult as well as children, to the death of the old woman no one truly mourned. It was finally broadcast in August 1958. But Thomson was privately writing to Baker, with insight:

> Dorothy, privately, I believe Jessie's only hope of writing another really good script is to start on her own life at the point where *The Childhood* ended. It is so dramatic and moving. I said this, but some ass has told her that a 'real writer' must be able to write about other people. My opinion is that she cannot, except in an autobiographical context. And what's wrong with that?'

He was partly right: Jessie had to write the sequel, to express the scenes of traumatic youth that Chatto did not want, and that up to now she had been unable to write fully for radio –

although *And That Unrest* had been a very moving account of the time in the Mental Hospital. Until she had achieved a coherent account of her young life after the Orphanage, she could not convince herself fully of her coherence as a person, from Elgin and Skene to Cornhill and Abriachan. Life became less disjointed after that, and the presence of Johnnie and the family testified to her reality and continuity as a person. Only after this account had been recognised would she be free enough to go on to achieve the wider range that was to come, instead of exclusively dwelling on the past. She wrote to Dorothy Baker in October 1957:

> Incidentally, you remember 'The Teens', and a script on mental illness you once read of mine? I have done them *completely* and *fully* now, not for radio, not for any medium, but for clarification. If you would like to read this, you are most welcome. I think it might interest you personally.

The past had to be written, and approved by understanding eyes, before Jessie could feel confident of it and of herself.

That hard-won self-confidence in turn produced a thoughtful non-autobiographical poem. The recognition of this final product of the '50s particularly gladdened Jessie's heart. This was a poem called 'Saturday Night', which she first sent to Peter Calvocoressi in 1959, for his amusement.

> Cry Hallelujah in Ansell Street
> For your souls' sake!
> Where old men cluster round its stalls
> Like sores brought out by heat.
> Fumbling with radio parts and second-hand tools
> For the joy of touch and feel
> Till in their attitudes so consecrated
> Junk takes on quality of instant worth
> Though not of value
> The old men seldom purchase.

No more than Mrs Eck appears to sell
Looming in large indifference
Amongst the cast off clothes
There's no demand, she reckons, for dead men's shoes
Or Ladies hand-me-downs
What with Italian suede and sailcloth
Going to their heads.
There's no demand for anything of quality
Mrs Eck confirms
Nodding assurance to herself distorted
In the Cut Price grocers' window
Along with OMO DOWN TODAY
And SUGAR SLASHED AGAIN.
Only the woman shouting Marguerites
Tenpence a Dozen!
Retains cool confidence
Cutting the last bunch down to Sixpence!
With fine finality
Knowing the day's full profit
Allows the night's last loss
And gathering herself together with paper and twine
Takes one last look and makes for Fred's
Fried Fish To Carry Home
Conscious the world is nigh its end.
Mr Breen firefull and hellsure
Startles the quiet.
Shouting a personal Christ. Walking the gutter
Beheld by Mr Breen himself, just forty years ago
At Manchester.
They don't believe him quite.
The folk who have hung around the stalls so long
Loving the lazy lie the leaping legend.
Laying the odds on miracles more complex,
Never in *Manchester*! Their minds protest
Keep Him in Galilee.
Dim memory urges walking the waves.
Amen! Amen!

> Gintsy, half-witted, follower of orators
> Street corner clown
> Breathless from chasing salvation's trumpet gleam
> Down half a lifetime
> Acclaims its glint again
> Amen!
> She might as well shout Fish!
> Live eels today!
> Drowning her cry, in the oyster chorus,
> Amen!
> The old men glance upon her without eyes.
> Pondering her image within their being.
> The strange familiar.
> Ah men.
> The new creed echoes round their orbit.
> Top Ten. Without commandment.
> And the saints cha cha-ing in
> Rocking their souls in the bosom of Abraham
> Confusing the ancients.
> Tom Dooley for the tree tomorrow,
> – 'Reckon you're going to die' –
> A kind of Christ.
>   Outwith poor Mr Breen's provincial prophecy
> – 'Hang down your head and cry' –

The indomitable Miss Bella Walker was urgent in appreciation:

> Broke my left arm just after I got your wonderful poem –
> 'Top ten and no commandment'. It has thrilled me more
> than anything you have written. It is a *complete interpretation*
> of life today – alas! Sending copies to Dr George McLeod,
> Sir Thomas Taylor, Sir George Waters. *Now collect your*
> *poems and publish them.*

So many people liked it that she submitted it to *New Poetry* on the
Third Programme. It was accepted, and broadcast on 23rd April

1960. When a cheque in payment arrived, she wrote again to Calvocoressi:

> You could have knocked me down *without* a feather! Ten pounds for poem – and me giving away the first fine careless rapture of it to noble firm of C&W for nowt! The thought now makes canny Scot in me come out in Goose Gogs!

But she signals very clearly that the above is mere badinage, and how much she values the understanding and support of Calvocoressi, and of Dorothy Baker, when she continues:

> But that isn't important. Dorothy rang to ask me to hear one of the other poems in some programme, which she read over the phone. I'm always moved, in a wondering, humble kind of way, because she does value my opinion, and shares hers with me. Then she read introduction to mine . . . 'with fine observation and *loving* irony'.
>
> And here is *core* of letter! She said all the poems in this programme deal with contemporary life. But in the main are gloomy, and have hate. But mine retains 'affection for and despite'. We had a long news about that. It seems to me that satire is like the hard ugly scab that forms over a sore. And, in a kind of way, protects that sore from the pain of exposure. In art, it's the pain of loving too much that one protects from exposure. Or at least I do, with satire. I feel too, that however hateful and uncongenial *reality* is, that one's spirit is only ever in peril of becoming wholly arid, when it ceases to have tears for the *idyll*. (That's surely a paradox?)

This seems to touch on a central belief of Jessie's, belief in 'the idyll', which she never fully articulated on paper. But it surfaced again the year before her death, in a letter to Alistair Campbell in Elgin, when she was discussing entries for a poetry competition and incidentally reminiscing about her past:

One of my greatest pleasures when I was a Producer on *Woman's Hour*, London, aeons ago, was my monthly feature 'Voices and Verses'. Sometimes I used living poets reading their work. Sometimes I sat in a cubicle, surrounded by the vast finest recordings of poetry in the world, listening and choosing from infinite treasures. It was always a popular programme, possibly because the human spirit needs the idyll.

The '50s had seen a slow increase in Talks material, plus *The Childhood* (2), and *Green Glass, Goblin*, about being Night Charge with the spastic girls, and the first broadcast of *And Barley Rigs*, the radio version of *Glitter of Mica*. Jessie had shown she *could* write on subjects other than her own early years, although that still often needed expression. The next decade would see more.

PUBLISHING

Since 1941 at least, Jessie had been, however sketchily, writing or trying to write a novel. Sometimes it was an early version of the novel which did turn out to be a classic, *The White Bird Passes*, which was finally published in 1958. Sometimes it was the Abriachan story, the one about the boarded-out children, which never, in fact, got published as a novel. It was a typescript of this manuscript, then entitled *The Hill*, that Christina Foyle, then Jessie's agent, sent to Chatto & Windus in 1954. Chatto had turned down *The Hill*, but had made some encouraging noises. Then the success of *The Childhood* (2) on radio was outstanding. It was repeated time after time, on the Third and Home Services. Jessie sensibly decided that her own story was perhaps the most appropriate for a first novel. In 1955, then, she wrote to the firm, offering the first part of *The White Bird Passes* and telling of a forthcoming broadcast she had recorded, about the Orphanage years. Chatto was a small 'hands-on' firm at this time. All the directors, Norah Smallwood, Ian Parsons, Cecil Day Lewis and Peter Calvocoressi, quickly got involved, and read and discussed various versions of the manuscript.

Again, Jessie was lucky in many ways. Her basic quality was detected, and the firm tried hard to help her, although, not being privy either to the events of her youth, or the labyrinthine reworkings the experiences had already undergone in magazine and radio, they were at a disadvantage. They could not know at the start how much Jessie's writing represented her own self-therapy, or how profoundly they could shake her by a casual suggestion.

Very soon, it was with Peter Calvocoressi that she generally corresponded. As she had done with some BBC producers, mostly male, both in Scotland and in London, she set about charming him with her letters. Peter Calvocoressi was to become in many ways her ideal of a man. What would he think about this, or say about that? she would demand of Avril. He was a gentleman in every sense, with a backgound of Eton and Balliol and the Bar, but no hint of the kind of understated 'effortless superiority' that Jessie would have detected in seconds. He was very handsome, and extremely responsive to literature. Scholar, historian of world affairs and publisher, he treated her with exemplary sensitivity always. Long after he left Chatto, they remained in touch. For years, until about 1983, they would meet for lunch every three months. He wrote to me in 1996:

> Besides being exceptionally talented as a writer she was an exceptional person; although, having said that, I find it hard – and have always found it hard – to sort out into words what made her so different and compelling. I lost touch with her soon after my wife and I left London some 13 years ago and my visits to London slackened off. I constantly regretted letting this happen but did little or nothing about it . . . It was one of the peculiarities of our friendship that we met almost exclusively for lunches in pubs – more drink than food, although she forced me to eat as well as drink – and just the two of us.

The efforts to complete *The White Bird* were terribly difficult. Often author and publishers were at odds, and failed to communicate satisfactorily, and it all took time, which in Jessie's case was exceptionally precious and hard-won. The publishers liked the Elgin section, but the Orphanage less so. They went on to suggest she write more of the story: what happened to Janie next? But when Jessie rather unhappily acquiesced and worked hard to produce more, they did not like the new parts, and felt a profound discontinuity between the first part and the rest. In the end they offered to publish Elgin-and-cut-down-Orphanage, and forget the rest. Unsurprisingly, Jessie was very unhappy: she would not know what to do with the new material she had worked so hard on. One wonders if this was a major reason why she shied so determinedly at every later suggestion of autobiography. On a more mundane level, it very probably explains why Jessie was so amenable to David Thomson's suggestion for a radio sequel to *The Childhood* (2), and was able to produce it relatively quickly: the material had been thoroughly prepared. In the end, Chatto said Jessie should feel free to try another publisher with her whole manuscript, but if she was unsuccessful, they would happily publish the childhood sections. Jessie was understandably fragile by this time, and once or twice flared up at imagined snubs. She wrote to Calvocoressi after he had made peace after one such misunderstanding:

> I feel if I had just *spoken* to you personally for five minutes, it would have been all clear, but publishers seem very remote people, and I have never dealt 'remote control' before. I had the feeling I was a bear sniffing the wild wastes, and you had all gone under the ice floes – a kind of Magoo myself, peering bewildered. The thought made me laugh, that's how I now think of publishers. But you are very nice ones despite the ice floes.

Things settled down, her correspondence with Calvocoressi was renewed, and even before the publication of *The White Bird*, she was getting into the writing of her second novel, *Glitter of Mica*, then called *To Cashel I'm Going*, and writing 'dry-runs' of it for radio, with some success. By July she was writing to Calvocoressi that the character of Sue Tatt was trying to take over the story, and they were having quite a struggle.

Meanwhile, reviews of *The White Bird* were excellent, on the whole. Compton Mackenzie had said 'Frank, honest and deeply moving'. In the *Aberdeen University Review*, Nan Shepherd wrote of the 'bubbling immediacy' of her voice, and the 'terrible authenticity' of the book, and of the artistry of her epiphanies. On the Scottish Home Service Alex Scott had headed a most appreciative panel of reviewers, and Calvocoressi wrote that the book 'had a wonderful press, and in particular a rave review by Pitman in the *Sunday Express* . . . We have high hopes that she will go far.' Robert Pitman had praised the novel for half a page, calling it 'a tender and tragic story', and predicting great sales. There was a host of newspaper reviews, with headlines like 'The little girl from the slums', 'The story of an Elgin waif', 'Jessie Kesson's Slum Heroine', 'A lass in Morayshire found it tough', and 'Childhood perception is recaptured in first novel'. Only the *Daily Record and Mail* missed the point totally, with its infamous banner headline: 'Daughter Shows No Shame'.

It is hard, looking back, to see why *The White Bird*, which was reprinted soon after publication, was to go virtually into hibernation for some 20 years, until Michael Radford's BBC film of 1980 and Paul Harris's new edition of the novel relaunched it on a more appreciative world. Certainly there is evidence in the files of Calvocoressi trying to get more than one firm to take it on as a paperback, but he was unsuccessful. Like all Jessie's prose works, it was unfashionably short. But rarely has a book with such an enthusiastic press sunk with so little trace. Best-selling paperbacks in 1958 included Alan Sillitoe's *Saturday Night and Sunday Morning*, Leon Uris's *Exodus* and Ian Fleming's *Dr No*, but I am not arguing about best-sellers. Angus Wilson's fine novel *The Middle Age of Mrs Eliot* received reviews similar to Jessie's in admiration, but it did quite well enough in paperback.

Chatto was a firm that was literary, old-fashioned, and averse to sensationalism: none of this helped. It also had directors with impeccable taste, but that did not help the marketing. Perhaps if Calvocoressi had not left Chatto in 1965, Jessie's books might have been more effectively marketed, and might have reached paperback. As it was, her books were in enormous demand in libraries, but she was not to become a fully recognised writer until 1980, and then not directly because of her written fiction, but through Michael Radford's adaptation of *The White Bird* for television.

Chapter Nine: The Sixties

The '60s started badly for the Kessons. Jessie had lost the job at Cowley, and what seemed to her a princely salary. She went back to Cowley to make a radio discussion programme with teenagers, doing the interviewing herself, and that went out on 30th May 1960. But jobs refused to fall into place. She told Joanna Scott-Moncrieff:

> My book [*Glitter of Mica*] is still not completed . And I need a regular wage in order to have the peace of mind necessary to complete it. I applied for a job as 'Motivation Interviewer'; was chosen as one of the 'Possibles for training'. But when I saw the other 'Possibles' I felt suddenly terrified. One never does see oneself! Middle-aged. Hearty. 'All girls together.' And 'Isn't it fun?!' Brandishing sheets of typewritten questions to be fired at an unwary public. Same public nicely classified on same sheets. Working class. Middle class, etc. Felt we would all have done fine in South Africa. I realised it was not for me. Said so to incredulous 'Field Officer', who seemed to think the job was God's Gift to indigent ladies!

She hoped, she said, for a job at *Woman's Hour*, offering to answer readers' letters or do recordings, on the grounds of David Thomson's praise for her Cowley teenagers. But nothing came of that.

In July 1960 she wrote to Peter Calvocoressi about her current job, which she loathed. She had been recruited into some kind of 'Park Police', but her accounts are more funny than informative:

> Spend one half of day looking under trees for 'Fungus', which I can't distinguish from foliage. So many deceptive

things spring from trees. The other half of day, peering under bushes, and in 'likely' places for instances of 'Indecent Exposure'.

She could not acquire the necessary relish, she declared. She went back to her old stand-by, Woolworth's. But things were going to get a great deal worse. By October she was writing to Miss Scott-Moncrieff:

> It has been a gey dark night of the spirit. Johnnie had a severe coronary thrombosis two months ago; was on the Danger List for weeks; is recovering now, a bit: but will not again be the bread-winner. Previously he had never had a day's illness in his life! It was a deep shock. I am working in my local Woolworth's, which keeps me and Kenneth fine and meant I could visit Johnnie in hospital every night.

She foresees the need to sell the only house they had ever aspired to own. They had to sell in 1963.

In June 1962 he had another major heart attack. Jessie, in despair, wrote to the BBC, who were to repeat two plays, asking if she could get her fees in advance:

> I am anxious. My husband has been ill since the beginning of April, and I have been unable to go to work. My mortgage is now overdue . . . Could I *possibly* get my fee in advance to meet my rates and mortgage. And if I can, do you think I could get it soon, as I am overwhelmed with worry.

Most exceptionally, they agreed.

But Johnnie's state of health, sometimes his nursing needs, and Jessie's earning power were to be constant worries from now on, although Avril has suggested Jessie was somewhat overanxious and overprotective. When he came out of hospital, she was nursing Johnnie at home, and meantime at work nursing a very old lady of means, she told Calvocoressi in 1962, and it is easy to detect a degree of desperation here:

I am torn between looking after Johnnie and an old (90) blind and mental lady in Hampstead: Johnnie for love, and the t'other for £3 – my God, it's earned! My weekends – 24 hours solid – are spent enclosed with her in a room where no amount of disinfectant cancels the smell of old age and urine, handling the unspeakable with that awful progression of minutes on my hands. It's like walking a tight-rope, seeing to her wants and yet not upsetting the downstairs staff by her needs. And of course the old lady's ever varying humours can make or break each second of my day. I veer in her eyes between being 'a jewel' and 'a perfect fool' – the only kind of perfection I seem to have reached! . . .

But there is a world of pain in me. I can never help thinking of other olds I have known who would have given a mort for a tithe of the care this old lady gets and the material comforts she can afford, and the worst bit of it is, I think of the *infinite* patience her £3 buys from me, when I have not that patience with Johnnie, who is equally sick, dear to me, and by his nature *far* more worthy of it.

He had an attack last night, but has slept well today. I go to see him heart in the mouth, listening for his breathing. He was so still, his face in profile, drawn and fine. I had never seen him so. And I knew *surely* I had in life seen how he would look in death, my very dear. We are not by our natures ever able to demonstrate the true depths of our caring, that's the worst of it: there are no words. Except that I'm going to try my best to have more patience.

According to Avril again, Johnnie in a relatively short time regained his former good health, and after 1962 remained in full employment until his retirement in 1970/71. He was working with bill-posting for London Transport Underground, although never earning a great deal. Jessie agonised over his health after his retirement when they went to Scotland and he undertook light maintenance work on a farm, and she stopped him. Perhaps she never recovered from the shock of the two major heart attacks and the possibility of losing him. Her dependence on his quiet presence was greater than many people realised: he had been the only dependable, lasting rock in her life. He was certainly well enough to work long after official retirement when they returned from Scotland. Jessie set up two Abbeyfield old people's homes in 1975–76, and Avril records that he helped her full time in that period. Until about 1990, when he was 85, he remained in good health, apart from worsening deafness, which was a cause of real frustration to them both.

Money was a permanent worry. When in September 1962 Peter Calvocoressi offered Jessie a copy of the contract for *Glitter of Mica,* she replied she wasn't bothered about the contract, but she *would* like the rest of the advance: 'Do you think you might charm the cashier into willingness and eagerness?' Apologising for his lack of thought, he did so at once.

Jessie's health suffered too. She had been a heavy smoker since Skye, and years of hard, hard jobs and the constant attempts to keep up with her writing took their toll. She was liable to bronchitis, and several (undated!) letters report she has been staying with Avril to convalesce. In the mid-'60s she went into 'retreat' for a bit, exhausted by the years of constant pressure. Typically, though, she found her own way out by taking up a new, less physically strenuous regime of life-modelling, and typically, when Stewart Conn pursued her with pleas for her writing, she responded. But they were painful and muddled years, the '60s. There were so many house moves, so many jobs, fewer letters than before and rarely dates on any of them. I cannot pretend that this account is complete or coherent.

Jessie made entertaining letters out of her endless pursuit of post-Cowley jobs, but it was a depressing process being a spy in the park, or failing a speed test for a news typist post, or being interviewed by a hearty lady for a post as 'Motivation Interviewer'. She was thrilled by an offer from a newspaper of a weekly column at 15 guineas, until she discovered what the Editor had in mind:

> Column? *Up in Air*! Not for 50 guineas per 750 did I want to write the type of thing Editor wanted me to do. Said so, though, in fairness to him. Would rather work in

Woolworth's for Christmas Rush – probably will have to anyhow! Old stand-by firm of mine, Woolworth's – *always* seem to get Paint and Polish counter! Tide, Daz and Omo – probably because I've got strength to tear them open – the cartons, I mean.

Sometimes a rush of things happened at once, and things looked better. Working at Woolworth's, she wrote to tell Calvocoressi in December 1960:

It looks as though Jessie Kesson may not be lost to thee and thine! All kinds of things happened to me at once . . . Ellis Powell, 'Mrs Dale' of *Mrs Dale's Diary*, a crony of mine, has received innumerable requests for her *own* Diary, from the Glossies, but has never consented, since she wanted this written by someone she knew well; and who was, *her* description, 'a good writer'. *Me* she has chose! I'd far rather do this, and keep my house, than work with any kind of Social Workers again. Then Edinburgh BBC sent me a telegram requesting recordings for their magazine programme *Scope*. Then the Scottish press sent me two books to review. *Is Chastity Outmoded?* Dr Eustace Chesser. And *A Law For The Rich*. Reforms in Abortion!!! Why these particular themes should land to me, I puzzle . . . Then BBC commissioned a new play for Third. And last, but not least in interest to you, I am sure, Third are broadcasting a series of programmes, which they consider are their Classics. The dramatised version of *White Bird* [*The Childhood* (2)] is being remounted and reproduced on 17th January. This will be the *seventh* time it had been broadcast . . . I still thrive and flourish in Woolworth's, how good they all are to me. And what fun we have.

The Diary did not happen. No more book reviews were requested. Security was not in sight.

With all that was going on, Jessie was still alive to the needs of old friends. Chrissie Hubbard, her old friend and drinking crony from Elgin, decided to come down to London in 1962 to see whether she wanted to live and work there. Jessie insisted on offering her a semi-permanent home. She stayed at the house in Wood Green, where Avril and the six-year-old Sharon were also staying, for several weeks before moving on, and stayed in London about a year before deciding Elgin was a better option for her. They remained good friends, and it was Chrissie who was startled, some years later, by Jessie walking around in her (Chrissie's) house naked, apparently unaware of windows and possible spectators: an unselfconsciousness born of long experience of nude modelling!

But Jessie was always able to put up a brave front in public. When in summer 1963 they went on holiday to the North-East, to Elgin and Aberdeen, she gave an interview to Helen Fisher of the *Press and Journal,* which offers a snapshot of a happy and successful extended family.

> Now they live in a house at Palmers Green where Jessie takes time off from writing and broadcasting to cook and clean the house – 'I've never employed help in my life – thank goodness I like cooking! – with their son Kenneth who works with a jewel importer at Hatton Garden, and their daughter – 'our beautiful daughter', who is a fashion model and is married to a deep sea diver and has a six-year-old daughter. When you hear this, and look at bright-faced lithesome Jessie, it's incredible to think she's a grannie!

Clearly Jessie continued to press for a job at the BBC, with no luck after 1961. Nan Shepherd wrote that she had done a reference for her in December 1962, but felt the post was 'less your type of work'. And in January 1965 Peter Calvocoressi wrote to her, clearly in response to her distress:

> I'm off to Geneva this week for the rest of the month. The *Woman's Hour* story is most depressing. It's such a terrible shame and waste of spirit. You deserve so much better from fate and the BBC. But at any rate the letters are a comfort . . . The easiest thing about the money (and it is

perfectly easy) is the enclosed cheque. I'll sort it all out when I get back. It's no good acknowledging because I shall be gone. Well, I hope 1965 is going to be a great deal better than its predecessor.

The Kessons' home in Woodside Road, Wood Green, was sold in 1963, but Jessie hardly had time to miss it. She wrote despondently to Joanna Scott-Moncrieff from the new address in Green Lanes, Palmers Green:

We gave up '46' with a world of reluctance, since it meant so much to us. Strangely, but mercifully, I don't feel it and haven't missed it, not even when I pass it on the bus. I have grown a shell of cynicism I think: I don't feel anything much, except, as always, for writing.

The next move, in early 1966, was the real retreat. When Stewart Conn at last tracked her down, because radio actress Effie Morrison had her address in Rosebery Road, Edmonton, Jessie replied:

Do forgive me for being so long in replying. The fact is I 'opted out' for a year. I needed to refuel, to do something entirely different. So I took up modelling. To my own surprise, got more work than the day held hours enough to do it in! No one at all, not even my publisher, had my new address. One evening I went to sit for a head sculpture; a BBC producer was there, knew me and that was that.

Subsequent letters to Conn in a scrawl miles from her usual neat script confirm that she really was pushed. She says she had no free time except at both their lunch times, and late at night, and certainly one surviving contract for Hornsey College of Art has her down on Thursdays '9.30–1, 2–3.30, 4–6pm'. She may be exaggerating the load somewhat, but with the weekend for housework and shopping, it seems fair to claim, 'I have only a few hours on Sunday to call my own.'

It was Avril who started the nude modelling. She had been posing for six weeks before her mother got wind of it, and there was a major scene. But Jessie was never one to waste a good idea, and soon she followed suit, and loved the work. The story 'Life Model' in *Where the Apple Ripens* is Jessie's most finished account of this experience, but she was very funny and interesting about it when we interviewed her in 1985.

The one job I got towards the end, but when I was a good bit younger, was the job I loved best of all. It was the only job ever I got paid for in my life for standin' or sittin' and thinkin' my ain thochts. I became a Life Model at the Art School . . . For aboot ten years and a very good model was I! In the sense of reliable, could always stand in poses, I could, and very few could . . . It was well paid. You'd no tax, you got your bus fares and a'thing. And, it was the kind of job when you went home at nicht ye didna take it wi ye, and ye didna' worry aboot it. I could concentrate on my writing, because I had no worry.[1]

There follows the story of the fellow model who finds the students pass out with excitement when she poses. So off and on this was one of Jessie's occupations for a decade. In interviews, and in the 'Life Model' story, she told her secret: when she had recited The Lord's Prayer under her breath three times, very slowly, she knew her hour was up. And she elaborated on her experiences to Dr William Donaldson in the '80s:

After years of modelling I know London well; all the different Art Schools, Inner and Outer London; from St Martin's Charing Cross Road, to Richmond, to Camberwell Green. Fellow model there was Quentin Crisp of *Naked Civil Servant* fame. The students couldn't stand him – NOT because of his homosexuality, but because he took the most difficult twisted poses. Fine, except that physically he couldn't hold such poses long, whereas I could stand immobile, foursquare, day long.

I did a lot of sculpture, mostly reclining poses which I didn't like, roasting me with the electric fires round me.

The tutor exhorting the students, 'Touch her. Measure. Don't be afraid.' Or gather them all round me, 'describing' me. 'Look at that great plane – at that roundness! By the time he'd finished 'describing' I felt as big as an elephant, and could hardly get myself to my feet.

I liked 'head' sculpture; much measuring, much physical 'touching', almost like gentle massage. Had my talent been Art, how much I could have learned.

In 1966 or '67, Jessie took on a new job, in Muswell Hill, one of the hardest ever. She gave an account to Dorothy Baker in 1968, in between making wistful enquiries about work, past and present:

I'm just recovering from a sharp attack of bronchitis. I find myself fairly exhausted after more than a year of night duty, and sometimes depressed. For there is no end product to this work, except the end itself, death. I know this, but worse, my old people know this, and the old are so demanding, and so selfish. I've seen them watch me struggle to lift a large woman off the floor, and then harry me for 'a drink', 'fill my hot water bottle', etc. And yet, I don't know what it is, but I find satisfaction in the work, although nearly all of it is uncongenial. But then 'women have always been in at the beginning of life, and at its end, doing the unspeakable things with their hands.'[2] If I did nothing else at all, at the last it's usually only myself with them when they die. I often think, this is perhaps the heart of the job: they know me, and in the last instants I take the place of their families who *aren't* there.

She wrote in the same vein to Molly Lee, who had been made Editor of *Woman's Hour*. She had written a short talk, which was used, but she was looking for more substantial work:

This is one of the most modern, purpose-built Council Homes for the old, but if you sent a producer along, I don't think they might get as much as I would, from the old people. I mean the right down-to-earth ordinary day thing. I'd like very much to do a small programme, with recorded illustrations. I actually wrote a short talk, but after one of the new old ladies was finding her way about the building, and said to me, 'I just cannot find my way in this Hotel.' I thought the old folks' *own* reactions would much better describe the difference between old people's homes now, from then.

For once, the next 'house move' was for a pleasant reason, although for someone working permanent night shift, no small undertaking. Here is how she described it to Stewart Conn, apologising the while because the move had necessarily interrupted her corrections for *Friday*.

A friend of mine, BBC Admin, had a lovely large flat, and I had a true appreciation of it. She had true appreciation of a Regency house in Richmond. She always said, 'When I get my Regency house you can have my flat' – the kind of thing one says, and the other accepts, and both realise it will never happen!

This time it did! Within a week, she found the house she'd been looking for, and all negotiations with the Agent for the flat for me completed in a week. And flitted. But you can imagine it didn't leave me a second, and I never lost one hour's work, but I *do* feel done in!

The new flat was at Lakeside Road, Palmers Green. It is not clear why they moved again, in another year or so, back to a different address in Green Lanes, but on the whole things were beginning to look up.

This was confirmed in 1968 by a splendid coincidence. Cecil Day Lewis had asked her permission to apply for an Arts Council grant to give her some time to write. Lo and behold, in the same year, a bursary from the Scottish Arts Council! The money meant a lot, but the endorsement meant even more, as she wrote to Stewart Conn:

> I have never suffered from greed – immediately sent the Scottish Arts Council papers to him [Day Lewis], out of courtesy, saying that I didn't want *two*. Would he mind if I accepted the *Scottish* one, as I felt a bit more justified, and besides I have no ambitions, nor I think the ability, to be *other* than a Scottish interpreter, which is enough in itself. . . And dearly as I love Scotland, felt warmed that England also cared.

The last years of the '60s saw Jessie working at a day centre for mentally handicapped Jewish girls in the Borough of Barnet. She was described as 'instructor in social competence'. She told Hugh Macpherson:

> I also worked for five years with mentally handicapped teenagers. It was an experiment, it wasn't the usual thing, in a very select part of London, Mill Hill. I remember the present that one of the classes gave me was a tape recording of all the poems and pieces that I'd taught them.[3]

This, presumably, was where she made contact with the London chief of Mental Health who was to provide a glowing reference for Tynepark.

The family, meantime, was blossoming. Kenneth left home to marry in the late '60s, and produced Jessie's first and only grandson, and Avril and her new partner Bill Wilbourne were living abroad in great luxury, as Jessie boasted to all and sundry. She was often aware of her convoluted feelings about money and class, just as she admitted that the Devon adventure had been partly prompted by the notion of farm workers becoming farmers in their own right. She confided to Dorothy Baker, in a letter catching up with the news in 1968:

Kenneth is a father to Graham, named after his favourite
historical character, that Covenanter, the Marquis of Mont-
rose, 'Bonny Dundee', a dear baby, with his mother's red hair
and Ken's wide grin.

Avril's little girl Sharon left home on Friday for Public
School in Sussex, and Avie misses her. So do I, but she
seems to love it already, and although my *basic* feeling was
sadness, my other feelings were mixed. I thought, as we
motored down in Avie's new E Type Jaguar, 'Nice. Public
School and all. A far cry from "the Lane".' I do wish I was
rational, and not torn between a feeling of snobbery, and a
feeling of inferiority: I suffer from both!

Jessie herself, of course, had sent Avril to a private fee-paying
primary school, which she certainly could not afford: her attitudes
had always been complex.

THE BBC

David Thomson had been right (previous chapter) when he said
Jessie should write the sequel to *The Childhood* (2). Although her
life was full of often desperate worries from 1959 to 1962, worries
over Johnnie's illnesses, her own ability to keep them afloat
financially, and the for once rewarded attempts to get a job with
the BBC on *Woman's Hour*, somehow she went on creating
important work that crystallised much of her traumatic past for
her. She wrote to Thomson in June 1961, after they'd had a long
talk, with a synopsis for *Somewhere Beyond*. In it she stressed the
difficulties of fitting in when she went to Aberdeen after Auchronie. Grammar School clashed with living in a Home for
Working Girls on Probation. The Hostel girls were 'the antithesis
of all the Orphanage had trained me to be': the Matron never
forgave her for not being on probation, and for getting more
education. And at school 'the same kind of problem confronted
me'. After Auchronie, 'I was at one and the same time older and
younger than the Grammar School girls'. She was flustered on
occasional visits to her classmates' homes by salad servers and

napkins: she could not take part in their tennis-dominated talk. By this time, Jessie's grasp of her own past situation was marvellous. And when she got to the Mental Hospital, she summed up the main four 'things' with skill and clarity, although her use of 'one' in this section may betray lingering self-consciousness:

> 1) The awful effort of holding on to sanity: that is being more normal than one would ever be 'outside': afraid to laugh too much lest one should be reported as 'Hilarious', afraid to be normally sad, lest one should be reported as 'Depressed'.
> 2) The loss of one's identity with the loss of one's own clothes, and people speaking at you, or to you, rather than with you.
> 3) The blankness when one met anyone from 'Outside' – workmen in Hospital grounds, staring at each other with curiosity, but without contact.
> 4) The never dying hope that one *would* get out, and yet the many times when one resigned one's self to the fact one would never get out were easier to bear! You can start to make a life when you accept it, even if it's half a life. It's uncertainty that is the corroder of spirit.

Somewhere Beyond was broadcast first in February 1962, and like *The Childhood* (2) it was repeated many times. It is hard to credit that its author, subject to all the strains and stresses of her early life, ever struggled to such a coherent account, which reduces the experiences to their essentials. Like its predecessor, it became a classic of radio drama. It is finely written, in two parts, reflecting the uneasy time the multiple misfit spent in the Aberdeen Hostel, with silent hostility from the Matron, and with a hint of criticism of Miss Bella ('Miss Erskine'), who connives in the matter of the girl's becoming a 'voluntary' patient, presumably knowing, as the girl certainly did not, that she would not be able to 'volunteer' to leave in the same way. Part One most economically leads up to the scene where Ginny experiments on Mary's appearance with borrowed clothes and heavy make-up, and Matron's reaction causes Mary to attack her, with the inevitable consequences. *And That Unrest* (1951) had been a fine and moving account of Mental Hospital and Mary's feelings, but now this is integrated physically and emotionally into her whole disturbed and disruptive experience, so that a late scene, with two friendly nurses getting Mary ready for the Patients' Christmas Dance, forms a mutedly hopeful balance for the previous catastrophic one. Jessie's favourite technique of using an older Narrator to reflect on the experience of her younger self, is particularly successful here: it stresses the young Mary's passivity, her being 'patient'.

Woman's Hour had been one of the programmes specially targeted when Jessie began her assault on BBC London. She had accepted whatever they offered her in the '50s, theatre reviewing; contributions to talks series like *Something that Shocks Me*, *My Strangest Dream*, *Learned from Life* and *The Day I Met Myself*. Despite all her worries over Johnnie, the two periods of six months when she worked for Talks were extremely happy. Joanna Scott-Moncrieff had been most sympathetic when she heard of Johnnie's coronary thrombosis in October 1960, and wrote suggesting all sorts of ways Jessie could do odd jobs for *Woman's Hour*, such as 'a light-hearted account from your side of the counter [at Woolworth's] of the customers you see'. But she knew of Jessie's ambition to work for the programme, and after another letter in which Jessie offered to answer readers' letters and learn to produce, at last in April 1961 Jessie was offered 'a temporary engagement as a part-time Producer in Talks Division'. Her work would include 'written and spoken contributions to *Woman's Hour* . . . for 2½ days a week.' The first engagement was from 24th April to 15th July 1961. She was still there in September, when Scott-Moncrieff wrote to confirm that the BBC was 'unlikely to extend' her contract much after the end of the year: 'we like to ring the changes'. In October, she wrote to Scotland in search of a job, but there were no vacancies. And in 1962 Nan Shepherd wrote that she had done a reference for Jessie for a BBC job, although it hadn't sounded Jessie's kind of thing.

Jessie continued to do whatever she was offered while on contract, as she learned as much as possible about production,

doing a live interview with Miss America 1960, and giving talks
about women's magazines' Christmas suggestions, the first time
she had a baby, and her happiest Christmas ever. But she had a
desire to offer listeners sterner stuff, and this manifested itself in
two series she created for the programme. *Twentieth Century
Women*, the second of these, does not survive, because it was
never exactly written. Jessie described the Plan to Peter Calvocoressi:

> in my new contract I'm doing *Twentieth Century Women*
> ('Grey Eminences') . Means about three days only in BBC.
> One to lunch the 'Eminence' – nice, this. Two to absorb the
> essence and compile the questions for the Interviewer, give it
> form of course, and Three to produce the feature. The first
> goes on Sunday, 8th April – Freda Gwilliam; the second
> Viscountess Davison MP; third, Leila Rendall of Caldecott
> Community.

She hoped to include one of her personal heroines, Victoria
Sackville-West – 'My goodness I *have* been lucky.'

Asides in various letters show how Jessie particularly admired
and longed to emulate writers such as Iris Murdoch, Muriel
Spark, Elspeth Davie, Kathleen Raine and Virginia Woolf. She
had a free choice of subjects in the series, *Glimpses of Great
Women*, broadcast in 1961. It was very successful, and was
repeated twice in 1962, on *Woman's Hour* and *Home for the
Day*. Here, the choice of subjects was her own. This, and her
treatments where the scripts survive, tell us a great deal about her
fundamental beliefs and aspirations as a woman artist, and also
about her extraordinarily wide range of reading, in an already
impossibly full life. Her choices were Emily Brontë, Marie
Curie, Dame Nellie Melba, Mary Slessor, Anna Pavlova and
George Eliot. None of these is most famed for domestic virtues,
or for motherhood, although Curie, like Jessie, had two children.
In view of what we know about Jessie's early life and aspirations,
it is fascinating to see what she stressed in these 10- or 12-
minute 'glimpses', both what she wrote, and her selection of

material and quotation. There is a degree of implicit identification with the subject in every case.

Emily Brontë was firstly 'motherless'. With her siblings she shared a life of the imagination, but she went further into Gondal. Like Jessie, she was intensely identified with the countryside, and aspired above all to poetry. A (male) teacher asserted, 'She should have been a man. Her strong imperious will would never have been daunted by opposition or difficulty.' (Jessie always wanted to write as well as a man, and to be thought of in this way, and much admired George Sand.) When Charlotte discovered Emily's poems, she wrote, 'Something more than surprise seized me . . . a deep conviction that these were not common effusions, not at all like the poetry women generally write.' The script closes with Charlotte's words:

> I have never seen her parallel in anything. Stronger than a man, simpler than a child. Her nature stood alone.

Marie Curie, Jessie told us in interview, was the subject she had chosen to write the pageant for the Elgin Townswomen's Guild that brought her the £20 that allowed her to venture forth to London in 1951.[4] In 1961, it is instructive to see what moved her to tackle the subject again. She begins with nationalism, with Marie's discovery as a girl that she is a Pole living unfree under Russian rule. But to counter that, perhaps like Jessie at Skene, Marie discovers that she loves school, and she remains attracted to the 'austere discipline' of classroom and, later, laboratory. She has infinite determination in a life of much self-sacrifice (delaying her own higher education until she has worked for years to ensure it for two siblings). 'We must believe we are gifted for something. And that this thing, at whatever cost, must be obtained.' She resolved that one must 'never let oneself be beaten down by persons or events'. Unlike Jessie, she found a soulmate, a 'marriage of true minds' in Pierre Curie, but together they underwent 'heroic' years of work and poverty in their search for radium. Humanity needs 'dreamers' who will make 'tenacious efforts' without regard for material gain.

'Tenacious efforts' were also made by Melba, who struggled against her Scottish Presbyterian father to make a career in singing, only to fail conspicuously at her first appearance at Covent Garden. But when she had to work she did so with dedication, and when she took a new name it was from her native Melbourne (like Ness from Inverness), and for Jessie her life is summed up in the phrase 'pathos in austerity'. Her eventual success was threatened by public rumours and obloquy. She almost gave up, but read 'a book of short biographies of great men': identifying with them, seeing 'the persecution of those who had made a name for themselves', she continued to sing. No hint in Jessie's 'glimpse' of any other personal life. A fragment of report from the Audience Research Department says,

> The item that aroused most enthusiasm was that concerning Dame Nellie Melba, which was given a rating well above average. The recordings of Melba's voice were particularly welcomed, and the spoken part of the programme was also thought exceptionally interesting. Here was a woman who was indeed worthy of inclusion in the series Glimpses of Great Women, listeners said, and many regretted that the item was not longer.

Sadly, only the introduction to 'Mary Slessor' survives, telling of her birth in Aberdeen in 1848, and her early work in Dundee, before setting off for Calabar as a Missionary Teacher. But Audience Research says it did 'outstandingly well':

> Two or three listeners said they had no interest whatever in missionaries or took the view that 'good' women are invariably dull and tedious to hear about, but the vast majority were greatly impressed by the story of Mary Slessor's humble beginnings in a Dundee slum, her drunken father, and her tremendous courage in being the first woman to penetrate the unexplored hinterland of West Africa. This, said listeners, was a wonderful story about a fine character; it was beautifully presented, really bringing

Mary Slessor to life, and made an inspiring end to the programme.

Of 'Pavlova' nothing survives. But the subject of all of these *Great Women* who was nearest Jessie's heart was probably George Eliot: five years later, she still longed to expand her treatment to a full length programme.

Her sense of identification with Mary Ann Evans is clearly strong. She is understandably moved by her childhood, and its transmutation into that of Maggie Tulliver in *The Mill on the Floss*:

> The vision began for her, as it does for all great creative artists, with the beginning of her own consciousness, as a small girl at home with her family in the countryside of the Midlands. Time and imagination were to transmute that home for *us*.

Jessie's own 'ootlin' status, and one suggested title for the never-to-be-written autobiography, *A Different Drum*, help her to respond to Mary Ann's suspicion even in childhood, 'that she might be a plant of an alien species'. The Narrator comments,

> Like all children who earn the disapproval of those whom they love, by faults in their nature rather than in their conduct, Mary Ann Evans longed for approval.

When she was deprived of emotional satisfaction, 'books became her passion and means of escape'. Jessie stresses her need for approval, which she so clearly shared, when Evans talked of 'my besetting sin . . . my ambition, and a desire insatiable for the esteem of my fellow creatures'.

This need for approval led Mary Ann to adopt the religious beliefs of her supportive schoolmistresses, until a crisis of intellect and faith forced her painfully to renounce a religion 'based on the hope of future rewards'. This enhanced her loneliness. She experienced 'a depression of the mind's eye', and felt 'alive to

what is certainly a fact – that I am alone in the world . . . I have no
one with whom I can pour out my soul, no one with the same
yearnings, the same temptations, the same delights as myself.' At
least she had not made the mistake of marrying before finding her
desire. Her eventual relationship with George Lewes is described,
perhaps wistfully, as 'a marriage of true minds'.

Jessie made friends at the BBC. For the first time she was in the
company of like minds, and she blossomed. She and Avril loved to
turn up at the 'BBC pub', the Stag's Head, and sit drinking and
talking to Dorothy Baker, David Thomson, Lawrence Gwilliam,
Burns Singer and sometimes even Dylan Thomas, undergoing
what he used to term 'capital punishment'. She was overcome by
the fuss made of her when she left *Woman's Hour*. To Calvocoressi
she wrote:

> The end of my *W.H.* was marked with the loveliest imagi-
> native things I've ever had: a bottle of 'the Water of life' from
> my Rosemary; *The Land* (Sackville-West) from Genevieve
> who worked with me on the features, a beautiful briefcase
> from producers and secretaries: a sausage roll, gratis, from
> Renee, trolley girl – and of course a new contract!

There is a noticeable gap in Jessie's working with the BBC in any
capacity, after she left *Woman's Hour*. *Somewhere Beyond* went out
in February 1962, and the next new play was *Friday* in July 1966.
Of course she would be distracted by the run-up to the publication
of *Glitter of Mica* in 1963, but Jessie herself admitted that she had
rather retreated from the world for a while. And she admitted it
only to Scottish producer, playwright and poet Stewart Conn,
who undertook a real search for Jessie in March 1966. He knew of
her at this time only from her work, which he very much admired.
His admiring request for material was a real and necessary tonic
for Jessie, who, if work had left any time for it, was licking
unknown wounds. (One possibility was disappointment in the
reception of *Glitter of Mica*, which she was always to consider her
best work.) She wrote back: 'I opted out for a year. No one at all,
not even my publisher, had my new address.' She had already been

hovering between two ideas for a feature Dorothy Baker wanted for Third, and now offered one of them, *Friday*, in a new format, 'Evocation of a first love affair. Begun, contained and ended in one day.' This is, I think, the finest rendering of the situation outlined in the short story 'Stormy Weather' in *Where the Apple Ripens*. Here sky-watching, rain-fearing Isabel schemes to meet her boyfriend at Bible Class, but Matron finds his letters and puts a stop to it. As we saw in Chapter Three, this is very much based on fact, when as schoolgirls Jessie and her friend 'Bertha' schemed to meet two young boys: it is even remembered by Jessie after the Skene School Reunion in 1987, when she saw her 'young man' with his wife of some 50 years, and could meet both their eyes, because 'nothing happened'.

Conn was lavish in praise, expert at wheedling material out of her, and gratifyingly trusting, having received only half the script. On 11th May he wrote, unprecedentedly:

> I am absolutely thrilled by what you have sent. Your word 'evocation' is singularly apt. And you are guaranteed all my emotional response, and, I am sure, that of the listener.
>
> I am willing to accept it without any further correspond-ence or re-writing. This means, as we both of course realise, that I am taking the second part of the script on trust.

He stresses 'my belief in what you write' and 'my eagerness to produce a play by you'. While Jessie had been blessed from the start by supportive and keen-eyed broadcasters and publishers who had spotted the essential quality of her best work, they had never accepted work unseen: they had often demanded cuts and rewrites, as happened over *The Mourners*, or made suggestions of writing more, then cutting it all back, as Chatto had so spectacu-larly done over *The White Bird Passes*. Conn was a revelation. In March 1967 he wrote that London had accepted *Friday* and would repeat it, and that the Third had agreed to Dorothy Baker's suggestion of a new production of *And Barley Rigs*, produced by him. If a certain apathy of response to *Glitter of Mica* was part of the cause of Jessie's retreat, this must have been a salve to her self-esteem. By this time Conn is unsurprisingly becoming one of Jessie's Significant and Trusted male correspondents. He was also highly valued by specialists who saw from another angle what he was doing:

> Despite its unhurried pace, the Edinburgh studio produced good work over the years, particularly in the department of radio plays, with Stewart Conn conducting a one-man campaign to save the national drama from virtual extinction.[5]

And Barley Rigs had been first broadcast in August 1959. It was a 'skeleton' form of *Glitter of Mica*. Those who have read the novel will be very surprised at what it does not contain. It is a well-wrought play about two themes and two generations, represented by Hugh Riddel senior and his son. The themes are first, the degrading living conditions under which cottared farm workers lived in the father's time, and second, the sexual unhappiness of both generations, with lusty men married to frigid, chaste and ungiving women. Here Hugh has no daughter Helen, and there is no suggestion of the 'three generations' in the novel, of which Jessie was so proud. Charlie Anson is a character, but instead of hating Riddel and refusing to second him for election, he is proposing him: there is no history of mutual enmity. Sue Tatt, the lady of easy virtue who threatened at one stage to take over the novel, is much mentioned but never appears. In many ways it is a much neater work than *Glitter*: it lacks the melodramatic plot tensions supplied by Hugh's fatherhood of Helen and his hatred of Anson, to concentrate more on conditions in agriculture, oppressive community and general and sexual frustrations. But long passages have to be given to the Narrator (how Jessie longed to be rid of this device in her radio plays!), or to Anson's soliloquies to his dog, and readers of the novel will certainly miss the beguiling character of Sue Tatt. Conn's new production was to be repeated many times more, to appreciative audiences. But it fared less well in *The Critics*, who were less than kind, and complained about accents. Another blow to the favourite story.

She wrote to Conn how vexed she was on his behalf, and added, 'it really is better – or at least I'd rather be slain than be still-born!' He replied stoically, 'I thought the Critics waffled on as is their custom,' suggested they lacked understanding, and concluded, 'It's funny how accents can be accepted from all over Britain except Scotland!'

His enthusiasm meant no interruption to their co-operation. Conn was delighted with *Until Such Times*, the play that concentrates on small girl, Grandmother, the Invalid Aunt and the visiting 'Aunt Ailsa', a much fuller rendition of the story outlined under the same title in *Where the Apple Ripens* which is also much sparer than earlier versions. Jessie's synopsis indicates a greater measure of distance and control of her material than was possible for her when dealing with these experiences in the raw:

> It is the portrayal of an old woman's conflict between her duty to her chronic invalid daughter, and to her small grandchild.
>
> The invalid and child become bitter antagonists for first place with the old woman.
>
> In the end, it is the old woman who *ought* to have succumbed to the pressures on her, who alone survives intact.
>
> Spiritually and physically their lives are small and enclosed. All the windows of their home look out on a great wood; except one, which looks on the road, so that nothing external can happen, but they are prepared or forewarned; or few people enter their world, without again, they are prepared.

Conn wrote expressing his delight:

> And I can't say how grateful I am to you for sending in a script which I believe to be of such quality and (an important point to me) not a recapitulation of what I have seen of yours previously, but a moving piece of writing containing its own individual statement.

He was right about the quality. Like the *Friday* play, this is an assured and finely controlled piece of writing. He was not to know he was wrong on the novelty of the theme, as we saw in Chapter One. He reported on 21st August 1968, after the recording, that the play proved 'one of the most rewarding radio experiences I've had'.

He asked for more, and Jessie was in a position to supply it, because Cecil Day Lewis had applied for a grant for her to the Arts Council, which coincided with the award of a bursary from the Scottish Arts Council, giving her some time to write. She already had the story which was to become *Where the Apple Ripens* in mind:

> Yes, I would like to be commissioned for a Scottish play. I have never yet sat down thinking, 'I will' or 'I must' write a play. It's always something like a stone in my shoe, troubling me, before I write. I've had just that for some time. It's my novel, but I feel, as I've done with my other two novels, as you possibly know, that they *do* take well in what I call to myself 'skeletal radio form' before the full portrayal.

Little did she know at that stage that she would outdo herself this time, writing two different radio plays about the same set of characters before she could distil both into the shortest, possibly best-crafted, novel – or novella – she had yet produced. But that process will be picked up again in the '70s.

PUBLISHING

Jessie's fiction for the most part proceeded very slowly in the '60s. Johnnie's illnesses were central to everything in the crises of 1960 and 1962; and 1961, the 'golden year' at the BBC, passed all too fast. It was astonishing, indeed, that she was able to complete and deliver *Glitter of Mica*, which was begun before the publication of *The White Bird Passes*, to Peter Calvocoressi at Chatto in September 1962. After that, as with work for the BBC after *Somewhere Beyond*, there is a considerable gap during which she struggled doing permanent night shift with old folk for five years.

Glitter of Mica was promised in the *Press and Journal* in July 1963, in an interview with Helen Fisher:

> She began by telling me she kept nothing of her writings because she had done nothing that pleased her. But now she said: 'Maybe this is it . . .'
> It is a novel based on the life of an Aberdeenshire cottar. It is not autobiographical. 'I've made it from dust,' she said. 'It's only 180 pages long, but it took me four years to finish. I didn't want to part with it. Once it went to the printers and came back in proofs, I felt I'd lost something.'

When someone asked if her husband was the model for Hugh Riddel, she denied it, and confessed to Peter Calvocoressi that she herself was the model. In conversation, Avril Wilbourne said, 'Sue Tatt reminded me of Mum really,' but a minute later corrected herself and affirmed that Jessie 'was as much Hugh Riddel as Sue Tatt'.

Jessie took great pains over every detail of this novel. She wrote to Cecil Day Lewis saying that when she read over the completed manuscript the punctuation was so bad she wrote it out again in full. When he sent her the suggested blurb, she wrote to Peter Calvocoressi:

> I was pleased to be allowed to see it, pleased with contents. Thank Mr D. Lewis for me when he returns. Have only one suggestion re blurb. *I* know that Mr D. Lewis uses reference to 'vernacular' in its *widest* sense, but 'skippers through' might not realise that. And nothing is so off-putting to many *English* than the thought that they might have the Scots language to contend with. I've found this time and time again re radio work. Always the apprehensive question is – 'Is it in *Scots*?' I *do* hope you will all agree with me on that point.

She was right, and they did. This is a perennial problem for Scottish writers, whether they write in Scots or not (and Jessie usually did not): somehow English readers expect to be deterred

by obtrusive linguistic Scottishness. She sent the typescript to
John R. Allan, Maitland Mackie's brother-in-law, farmer, broadcaster and distinguished writer, in case she had blundered on any
small technicalities, and incorporated his suggestions. And she
was undecided over the title for some time:

> O and by the way. The title of the book itself is not to be
> *Barley Rigs* – too misleading, like an Agricultural Manual.
> But *The Angry Airt*.

She quoted two stanzas of Burns's 'O wert thou in the cauld blast',
as far as 'to share it a'', and commented:

> And of course it is *such* a sharing. In that – as writer and
> person, I do – and have – shared it *all* with them. So there
> couldn't be an apter title.

But later it became *Glitter of Mica*, first words of G. S. Fraser's
poem, 'Home Town Elegy (For Aberdeen in Spring)'. She told
Cecil Day Lewis that she had written to Fraser for permission to
use it, and these lines, below the simple declaration 'For Elizabeth
Adair' on the dedication page:

> This is the shape of a land which outlasts a strategy
> And is not to be taken by rhetoric or arms.

When the proofs were ready in May 1963, she sent a set to Joanna
Scott-Moncrieff, not, she said, for *Woman's Hour*, but for her own
interest. Miss Scott-Moncrieff's brother George had coined the
word 'Balmorality' in a widely known essay in 1932.[6] He blamed
Queen Victoria and her followers for the fetishes of tartanry and a
falsely sentimental view of Scottish history. Slightly misinformed,
Jessie wrote:

> It is, I hope, an antidote to 'Balmoralitis' and the 'Kail Yard',
> which is why I thought you might like it. And the cottar
> world has never been done before.

Glitter of Mica was not a great success. It is indeed an antidote to
the Kailyard, and I have argued elsewhere that it is a very fine
novel,[7] but it must have seemed rather old-fashioned, in subject
matter at least, in the year that Philip Larkin called 'Annus
Mirabilis', when 'Sexual intercourse began . . . Between the
end of the *Chatterley* ban/ And the Beatles' first LP'. In that
fast-moving, even 'swinging' world, this subject matter must have
seemed not immediately 'relevant', as the cry was at the time.
Certainly it is not immediately attractive: Caldwell is described as
'bleak' several times in the first few pages. It is, as Jessie claimed, a
first, in dealing with the especially precarious and downtrodden
lives of cottared farm workers, especially in the '20s and '30s. It
was published in September, after a summer of civil rights unrest
and killings in America, when the Profumo Affair was making
headlines in Britain, along with the Great Train Robbery; when
the Beatles were scoring one of their first big successes with 'I
Want to Hold Your Hand' and the bestselling novel was John Le
Carré's *The Spy Who Came in from the Cold*.

Although the book is strong in humour and fortitude, it
presents a bleak picture of human life, where now it is unbeliev-
ably difficult to become Hugh Riddel's ideal, 'a bonnie whole
man' (109). Jessie simultaneously chronicles and criticises a whole
agricultural parish, its class rigidities, its social inequalities, its
grim and joyless marriages and coarse and crude sexual attitudes.
By retracing Hugh Riddel's childhood memories, the novel also
acquires a dimension of history, recounting the barbaric conditions for farm workers before the Second World War, and tracing
the failed relationship of Riddel's parents as well as the catastrophic privacies of his own marriage.

His educated daughter's ill-judged and desperate sexual affair
with an unpleasant ambitious crofter is also bleak. This was one of
Jessie's main objectives. She always promised to write a film script
based on the novel, and was disconsolate when Michael Radford
said it would not easily adapt to film. She said to us in 1985,

> this is . . . a record, a time that'll never – you know, that is
> worth holding on to. It's worth holding on to the changes

that came over the farm work, the changes that happened to
their families; the girl at the university; a hundred things –
the nearly uncivilised way we lived in those days.[8]

She also wrote to Dr William Donaldson, when he was preparing
a new Introduction for the 1980s, and asking for her help. Here
she talks about the way the novel expressed her attempted
description of her personal development, the result of her bizarre
girlhood:

> I tried to explain it through Hugh Riddel in *Glitter of
> Mica*. Where he is trying to explain it to *himself* through
> Burns:
> One foot on the steps of the Castle, the other in the
> midden. And never both together. Just about the loneliest
> thing that can ever happen to a man.
> *Socially* a misfit. Mentally (intellectually) too; not fitting
> in to *either* environment, and thus creating your own, and
> seeming to become that dreadful word, dreadful thing, a
> 'character'.
> Like 'simple' folk become. 'Gowks' if you like. To me, the
> best word for it is that old word, a 'Natural'. Who are secure
> in themselves, because they have 'created' their *own* envir-
> onment, but disturbing to other people who cannot 'place'
> them.
> The difference with *me* is that I am neither simple nor a
> Gowk, but the process is the same. The No-Other-Man's
> Land just as vast.

I found this sketchy explanation profoundly enlightening – on the
fourth or fifth reading. She is beginning to formulate here, I
think, the idea she elaborated to us in interview:

> 'Queer fowk, who are oot, and niver hiv ony desire to be in!'
> Every work I've ever written contains ae 'ootlin'. Lovely
> Aberdeenshire word. Somebody that never really fitted
> in . . . Now, I know myself at last and it's just in one line

in that book where fowk were oot who never had ony desire
to be in.[9]

Like that of *The White Bird Passes*, its structure is unusual and
ambitious, telescoping events into a very brief span, while finding
room to enter and interpret each major character's thoughts and
feelings.

The reviews were mixed, and Jessie remembered them rather
selectively. She wrote to Dr Donaldson that the book had good
reviews in England, and sold out. But at the time she was
disappointed by the small number of English reviews. They were
few and on the whole short. And sales slowed fairly soon. Scotland was much better. An anonymous critic in the Edinburgh
Evening News said, 'Were it not for its abundant good humour, I
would compare it to Zola's *Earth*. It is certainly as good'. Alastair
Macrae in the Glasgow *Evening Citizen* compared her to Lewis
Grassic Gibbon, and called her 'a word artist of exceptional
stature'. Jessie's friend Burns Singer reviewed it in the *Times
Literary Supplement*, the best of the 'English' reviews:

> It is a perfectly controlled and beautifully balanced look at
> the enormities of life and death.

Moultrie Kelsall, who had known Jessie as a broadcaster from her
first audition, reviewed the novel on the air, and confessed to
some disappointment, finding it written with 'slightly clinical
detachment', as Jessie did remember, and reported to Dr Donaldson, but she was willing to forgive, because of the other phrase
she had remembered for many years:

> Genius is a word one hesitates to use, but I've known since
> first I met her that there's a streak of genius in her.

Dr Donaldson asked questions for his Introduction, and she did
her best to help. Although virtually in note form, this passage
helps to illuminate the book:

No. It wasn't optimistic. The White Horse will survive –
until the atom bombs fall – as will Soutar Hill. But the
human condition doesn't change (I'm not speaking about its
circumstances). Always wriggling under the darkness of the
stone. There will be the sex problems, the status problems,
i.e. Helen Riddel; all the words we speak – in place of the
ones for which we have no utterance. Speaking, but not
really communicating. I wanted the landscape itself, lonely
enough in itself, to 'collaborate' with the individual alone-
nesses of the people within it. I don't know whether I
succeeded in that. But that is as near as I can get to
explaining it.

In another letter she contrasted Woolf and Lawrence, who had
deliberate intentions in writing, with Emily Brontë and Katherine
Mansfield who had 'no reason' for writing, except the one,
'something inside them that had to get out'. The latter was
her case too, with *Glitter of Mica*.

But, having said that, I think I have just this minute realised
at least one of the reasons for writing it, a tremendous
feeling for the land itself. Innate in me from my very first
consciousness . . . I have always felt far more for places than
I have for people. I carry climates within me. So I think I
began, intended *Glitter of Mica* to be a celebration of the
land itself, such a *wide* land, in which its people seemed to
me to be captive within. Its people had the 'spiritual'
fecundity of the land; hence their absorption in the topic
of sex. At the same time John Knox glowered over their
shoulders. I think myself would describe *Glitter of Mica* as a
love/hate thing. I felt both deeply, as I wrote.

It is understandable that Jessie could feel rejected and misunder-
stood on the publication of the novel. No one seemed to value
what she had done, entirely: even her beloved Nan Shepherd
found it unnecessarily 'coarse'. After this, it was some time before
she found time, energy and zest to write anything major, for radio

or for book publication. And, by the time she did, with the novella *Where the Apple Ripens*, Peter Calvocoressi had left Chatto, and she had again ignored the rules of the market place by producing something 'the wrong length'. Her relationship with Chatto had been mixed: old-fashioned, treating authors personally, the individual directors, most notably Calvocoressi, had been exceptionally supportive and friendly to Jessie. But they were not sharp-edged when it came to business. After the reviews of *White Bird*, it was astonishing they could not persuade someone to do a paperback edition, and if *Glitter of Mica* failed to make much of an impact, some of the blame must rest with the firm. Arguably, the next time they were of use to Jessie was when Cecil Day Lewis applied to the Arts Council for her to win a grant, to give her time to write; and that was not until 1968.

Chapter Ten: The Seventies

A SCOTTISH INTERLUDE

By 1970, the Kessons were alone together again, both their children having married and left home. It was therefore open to them, if they chose, to venture out of London for a time, although the presence of family and grandchildren in the south would always have a powerful pull on their affections. In 1970, Johnnie turned 65 and became a pensioner. And because of this, Jessie's old friends, Anne and George Gray of Smeaton, East Lothian, who had known them since their days on Maitland Mackie's farm in 1940, offered them a cottage on the estate at Smeaton, at what Jessie described as 'a peppercorn rent'. This sounded idyllic. Cauldside Cottage is particularly pretty, and set in open farm land perhaps a quarter of a mile from Smeaton itself. The Grays had demolished the 'Big House' when they inherited, if only because it was *so* big, and they could never have afforded to furnish it, even with carpets and curtains. They live in a beautifully converted old farmhouse, which has its own separate guest apartments – something that Jessie or both Kessons often took advantage of, in later years, whether on holiday or just overnight, passing through.

The whole estate is beautiful, but there is a wooded lake of stunning beauty, just the right size to stroll round of an evening. It seemed like a dream come true. Jessie wanted to give back to Johnnie all the attractive aspects of country living without the conditions he previously endured on the land, and bought him a dog, preparing for happy years ahead. She wrote an optimistic letter to the Day Lewises, beginning, splendidly, 'Dear Jill and Mr Day Lewis . . .' (She had become friends with actress Jill Balcon at the BBC but, as her publisher, she treated the Poet Laureate with more respect.) The letter dilates on the prospect:

An old friend, a Scottish landowner, has given me a farmhouse, in East Lothian, for my lifetime. Johnnie, well past retiring age now, is real worn; so we go home at the end of August, to Scotland. A garden, a collie dog, a cat, some hens scratching at the back door, that's what we'll have. How *much* we have missed such things, being country people.

It is unclear, now, whether Johnnie ever really wanted to leave London, where he had been happy for many years. The impetuous Jessie took a precipitous plunge, and for a while it seemed it was going to be an idyll indeed. All she had to do was to find a job to support them. But here the first difficulties presented themselves: it was a long way from Smeaton even to a bus stop; and there was no sign of an appropriately paid job for Jessie becoming available, even though she was *not* being fussy. The difficulty that did *not* present itself was Jessie's secret unspoken dream. For many, many years she had been homesick for Scotland, and now she was dreaming of renewing old friendships and making new ones, even such writers and artists as she had hoped to find in London in 1951. Then, her friendships had had to be mainly epistolary, except for her exuberant year working directly for the BBC, and work had handicapped her very much in developing the artistic social life of which she had dreamed.

Now, at Smeaton, she was very isolated. Scotland was bigger than she remembered, and this was not her part of Scotland. They always used public transport, which was not wonderful, so the very thought of going to Edinburgh or Glasgow, let alone Aberdeen, was intimidating. And Jessie admitted to Stewart Conn that she had been fearful of intruding on anyone, and kept fairly quiet about her presence in Scotland. Her confident exterior so often hid a woman full of misgivings and lacking in confidence. She only met Conn himself once towards the end of her stay, though in letters she had confided and treated him as an old and close friend. She confided, for example, that John Foster was her father. Without Conn's benign and supportive nearness, she would have been lonely indeed.

It seems clear that contradictory impulses in Jessie herself helped to make her time in Scotland problematic, but it also just seemed doomed. Everything happened in the wrong order. When unhappy, during her stay, she tended to blame the lack of jobs, the Grays, who were forced to ask for the cottage back, even Avril and her second husband Bill, who were in Teheran, and asked Jessie if her granddaughter Sharon could stay at Cauldside and attend a secretarial course in Edinburgh. But it seems to have been a real chapter of accidents, with events not conspiring, but just in the wrong order.

What survives of Jessie's job-seeking makes a saga in itself. The pair were established at Cauldside by December 1971. Much of the saga is to be found in Jessie's letters to Stewart Conn, starting with this, fairly early in 1972:

> I was so *excited* about returning to Scotland. I've got a most lovely, reasonably priced cottage. But work is my problem. I need at least a *part-time* job. This I find impossible to get, at least in any way commensurate with my London job.
>
> However, I was down in London for a fortnight very recently. They have not managed to replace me in my job there [with mentally handicapped Jewish girls]. So it's open door for me still. However, this has done two things for me. I was *eaten-up*, for *twenty-one* years with homesickness for Scotland. I'm cured of it at last. Also, it's given me six months to get on with my book [the novella *Where the Apple Ripens*]. I'm well through it. One of my Directors – Chatto & Windus – has just been appointed Chairman and Editorial Director of Penguin. Even so, he's going to see my work through with Chatto & Windus . . . So I'm taking the good of the summer to finish my book. And unless something really reasonable turns up in that time, will return south.

At the end of May she updates him:

> I was to have returned to London today, but my son, born in Scotland, but with no memory of it, wants to come for two

weeks in July, a small request to make; so I've decided to stay
until he has his holiday. There's nothing else to keep me.
After nearly nine months here, I cannot get a suitable job.
I'm not in the least too proud to wash dishes or scrub floors,
it's just that the remuneration for so doing isn't enough! So!
I've dusted myself down, picked up all the little bits of
myself, and think I feel whole enough again to pick up that
gauntlet! [The metaphor of disintegration above is very
telling.] I feel unaccountably sad. I had hoped so much,
to see some of my old friends in these past months. But I so
dread 'intruding', and want to slip away from Scotland, as
quietly as I returned to it.

But at last the prospect of an appropriate post loomed ahead, only
to be frustrated by a kind of religious bureaucracy. Jessie wrote to
Conn early in June:

I still *half*-hope, I must be the original optimist! It's in-
credible! One job, for which my qualifications and experience and *References* (from London's Senior Medical Officer)
really qualified me for, fell through. I didn't have a reference
from a Minister of the Kirk!! I haven't known a Minister
personally since I was fifteen, and said so – end of job. In
London, the last thing that concerned them was whether
one was a Hindu or a Heathen!

The post was at Tynepark, a school for List D girls in Haddington, run by the Church of Scotland Committee on Social Service.
   Inside a month she had run out of money altogether, and had to
send an SOS to Conn for the second half of her fee for *The Gowk*.
Under so many strains, she began to agonise again over Johnnie's
health. He was doing light farm-maintenance work for George
Gray. She was doing nothing but job-hunting and trying to write.
And so she wrote to Conn in an agony of guilt, worry and
frustration in November, saying she was watching her husband
suffer, and, she believed, die. She made Johnnie stop work in
December, but refused to go back with the family, who had come

to take them back to London. And suddenly things looked up. She was soon writing to Gordon Emslie at the BBC:

> I still persevere! I can't bear failing. You may remember I was *half*-considered for a job which I could do, and do well, but under the auspices of the Kirk of Scotland! The one thing I couldn't produce – and so necessary – a Minister's reference. I don't even know a Minister.
>
> Anyhow, at long, long last, they've put me on the short list. I shouldn't, I suppose, have been told, but one of the Committee Members, who will *not*, incidentally, be on my board, saw my references, which they sent to London for . . . Apparently Dr Greenburg, Chief Officer Mental Health London, wrote: 'how fortunate you are, to be given the opportunity of using Jessie Kesson's services,' . . . It cheered me, gave me some of my waning confidence back. I may not get the post, but that 'Burning Bush', so beloved by the Kirk, shall not consume me after all.

In March 1973, a brisker, happier Jessie wrote again to Emslie:

> The Board gave me the appointment three months ago by 'Unanimous Decision'. Since my job is an experiment, it *is* difficult. Not enough hours in the day for all I want to do in it. But I love the work.

But the next problem was to be with another bureaucracy. Jessie was told by the Social Work Services Group that she could not be paid as a teacher because she had no qualifications on paper. Given the nature of the post, and of Jessie's unrivalled experience, including all she did at Cowley, this was clearly pedantic in the extreme. Her local MP, John Mackintosh, wrote twice to Hector Munro, the Secretary of State, on her behalf before things were sorted out.

But the problems were not over yet. Jessie had said from the start that a suitably remunerated part-time job would suit her perfectly. But as she described the job in January 1974, it was far from part-time:

A 70-hour week; a day off once a fortnight, teaching psycho-drama in an approved school. 'Situation drama' some call it. Not me! The 'situations' are aye dramatic enough, without artificial setting up on anybody's part! On top of that a *six-mile* walk every day to the Bus, before I even begin. Still, I've thrived on it, and loved the work.

Tynepark was run as a therapeutic community, where teamwork was of the essence, and authority was shared by staff and inmates. It was run by pioneering psychologist Max Paterson, and broke new ground in many ways. Archie MacLullich worked with Jessie. 'Sweeping up,' he said, was her role, but for once we are not talking housework.

I could not continue at that pace for another year, particularly winter, so gratefully accepted Edinburgh Corporation's offer of a three-day week. Same type of girls, but at least giving me time to breathe . . . *Very* sorry to leave my school, and my colleagues . . . but happily my 'old' girls come to my new job, so the contact isn't broken!

Evidence of her enjoyment is seen in this little poem, which Jessie sent to *New Society* in March 1973:

Moment of Communication
With List D Girl

F*** off!
She said,
Dismissing me
and my persuasions
with a contemptuous stare
that crinkled to a smile
of small surprise
When I
in anger roared
F*** off
To *Where?*

Thus the job was not ideal for Jessie, but Jessie was ideal for the job, except in one particular. A persistent story records she was in charge of a shopping expedition to Haddington in a van. When the girls reassembled to go home, they had had a massive shoplifting spree!

Clearly it was these two jobs, at Tynepark and Seaview, that inspired Jessie to write her radio and later television play, *You've Never Slept in Mine*, and her own youthful experience of a hostel for girls on probation only deepened it, without its having to be a kind of personal exorcism as well. Like the earlier *Green Glass, Goblin*, and the later *Dear Edith*, this play testifies to a real involvement in the work she did and real understanding of humans diminished by institutional status. But when I asked about it at our 1985 interview, she played this down:

> As you say, my other jobs were all about the . . . have-nots or whatever, and I would *like* to say, 'Ah yes, I had a great feeling for them and a' that.' Actually I did the job very well and I *did* have a feeling for them . . . It wis mair money, ye see . . . The two jobs that I loved was I was six years wi' mentally handicapped teenagers. That I loved! And I taught them their little plays and a' thing, that's what I mean, I get on well with the young. And at Tynepark, but wi' the ither jobs, like wi' the old age and a' that, really, it wis just because they paid well. They paid the amount of money I needed at the time.

I am convinced her involvement was greater than she was willing to admit that day: she seemed determined to avoid on the one hand being said to take jobs to use simply as material, and on the other presenting herself as a latter-day Florence Nightingale.

Jessie's accounts of the next events vary considerably, not just from time to time or correspondent to correspondent: she kept the draft of a letter to Stewart Conn, which differs considerably from the one she sent in January 1975. In the draft, she writes from another cottage, at Seton Mains, Longniddry, saying she had been just about to return to London, and had given up her cottage: 'After three years I knew Scotland hadn't very much for me, in the impetus sense. They've been solitary years'. Then Avril had asked her to have Sharon to stay while she did her secretarial course in Edinburgh:

> I was of course delighted to do this for them, and to *have* Sharon, but of course it meant my own plans went by the board. I had given up my cottage, so I had immediately to set about finding another cottage . . . However, Sharon finished on December 22nd . . . and has now returned to her parents *intact* (in all senses of the word) . . .

In the letter she sent, she introduced a note of blame for the Grays:

> We had been *lured* from London by the prospect of a beautiful cottage, at a reasonable rent, for as long as we wanted to live in it. The one thing that was true, was that it *was* a really beautiful cottage.
>
> However, the son and heir of the Estate got married, and 'our' cottage was the one he chose to live in!

In this account, she was about to leave for London when the request about Sharon came in, and she had to find another cottage, 'one I would *never* have left London for!' In the end it was a chapter of accidents, and blame doesn't really come into it, but using Avril to 'blame' to the Grays, and them as culprits to Avril, may have helped her vent her frustrations. As Jessie said in an interview with Hugh Macpherson, 'I think we all, certainly I myself am guilty of the same thing: we adjust our letters to fit in with the nature of the recipient'.[1] It was still rankling when she wrote to Conn in February 1976:

> how I was tempted north by a lovely cottage, how it was taken over by the son and heir of the Estate, and I had to

find another, too far away to continue my job in List D school, a job I'd loved – and of course now never the cottage I came north for, damp, dark, etc.

Anyhow, son and heir didn't stay long in it. It is now vacant . . . It is ironical.

Continued excellent relations with the Grays as well as her beloved daughter seem to point to Jessie's realisation that much of this was just gesture politics.

But, as she said herself, the main purpose of the letters to Emslie and Conn was to explain her emotional state:

> I didn't quite know how sad I'd be leaving my girls, nor indeed how upset they would be; we've had such a close relationship. I never once had to raise my voice. You never see results in the work, so always feel a kind of helplessness. My own *private* impression was the system was creating a race of takers, rather than givers.
>
> How disarmed I was! They had spent their pocket money to buy gifts for me, and there was nearly a free for all, as to which girl was to give them. I could hardly bear that, have always found it so much easier to give than to receive.

Her random papers also enclose emotional farewell pencilled notes from a couple of girls very sad to lose her, and making promises or resolutions about their future conduct. Here is one, crudely but carefully pencilled:

> Dear Jessy,
> I hope you will forgive me for the cheack I use to give you And I won't take **sniffer** any more. Well see and look after yourself well I will miss you very much tonight I don't think I could go to sleep just thinking of you please don't show know one else this because they will think I am just a baby. But I'm not well Jessy Good By and God

> Bless you and
> Your Husband.
> I hop you settle
> at home ok
> Well it has been
> great here with you
> all my love
> Cathy
> + Major my dog

Jessie may have applied for several posts in the south: an interested letter of response from the Cotswold Community in Swindon testifies to one, but the post she accepted was that of setting up a new Abbeyfield old people's home in Osterley, Middlesex.

BACK TO LONDON

She told us in our 1985 interview how they set about going back to London. It seemed like almost a variation on the first foray in 1951.

I get *The Lady* and in *The Lady* I see: cook-housekeeper wanted for Abbeyfield, for a new Abbeyfield, you know, for the old fowk, so I apply. A' the wey fae East Linton . . . So I gae doon, I get the job, I come back. I have a friend that worked in Tynepark, she's one of the house-mothers, and I hired a nice van and I had my Labrador dog and my cat and Johnnie and a' thing, and Eileen my good friend who was having a week's holidays onywey fae Tynepark, and a good driver, she drove us a' doon. I arrive at this Abbeyfield, it wis aboot six at night, a lang journey, and then there's eight auld wifies and there's the committee lady, 'I am so pleased you've come. Now,' she said, 'you'll easily find your way around here.' Here's me wi' eight fowk that I've niver seen in my life to cook for, and nae kennin' faur the meat wis, and there's a big major comin' through lookin' for his supper and I haed to dae it.[2]

Jessie and Johnnie worked together to set up the new Abbeyfield at St Mary's, Osterley, but none of her accounts mentioned that he was working for her full time: it was Avril who mentioned this. The task was abrupt, driven by haste and with many responsibilities. As usual, Jessie was up to all this, but she was almost 60, and it took a great deal out of her.

In February 1976 she wrote to Conn and Emslie:

I had to set up and run a new home here for a Charitable Trust.

'It is finished!' is the cry!

I spent months in the company of builders, electricians, plumbers, carpet-layers, plus calming and caring for residents, uprooted and alien . . . The house is being officially opened in April, Bishops and Archbishops: all is ready for them *now*, and I can do my own thing.

Happy to be back in London. My Grand-daughter got married 23rd December; she lives here in London. My son expects my second grandchild this month; he too lives here in London, and Avril and Bill return to their own home here, from Teheran, in April. I missed them all very much.

This was very important to Jessie: the family was a great joy, and while she felt that she had rather missed out on her own children's childhoods, with the need for full-time jobs and her drive to write, she was more relaxed with her grandchildren.

I've had more pleasure from my grandchildren . . . Another thing it's great, ye've the best o' them, them playing and that, and then when they start their grumbling because o' their teething, 'Mam', you know. (L) Oh but I, oh we always were very very – always got on. We are a very, very close family. Always great affection, great love for each other.[3]

The following year she set up another Abbeyfield in Muswell Hill.

Her longest account of the work and the working conditions she experienced is in a letter she sent Nan Shepherd in July 1980. It is a long letter, because she knew the Lady in the Train was very ill but, as it was inspired by Shepherd's being moved into a 'home' in Torphins, it might be described as rather tactless, as it goes on and on about the working conditions *she* experienced. Some extracts:

> When I say 'set up', I mean purely on a basic level. I got the place ready for my women, all of whom had sold up their own private houses. Gradually getting acclimatised to this new way of life, their worst problem was which of their possessions to take to their new rooms, which to reject.
>
> Then down to my job as Cook/Housekeeper. Two hot meals a day. Lunch 1 pm. Two vegetables compulsory (apart from potatoes). Supper/High Tea 7 pm. After Supper I gave them their milk, bread, marmalade as needed for their Breakfast, which they saw to themselves. And every Friday Night their 'rations' for the week, tea, sugar, butter . . . My working conditions were almost Victorian . . . No set hours to my week; on call night and day . . . Our food was free, our bed was free. But since I was allowed only a certain amount of money for each Resident's food, I found myself so often in the position that mothers with families do find themselves in, confined to scraping the pot myself, so that my residents would have enough. I never ate so poorly, not even in my poorest days . . . I used to simply fall on to my bed, shoes and all, with sheer fatigue at the end of the day . . . I had no illusions about my residents. I could have literally died in my tracks setting out their suppers, and they would have continued eating. And yet I was fond of them, and they of me . . . They have had *six* different Cook/Housekeepers since I left.

She really was worn out after these two jobs. She was now over 60, and her letters from now on more and more indicate times of stress or great fatigue, in between times of the energetic old Jessie,

as bouncy as ever. She retired into herself for a while now, to
recharge the batteries, and lost touch with people for a time, as she
had done in the '60s. But by June 1978 she was writing to Stewart
Conn from the new flat in Muswell Hill:

> I truly was physically and mentally drained after nine
> months with my old ladies.
>
> I had also promised to look after Kenny and my two-year-
> old grandchild, and his wife, when my next grandchild was
> due: she's young, fragile and not all that able to cope with
> *two* young babies.
>
> After *that* was over, all I could face was a small place of my
> own and time to think my own thoughts, and rest a bit.
>
> I have done so, and surfaced.

She surfaced indeed, enough to be tempted in November to return
to her old favourite activity of life modelling. She did six hours'
work at the City and East London College, for GCE Arts and
Crafts Examination classes, but that seems to have been all. Her
realisation that she was rather old for it all, and even perhaps that
she was being employed for old times' sake, would explain the
basic situation in her short story 'Life Model', where the ageing
model realises that she is only being offered work 'for old times'
sake', and refuses it for the same reason.[4] She also rose to an
emergency when a friend aged 31 committed suicide, leaving a
helpless aged grandmother whom Jessie cared for until permanent
arrangements could be made for her. This would seem to be the
same case as Peter Calvocoressi commented on in shocked terms,
that the grounds for the suicide was being awarded not a First but
a Second Class degree.

In 1979 she re-established contact with cousin Mina, and with
the Grays, reporting her doings to both. She told Mina that the
Grays had come to London and taken her to see *Evita*. They had
'pleaded' with her to return to the cottage at Cauldside, and she
was sorely tempted, but Johnnie was strongly opposed: 'one thing
I *do* know; I wasn't ready to return to Scotland when I did'. After
the Abbeyfields, she said she had decided 'to give my attention to

my writing – I seem to have been giving it to 'Old Needies' and 'Young Needies' most of my life'.

To the Grays she reported in November 1979 on the excitement attendant on her visiting Scotland with film director Michael Radford, when they were prospecting for locations for his BBC film of *The White Bird Passes*. Although she was so tired, she was also clearly exhilarated, but returning to the scenes of her youth would always be a very emotionally demanding experience:

> The thing was, I felt shattered. Emotionally and physically. Due to the tremendous hospitality of old friends, *plus* the equally tremendous hospitality of people who claimed to be old friends!
>
> On top of which the Town's local simpleton took a tremendous crush on me. Confusing me with Betty Grable (the film star). Bombarded me with baggies of sweeties, and didn't give me a minute's peace, even while I was doing recorded interviews! That could only happen to me!!

But meeting Michael Radford was arguably the most important thing that happened to Jessie in the '70s. He was an aspirant film director aged 29: she was a woman in her 60s with a fine work record for radio, who had published very little in her chosen field of written fiction, and whose work was undervalued. They would change each other's lives. Radford said to me in February 1998: 'I curse the fact that there was such an age difference between us.' If she had been younger, he said, 'I could have turned her into a great screen writer.' He was quite convinced she had 'missed her vocation', and that she could have made 'millions of dollars, I promise you'. He much regretted that she had been so long ignorant of film, and ambitious about television. To him the difference is crucial.

Both her personal and her professional life were enriched by their meeting: they became very close friends, and he was a confidant with whom she became able to share anything. He sees the defining moment in their relationship as happening on that visit to Scotland to look for locations for the BBC film. He had already realised that she could be 'very, very difficult to many people' because she was 'very fiery'. There was one pivotal scene which secured their relationship. They were at Skene, and had visited the Orphanage and the graveyard, and she became very emotional. She told him how it had felt to be called 'girl Macdonald', and became furious with him when she thought he did not understand. She was very rude, and he also became very angry. Then came what he sees as 'the defining moment': she flung out of the car, and 'set off to walk back to London'. Overcoming his own anger because 'I understood the hurt', he went after her and put his arms round her. After telling me about it, he immediately tried to undercut his own insight and impulse by laughing and saying, 'I saw the film disappearing down the tubes', but his instinct was sound, and from then on their mutual trust was secure. He still regrets that he missed seeing her by one day before she died: they were 'close, close friends'.

Jessie's personal life would never be the same again after the film of *The White Bird Passes* and her accompanying interview were televised for the first time in 1980. The film helped, as Radford said, 'to rescue her from oblivion' and to 'give her the kind of dignity she craved' – although he is quick to point out that 'it was two-way', and 'without her I wouldn't be a big film director'. She was treated thereafter as a celebrity, and felt she was recognised as a writer, professing herself puzzled by a review that said, rightly, that she had never had appropriate recognition. For her last 14 years she would enjoy the celebrity she *had* achieved, and more than deserved.

THE BBC

> Largely due to the work of Stewart Conn and the late Gordon Emslie, in radio there was throughout the 1970s an encouragement of playwriting often venturing to the frontiers of the medium. A considerable amount of Stewart Conn's most interesting work has been on Radio 3, and has not had the attention it deserves within Scotland.[5]

By 1970, Jessie had been writing for radio for 25 years. As we have seen, she had returned repeatedly to aspects of her own fractured experience in early life, effectively writing her self, her continuity, assuring herself of the myth she inhabited. She had been doing this since 'Railway Journey' in 1941, her first attempt to make sense of the 'disintegrated personality' she had been labelled with in the Orphanage. She compulsively returned to troubling experiences, until she had achieved full expression of them. This sometimes gave producers have a sense of repetition: even in 1951 the supportive Elizabeth Adair had been relieved that her adaptation of Sholokhov, *Forty Acres Fallow*, was not more autobiography. But after David Thomson's encouragement to write *Somewhere Beyond*, the sequel to *The Childhood* (2), and his fine production of it in 1962, Jessie seemed to an extent liberated from the need to 'write herself'. As far back as 1959, shortly after the successful publication of *The White Bird Passes*, she had written the non-autobiographical *And Barley Rigs*, with its male central character Hugh Riddel, and she developed it into the novel *Glitter of Mica* which she finished in 1962. She was particularly proud of that novel because she had shown herself that she could create a story not her own. It was also a fillip to her confidence when Stewart Conn undertook a new production of *And Barley Rigs* in 1968. There was no sudden turning from autobiography to imagination. Her mind was too subtle for that, and she was wise enough not to stray too far from the worlds she knew. But all four of the major radio plays she wrote in the '70s break what is new ground for her.

Two of them, *In Memoriam* and *Thorn Blows Early*, are related to each other in a quite extraordinary way. They cover different aspects of the lives of the same characters. The main character in both, Isabel Emslie, was played by Eileen McCallum; her father in both by Bryden Murdoch. The first was produced by Stewart Conn and the second by Gordon Emslie, after a stormy beginning to their relationship, because Emslie neglected to communicate with Jessie, who got tired of waiting and demanded her script back. She accepted his apologies, and developed a good working relation with him as well as Conn, writing to them sometimes jointly.

These two radio plays, each outstanding in itself, were to become one seamless novella, *Where the Apple Ripens*. The title of *In Memoriam* reminds readers of the novella of the dark background to the young girl's emotional and sexual development, the death of Helen Mavor:

> There's this girl so affected by the sudden death through an illegitimate baby o' a classmate who remember, she had a great admiration for because o her poetry and a'thing, because she came fae a mair exotic world, a sort of hero worship if you like, or heroine worship it wad be. Now at the same time despite the fact that her feeling is deep and genuine, in a way horrified, she's jist going off to dae the same thing.[6]

She is only 'saved by the bell', as the postman arrives on his bicycle. In the final novella, the humiliation of the intended seduction makes Isabel resolved never to risk such exposure again. But the play exploits the other possible reaction: when someone has to go back for the milk pail, Isabel volunteers: '*I'll* go. I'll easy go . . . I'll be ready in a minute. I'm just off to brush my hair.' Jessie was without peer in rendering this dilemma: as she said in a theatre review on *Woman's Hour* in 1963, 'A very young girl is such a mixture of spirit and animal need.' The play went well. In a missing letter Conn must have apologised to Jessie for it being placed third in a Play Competition, but she welcomed it:

> I was almost sure *In Memoriam* would be accepted for production, but I didn't think of it in a prize sense! It didn't seem long enough, and it couldn't be 'padded', so I am surprised *and* pleased.

Thorn Blows Early is, in comparison, less eventful. BBC reader Chris Barlas includes a 'synopsis', while commenting: 'This is in no sense a linear play so that a synopsis is virtually impossible.'

The play deals in a very impressionist fashion with the sensibility of ISABEL who is at the centre. The sudden sexual awareness that comes with her first periods, the garbled information about sexual activity, and the horror that she feels at the idea of her parents having a sex life are the subjects.

The relationships with her brother DAVY, her MOTHER and FATHER and with her school friend, ELSE, are the paths by which she travels.

No word here of Helen Mavor or the sexually overactive crofter. Instead Jessie tackles the 'normal' home life she had never known, with parents and a brother. When I asked whether it was autobiographical she replied:

Obviously no, it wisna, if you remember it, it's aboot a young girl wi' her father a sma fairmer, and proper parents which I niver haed, and the relation I think between the parents is awfa good, I'm sure it is: instinctively I know that's how it would be. I didn't experience any of that, except I experienced the adolescent thing, a desperate need for love.[7]

When Jessie combined both plays into the novella, almost nothing was lost. It is perhaps her most accomplished work, but this achievement of 'the sma' perfect' was to mean great difficulty for Peter Calvocoressi in marketing it. She wrote to Stewart Conn in April 1976:

Book still with Peter Calvocoressi. As you know my writing is very condensed. (We were taught at school that was a good quality. My Dominie swore by the use of one word doing the job of two!) But, as publishing is just now, it's the 'Big' novel that sells. P.C. likes it, he's very like yourself in that respect, he has always liked my work: if anyone can get it published, he can.

The following March, she wrote to Conn again:

> This *was* to have been dedicated to you . . . John Calder is
> publishing it in Paperback/Hardback. New Writing series,
> along with work of some European writers, so that I won't
> be able to dedicate it individually. But the thought was
> there. Because you had so much part in it.

Conn, himself a distinguished writer, understood very well the
process Jessie subjected her work to, the need for every stage of it.
He replied to Dr William Malcolm in 1983:

> I certainly feel that some mention of her radio work, itself so
> outstanding over the years, would be not only appropriate but, I
> suspect, essential to any comprehensive assessment of her talent
> and achievement. She is certainly one of the most imaginative
> and accomplished radio playwrights I have come across.

The next play of Jessie's he produced was *The Gowk*, in January
1973. The final short story version of 'The Gowk', published in
Where the Apple Ripens, is perhaps the most anthologised of
Jessie's stories, and for good reason. It is a very strong story,
compressed even more than was the novella, into a mere 16 pages.
But both the radio play and the story have astonishing power,
underlined by Jessie's characteristic paring down and allowing
silences to convey the unspeakable. When Liz Aitken becomes
pregnant by her schoolboy boyfriend, she dare not tell her parents.
When Kate Riddrie chose to marry her husband Hugh, she also
perforce took on his defective son, who by the time of the story is
in his 40s. Liz eventually succumbs to the temptation to accuse
the Gowk of rape, and he is put away. The play ends with Hugh,
tried beyond all bearing, meeting Liz outside in the woods:

> I ken damn fine what you told the Board.
>   You try telling ME, try *that*, Liz . . .
>   Struck dumb, are you? Lost your tongue!
>   Some late in the day for *that*, Liz!

You see, Liz, Jockie wadna have kent where to PUT the
bloody thing!
(*Very Quietly*)
But *I* ken, Liz. I ken FOR him.

The play ends on her scream. Conn again:

Those plays of hers which I directed have all had a North-
East setting, and have shared a poetic intensity on one hand,
and a down-to-earth dramatic economy and immediacy, on
the other. I particularly recall two short pieces, *Friday* and
The Gowk – the latter of which in particular pivoted on an
action by one of the characters which was 'evil' in an almost
Dostoyevskian sense, albeit on a very different scale.

Jessie worked at length on a television version of the play, but
there is no sign that she completed it.

Jessie's final radio script of the '70s was again something new,
not dependent on her personal experience. But all her insights
into losing identity when you lose your own clothes, and being
institutionalised, are marvellously transmuted in *Dear Edith*,
which again became a short story in *Where the Apple Ripens*.
As she had used her work experience of caring for spastics and
polio victims in *Green Glass, Goblin*, so she now rendered the life
of an old lady deprived of her lifetime companion and diminished
into a home, something she had seen all too often in her work, and
understood perfectly in her imagination. The play is framed by
staff clearing out the room of the deceased Miss Creswell, and
switches between this and Miss Creswell's writing mental letters
to her friend Edith, with other old ladies, repeatedly fussing and
interrupting. Miss Creswell is only meaningfully in touch with the
past, and Edith. Her friend had said, 'If and when we become a
Burden to Others, we will find our own way out', and she initiated
a plan to save half their sleeping pills. It is not clear whether
Edith's own death was natural or contrived. Miss Creswell is now
desperately lonely and unhappy, and above all intruded on. The
play ends soon after her panic:

I used to like this small Bed-sitting room. My books, my
desk, my photographs. All my belongings. I began to
understand why the cells of Religious Orders are always
tiny. The walls not only bring you face to face with yourself,
and force your own thoughts on you, they bring the images
you *care* for. And the faces of those you love to talk
with. . . But now, Edith. Now the walls of my room seem
to imprison me. I feel like assaulting them with cries and
sounds. Breaking through them. And tearing them down.
Emptiness has taken hold of me. Like a terror. And hurry
seizes me. Like a panic . . .

In the story, the ending is more definite, suggesting either that she
lets go her hold on life, or even that she exits deliberately:

Dear Edith I have changed my mind. Not about my going.
The reason for it has changed, other people have become a
burden to me . . . [*WAR* 147]

Conn did not produce *Dear Edith*, although he had in no way lost
his enthusiasm for Jessie's work:

When Marilyn Imrie joined us in Edinburgh, I passed
Jessie's next script to her, for a change of director-perspec-
tive. The result was a fruitful partnership, sustained after
Marilyn's move to London. Outside the studio Marilyn saw
a lot of Jessie. And she relayed news of Jessie's worsening
health to me.

Marilyn Imrie was a young Scottish producer. Jessie was old
enough to be her mother but, as Imrie relates, it was possible to sit
down and talk with her of passion and emotion in a way that
would be hazardous with others of her generation. Once again,
Jessie was graced by a producer of great gifts and empathy. With
Imrie she would write on triumphantly through the '80s and
beyond. Meantime, just as she had more or less shaken herself free
from absorption in her childhood, the most important dramatisa-

tion of her career was taking shape, as Michael Radford prepared his award-winning drama-plus-documentary, *The White Bird Passes*. This would enhance her public profile dramatically, but identify her permanently with that first book, and the childhood so recently and relievedly put away.

PUBLISHING

A number of factors militated against Jessie's publishing much in the '70s. The directors she had known best had left Chatto & Windus, though she was to maintain at least irregular contact with Peter Calvocoressi. She seemed increasingly to be taking to heart her beloved Dominie's advice to pare to the bone, so that long worked-over ideas made into radio plays began to eventuate into shorter and shorter prose pieces. She even joked once in a letter to Peter Calvocoressi that a book could be reduced to a sentence, but it is unclear whether she was fully aware of the trend in her own work. Possibly she was beginning to write radio for its own sake, enjoying it more, and finding the published version less important. *The White Bird Passes* had been short, and *Glitter of Mica* especially so for the equivalent of a family saga. The third 'book', *Where the Apple Ripens*, was hardly book length at all, although, as indicated in the previous chapter, it seamlessly incorporated two different radio plays based on the same family. She would continue, almost to her death, writing hard for radio, film and television, but apart from the special case of *Another Time, Another Place,* another very short novel, she reduced all the subsequent work destined for published prose into short – sometimes very short – stories.

Where the Apple Ripens is a marvellously written novella, but even Peter Calvocoressi, now at Penguin, found difficulty placing it. When she gave him the story, or a part or early version of it, in 1972, he responded with pleasure:

> I like it very much. It is very much 'you'. The girl is a girl one immediately wants to know more about and what you have to tell about her is done in your best straightforward way . . .

a highly reasonable and strongly interesting story in which one's curiosity is aroused from the word go.

But he was not slow to express his irritation with her increasingly idiosyncratic punctuation, 'the staccato punctuation with so many full stops at the end of short phrases. Do you really gain anything by doing it that way?'

Since the marvellous archive preserved by Chatto now fails us, details are missing. Eventually Calvocoressi or Jessie herself managed to place the piece with John Calder, a serious, even avant-garde, literary publisher. But he only found it possible by printing the work along with new work by four other writers, in *New Writing and Writers 15*. This is why she was unable to dedicate it, as she had wished, to Stewart Conn.

Calder's Introduction explains that 'originally intended as an introductory series, it has increasingly become a series of collector's items'. Previous volumes had included a majority of European writers, with native English-speakers represented by Alexander Trocchi, Penelope Shuttle, Samuel Beckett, Edward Bond, and Elspeth Davie. Jessie appeared along with Heinrich Boll, Alan Brown, Michael Horowitz and P. J. Kavanagh. She is presented in the Introduction as one

> who for many years has been praised as a writer's writer, a highly individual talent whose natural style and sharp observation of character and event should by now have guaranteed her a place in the forefront of modern British literature.

Although the series, as executive Bill Swainson admitted in 1979, 'wouldn't keep a thrifty mouse alive', the volume was assured of wider coverage when it came to reviews. Jessie particularly remembered Blake Morrison in the *TLS*. In 1986 she could still quote his final sentence by heart:

> Ms Kesson's story of a Scottish girl's last days of adolescence in the 1930s is frankly nostalgic – she records many of the

hymns, rhymes and poems of the period – but the nostalgia is toughened by her witty presentation of a village community puritanical about, yet also fascinated by, the sexual morals of its young. Though the story ends on a bright note – the heroine, Isabella, seems to have been 'saved' from the local farmer's attempts to seduce her – enough has been seen of the adult world to prevent a coy lyricism from prevailing: if the apple has not been finally plucked, it has certainly ripened.

She appreciated his appreciation of the delicacy of the situation: after all, she had adapted her title from Browning to express this delicacy. In 'A Woman's Last Word', Browning had written:

> Where the apple reddens
> Never pry -
> Lest we lose our Edens,
> Eve and I!

Jessie changed it to suit her purposes, and many have failed to notice the poetic basis at all. She made it:

> Where the Apple ripens
> Never pry
> Lest we lose our Eden
> Adam – and I –

Her alteration of 'Eve' to 'Adam' is much less significant than her change from 'reddens' to 'ripens': the connotations of 'reddens' would be likely to remove any doubts about the outcome of the story, so she alters it, despite losing a rhyme.

Where the Apple Ripens got another set of reviews in 1985, when it was published with ten short stories as a slim volume by Chatto. Alison Fell in the *New Statesman* described Kesson as 'drenched in her subject':

No controlling authoritative eye here, rather a selection of intense, partial, shimmering views of a rural Scotland where

sensuality wars against Calvinism with an energy propor-
tional to the force of the repression . . . These are singing
stories, rich in landscape, dialect and poetry. Colette, daughter of a happier land, would surely have admired them.

In *The List*, Alan Taylor admired Jessie's treatment of 'the
threshold of womanhood' and Isabel's 'half-realised confusion,
aware yet unaware of the reality of the tawdry world she is about
to confront'. In the *Glasgow Herald* poet Douglas Dunn found the
poetry of her writing 'austere and piercing', and was impressed by
'its brevity, its intensity. Humour, charm and a warming presence
of affection, make it a memorable and beguiling story.'

Critics were divided about the amount of quotation, the
snatches of hymns, popular songs and children's games. I
admired Isabel's 'singing mind' in *The Scotsman*, and Douglas
Dunn found they pointed up 'the balladic tone of much of her
own writing':

> The effect is one of Kesson's tales reaching the reader like
> melodies coming softly through a half-open door and with a
> peculiarly spoken quality in their telling.

Poet Flora Garry was full of delighted recognition when she
admired the same technique in the televised *The White Bird Passes*:

> I thought I was unique and queer in living so much among
> tunes and songs and phrases. All my life I've been open to
> the passing and often ephemeral music floating in the air
> and associated with certain people, events, places . . . All
> through your writing I see this same association and it
> comforts me very much. I'm not the only one.

In *Books in Scotland* Douglas Gifford, long an eloquent admirer,
found 'the effect of over-emphasis on an otherwise revealing
device is annoying', and he also complained, as had Peter Calvocoressi, about an increasing tendency 'to italicise emphasis itself'.
But he still appreciated the novella acutely and positively:

This is what I mean in describing Kesson's consummate ability to catch the moment passing; that transitional, trembling point of awareness of life as painful yet delightful, dangerous yet desired. That opening funeral poises the story so appropriately between life and the fear of missing any of its possibilities. Dead Helen's zest for experience had taken her over the edge, into the darkness; and as always in Kesson, there is that sense of a pool of light beyond which the darkness lowers.

The problem of length remained. In October 1979 Bill Swainson wrote to Jessie to ask, 'What *Longs* do you have cooking?' and John Calder apologetically wrote in January 1982 in delayed response to a letter of Jessie's in January 1981:

> I have always intended to bring out *Where the Apple Ripens* on its own and will schedule it for our Riverrun Writers series, which is for short fiction. But it would do better if we could combine it with another text. Have you anything else short?

For a while, it looked as if Calder would take over all of Jessie's previous work, but by November 1981 Jessie was back with Chatto & Windus, now dealing centrally with Carmen Callil.

The outcome in 1985, of course, was the republication of the novella with ten short stories, which Carmen Callil felt tended to be slight, and to make for another slim volume. One combines gratitude for her interest with sadness that she missed the distillation of an essence that marked so many of them.

Chapter Eleven: The Eighties

1980 was a pivotal year for Jessie. This was because of Michael Radford's television adaptation of *The White Bird Passes*. James Hunter, Senior Producer of the BBC Arts and Music Department in Glasgow, got young director Michael Radford interested in *The White Bird Passes* and, in particular, the way in which the book treads that fine invisible line between fiction and autobiography. The initial idea, in Hunter's words, was 'to make a film documentary about yourself with dramatised episodes from your novel *The White Bird Passes*'. This clearly meant that Jessie would necessarily be involved in the undertaking in a major way. She acted as consultant when Radford was adapting the book for filming. She and Radford went to Elgin and Skene to look for locations. In the event, it developed into a film version of the whole novel, with an interview with Jessie at the end forming the documentary element.

The BBC early recognised that the programme would be a winner, and organised extended publicity, with Press Previews in Aberdeen, Glasgow and London, all of which Jessie attended. Paul Harris, a young Scottish publisher, brought out *The White Bird Passes* simultaneously, the first printing since 1958. Jessie was enormously stressed and anxious in advance, but the result was astonishing. It was a triumph. Hunter described

> ecstatic reviews from the press and public alike . . . a remarkable achievement . . . It really has been *the* highlight of BBC Scotland's output for many a long year . . . There were innumerable phone calls from people many of whom were still moved by your writing days after the programme.

Then he sent her flowers: 'Bravissimo. *White Bird* won Scottish
TV Drama award'. And Michael Radford remembered the Radio
Industries of Scotland Award.

Jessie was also inundated with mail. Total strangers who had
shared some elements of her experience wrote emotionally about
their own life stories as well as hers. People from long ago and far
away made delighted contact. For a while she was really famous and,
of course, she enjoyed the celebrity, the success. She and Michael
Radford were already working on another collaboration, which
would result in the novel and the film *Another Time, Another Place*.
But it was not an unmixed good fortune. As the '80s progressed, she
often became frustrated that her fame was tied up with *The White
Bird Passes*, the book that had cost her such efforts long ago, from
'Railway Journey' in 1941 to the published novel in 1958. Writing
herself had been hard, and repetitive, with many new versions, but
the self-therapy had worked, she had created her myth and gone
beyond it. I really think by this time she believed what she told us in
1985, that her early books were written very quickly:

> *Glitter of Mica* was a book I wrote at white-hot speed. I really
> did. Far mair speedy and completely than *The White Bird
> Passes* itsel'. This one came white-hot you know . . . I edit as
> I go along. I never, never go back and revise anything!
> There's certain words I'll say, Oh that's a missed word, or
> some of these things, but I *never* – I do it at the time . . .
> That's what I mean by white-hot.[1]

She wanted recognition for *Glitter of Mica*, which was not 'just'
her own story. She never ceased to want it dramatised or filmed,
by Radford or herself, or both. His verdict, that the novel was too
internal to adapt easily to film, and lacked the epic quality he
found in *The White Bird Passes* and *Another Time, Another Place*,
was not what she wanted to hear. The BBC gave her various
contracts for it, but it was only after her death that *Glitter of Mica*
was finally adapted for radio by Anne Downie, who had, with
Jessie's approval, adapted *The White Bird Passes* for the stage in
1986.

Although she at last gave up her 'hard jobs' in social work, and 'retired', she seems busier than ever in the '80s. Moreover, she was diagnosed as suffering from angina, which troubled her henceforth, and her chronic smoking habit ensured frequent attacks of bronchitis. She was, inevitably, more easily tired than in the past. She was asked to read or speak many, many times, most often in Scotland, at universities and literary societies. She was approached for help by a number of school pupils writing on her work for dissertations, and she never refused, although she complained about the time it took, and about the fact that it never occurred to them to send stamps to cover postage. She co-operated with postgraduate students, such as Andrew Monnick-endam, who was preparing a doctoral thesis for Barcelona. And she wrote helpfully to my M. Litt. student Letizia Accinelli from Bologna, who came to Aberdeen to study Kesson, largely because she had been so impressed with the film of *Another Time, Another Place*. She meticulously answered academics who expressed interest in her work. And she became a regular performer at the Edinburgh Book Festival, reading or taking part in discussion in the 'Meet-the-Author' sessions. A memorable letter to Jenny Uglow at Chatto's describes one projected visit to Edinburgh:

> I go to Edinburgh for a week for what is described as 'Women Live' and 'Spring Fling'. Very 'Women's Lib', a state which I've simply taken for granted as something natural all my life! . . . At 70 years it becomes a bit too much. But I never have the heart – or is it the courage? – to say NO.
>
> I can't see Iris Murdoch, whom I don't know but so admire for what I think is her aura of intellectual sophistica-tion – just can't see her 'flinging' around!
>
> Also, of course, vanity comes into it. I feel flattered that the young women – the young writers – always want my return: they are unquenchable. It's never enough! But ap-preciative, and a lovely audience really, so I shouldn't grizzle.
>
> I now get ready for a visit to my Oxfam Branch. I have

long since given up patronage of Balenciaga for my 'Public Appearance' wardrobe.

Still, partly as a result of the television *White Bird*, she re-established contact with a lot of old friends like Isabel Baird, Chrissie Hubbard, Mina Skea and Betty Wilson. And she made some important new friendships in these years, including Michael Radford, her radio producer Marilyn Imrie, Dr William Donaldson, and novelist Lisa St Aubin de Terán. And she made peace of a kind with Thelma Shuttleworth, nearly 30 years after leaving Cowley.

But she lost one old friend who was irreplaceable, and had been the inspiration and support of her literary career. Nan Shepherd was in her 80s, and frail. Eventually she had to leave Dunvegan, the house in Cults near Aberdeen where she had lived all her life. She had a pacemaker fitted. Jessie knew her life was precarious, but was enormously upset when it ended. Nan's friends had assumed she would hear by literary sources, but she was on the move, and knew nothing. Nan died on 24th February 1981. Jessie described it to Dr Monnickendam:

> I learned of it in a most shocking way. I was giving a reading to English Faculty at St Andrews University. One of the audience at question time asked your question, 'Who was the lady in the train?' I told him. He said, 'Nan Shepherd is dead. She died this morning.' I'll never know how I managed to go on with the rest of my talk. And yet I do know. I did it for Nan Shepherd, as she would have wanted me to do, and the last thing I could do for her.
>
> When the Prof of English wrote to me afterwards, he wrote: 'That was the best talk, the best reading I have heard in my four years at this University.'
>
> So, Vale, dear Nan Shepherd.

Jessie was hurt that she did not know in time, but she wrote to Nan's friend Sheila Clouston in April 1984:

My shock and sorrow was, I stayed overnight at St Andrews
with the English Prof. He knew I was affected by such stark
and sudden information. He rang *P & Journal* to find out
about the funeral. To discover it had taken place that very
day! And me so close to Aberdeen. I would have gone a lot
further than Aberdeen to say good-bye . . .

NEW FRIENDSHIPS

Jessie's relationship with Michael Radford was both close and
stormy. In this it epitomises and outdoes many other relationships
she made. He was young, admiring, handsome and enormously
gifted: no one but her was ever allowed to criticise him! But he
knew she was 'very, very difficult to many people – very fiery'. In
an interview in February 1998, he described that defining moment
of their friendship, when they visited Skene looking for locations
in 1979 and fell out and then, instead of displaying his own hurt,
he put his arms around her. They had not finished collaborating
on *The White Bird Passes* when they decided to push ahead with a
book-and-film of *Another Time, Another Place*. But Jessie repeated
her myth in our interview, that it was inspired by a random
conversation with Radford and Bill Forsyth after the *White Bird*
opening, during which they asked, 'What did you do in the war,
Jessie?' and she replied, 'Ach me, I fratted with the Italians.'[2] This
is bogus. In fact, she had already done a story version, and recently
a fine radio version of the story with Marilyn Imrie, before
Radford ever heard of it. But as he said, 'the best collaboration
was material that came out of herself, and that I could then take
and transform into cinema.'

Marilyn Imrie produced Jessie's radio plays from *Dear Edith* in
1979 to 1992, the last play being *Cold in Coventry*. Jessie
flourished in this collaboration, with *Dear Edith* followed by
Another Time, Another Place (1980), *You've Never Slept in Mine*
(1982), and *Three Score and Ten, Sir!* (1986). As suggested in the
Introduction, a cassette or CD of productions such as these would
be a most welcome addition to the canon of Jessie's work. As well
as recording the artistic experiences they created together, it

would show Jessie's preoccupation over these years with the loneliness and isolation of individual characters surrounded at close quarters by alien strangers, and the enduring difficulty of communicating with them and conforming to their ways.

Imrie became a close friend too, especially after she moved from Scotland to BBC London to start the radio serial *Citizens*. She visited them quite often, and was very fond of Johnnie too, who, for her, had always an impish smile. She found Jessie a good friend and a sympathetic and understanding ear. When she married James Runcie in 1985, she soon took him to meet Jessie, and they too got on famously. Runcie made a fine little cameo film of her for *The Late Show*, in which her mode of writing – blue Basildon Bond paper and a blue Biro – was contrasted with those of Jeffrey Archer, P. D. James and others. There she declared that although she could type, she could not type creatively, and that her slower, more laborious means of composition aided the quarrying of the words.

In 1980, two Scottish academics, Dr William Donaldson and Dr Douglas Young, were preparing an anthology of North East prose. Dr Donaldson wrote to Jessie to ask for permission to include some of her work in *Grampian Hairst*, and another epistolary friendship began. He has written widely on Scottish literature and history, and is a collector and composer of Scottish traditional music. Their correspondence is unique. They wrote with some formality and a tacit agreement that correspondence is for wit and entertainment. Eventually Jessie agreed to passages from *The White Bird Passes* and *Glitter of Mica* being included, and also let this be the place for one of her most popular short stories, 'The Gowk', to make its first printed appearance. In the course of the friendship they wrote with mock formality and great enjoyment and brio. When Jessie received her copy of *Grampian Hairst*, she rejoiced to meet old friends again, Burns Singer and Hunter Diack:

> Oh! and as for the work of Jessie Kesson, I felt she leapt out of the pages like a roaring slummocky quine wi pee streaks doon her legs.

Exaggerated simile, but a wee grain of truth in it.

The correspondence continued through 1989. They wrote about what they were writing and the problems of publication, about money worries and the frustrations of work, and eventually she asked him to be her literary executor. He agreed, and soon after, in 1986, she asked if he would agree to write her biography, if one were required. Again he agreed, but with some sensible conditions:

> First, though, I would think two conditions would absolutely have to be met before I felt myself equipped for this task, whenever it might fall to me to discharge it. 1) I would want to sit down with you and a good tape recorder and fill out a whole world of biographical detail either for use, or to provide me with a reasonably complete factual framework (you're not in the hands of an amateur, ye ken) so that I can distinguish your life from your works. However I might eventually approach the task I feel I need this kind of knowledge to do it properly. 2) I know next to nothing about the London end, your life and cultural context there. This is not an insurmountable obstacle, and most of the information could, no doubt, be assembled if and when needed. But if there are important people in that setting who may not see out the decade (chilling, aren't I) then I'd better see them soon.

Jessie took fright. He had laid his finger precisely on the problem, to 'distinguish your life from your works'. The subject was frightening and emotionally fraught.

She replied that she was apprehensive about tape-recorded sessions.

> I can't bear them. It was with reluctance that I eventually agreed to do a *short* recording for Isobel Tait's University archives. The mining down, the quarrying down inside one's self (which is necessary unless one simply waffles through it) . . . Yet I do want to give you all the help I can. Just as I

feel you are the person for the biography, because I respect your integrity, admire your scholarship.

Significantly, when I had approached her the previous year to do a recorded interview for the sound archive, she had prevaricated similarly, saying:

> Dr W. Donaldson, my literary executor, has probably more information than he will ever be able to use. He too has done an extremely 'in depth' . . . The only aspects that have not become public property are locked away in Dr Donaldson's desk.

She added a later note: 'You see what I mean! Posterity, if interested, has it *all* on record.' Thus she protected her past, even from her projected biographer. And enjoyed the correspondence, and the excuse for random reminiscences. And his gallantry:

> It's just *struck* me! All my personal/literary friendships have been with men, and long-standing. Which, I think, says something for the men, for their wives, and for me.

They fell out at least once, in 1983, when Jessie sent this poem-letter:

> Dear Dr Donaldson
>   And it's green for grief.
> No 'David Rorie'
> Have you been ill?
> Or have I in some way offended you? – That was
> certainly never intended
> *But*
> Busy?
> Weel that's aye in season
> An excuse
> But nae real reason.
> Eident masel, I aye 'made' time
> For courtesy's sel'

And this time, no reply needed; since forced replies lack
– grace.
Yours
Jessie Kesson.

On that occasion, peace was made, but they were to fall out
terminally over a relatively trivial affair. Dr Ian Olson, Editor of
Aberdeen University Review, gave me a fairly detached account. It
involved an occasion when Jessie was invited to some major event
in Aberdeen in summer 1990:

> She later wrote me (and Willie Donaldson – although I
> never saw his letter) an unpleasant letter abusing us for not
> turning out to this event, saying that she would have walked
> over broken glass (or some similar figure of speech) to attend
> had positions been reversed.
>
> My attempt to mollify her with the completely truthful
> explanation – that neither Willie nor I had (a) been told of
> the event by anyone (including Jessie), nor (b) been invited –
> evoked no response.

As Michael Radford says, she could be very fiery, and this time
there was no reconciliation. She had told Dr Donaldson in 1987,
'I am not conceited, but I am damnably proud.' This time,
perhaps, she had met her match.

Jessie had always longed to be on friendly terms with writers
and artists, so her meeting through Michael Radford with Lisa St
Aubin de Terán and her painter fiancé Robbie Duff Scott was a
milestone of the late '80s. St Aubin de Terán, as readers of her
novels and poems will know, has several romantic backgrounds
which have figured in her work. At 16 she married a Venezuelan
landowner and lived first in Italy and then in the Andes, where
she managed his estate for seven years. Her second husband was
poet George Macbeth. The death of her mother and the break-up
of her marriage to Macbeth precipitated a nervous breakdown,
which has greatly influenced her subsequent work. So here was an
admiring younger writer who wrote extensively about her own life

experience, as Jessie also did; who had deep feeling for her mother, as Jessie also did; and who had a serious breakdown, as Jessie also did. Although the similarities may end there, it made for an important relationship, and St Aubin de Terán was to become Jessie's literary executor.

Jessie met her in 1988, shortly before her marriage to Robbie Duff Scott. When the pair bought a flat in Venice, Jessie and Johnnie were to have a long holiday there, Johnnie and Robbie going by air, Lisa and Jessie by boat and train, for Jessie had a strong aversion to flying. She worried that the Kessons would be a drag on their younger hosts but, in the event Johnnie's health prevented the undertaking of the enterprise. The Kessons were invited to the wedding, held at Pittodrie House in Aberdeenshire because Robbie's father was very ill. The next lavish and glamorous occasion was a luncheon Lisa organised in Jessie's honour in October 1989, at the Monkey House Restaurant. Jessie obviously loved this kind of recognition, and the chats she had with Lisa and Alexandra Pringle of Virago, about contracts, terms, Public Lending Rights and each other's books.

The Kessons were also invited to the wedding of Michael Radford and Lisa's daughter Iseult. A large party was held at Lisa and Robbie's new home, Villa Quarata, at Morra in Umbria. The Kessons did not venture so far. A smaller Scottish event in Dunkeld, which the Kessons did attend, was in early August 1990. Duff Scott held several exhibitions in Italy, and it was arranged he would visit London to paint Jessie's portrait in June, an exceptionally busy summer. Lisa was meantime visiting Mexico to write a novel, and edited two anthologies, one in English and one in Italian, in which Jessie's work figured. Apparently only the great difference in age between the couples, combined with Johnnie's increasing frailty and deafness, meant that the relationship could not be enjoyed as fully as Jessie and Lisa could have wished.

THELMA SHUTTLEWORTH: A RECONCILIATION

In the late '80s one long-broken friendship was restored. Late in 1987, some sort of rapprochement took place between Jessie and her old friend Thelma Shuttleworth, of Cowley days, now living in retirement in Frinton-on-Sea. Evidence of this is scrappy, consisting of some of Thelma's letters with unexpected gaps, and drafts of letters Jessie may have sent in return, sometimes more than one before she was satisfied. There were also, apparently, some 'marathon phone calls'.

By sheer coincidence, I learned some background to the formidable Shuttleworths from Jill Balcon. She went to drama school very young, in 1941, and her protective father insisted she had a room in West Cromwell Road, where his secretary also lived, and could keep an eye on her. It transpired that these two adjacent large houses were owned and rented out by Bertram and Thelma Shuttleworth, who lived in one large basement room. Balcon said that in the '20s, Thelma was a teacher, and Bertram an unsuccessful actor. Balcon describes Bertram as small, bald, bespectacled and aggressive, and Thelma as seeming twice his height, and handsome in a dark way.

In 1941 Thelma, a good cook, would provide supper for those of the 'motley crowd' who wanted it for 2/-. But then came a time when the occupants had to care for themselves. The Shuttleworths were people of stern principle, and pacifists, and eventually they were both imprisoned, Bertram in Wormwood Scrubs and Thelma in Holloway, because they would not agree even to participate in fire-watching. More, Thelma went on to hit the tabloid headlines at Holloway, because she refused an order to take a breakfast tray to Lady Mosley, also resident in Holloway at the time.

By the time Jessie was reunited with Thelma, she was well known in a more exclusive circle. Thelma was now revered in the 'Inkling' literary world, composed of admirers of Tolkien, C. S. Lewis and Charles Williams, because of her long friendship with Charles Williams. She quotes his spiritual writings, and those of others, in letters to Jessie, and details her own corporal works of mercy, and offers bracing advice: 'Remember! There are so many reasons for being sorry, but none for being sorry for oneself. Not nohow.' They discussed past times, and friends in common. Thelma wrote in February 1988 about Jill Balcon and Quentin Crisp, for example:

We knew Jill Balcon or ever we knew you, for instance. I befriended Quentin from the moment I set eyes on him at a party in my house circa 1940, he coming through the door 'like Mercury, new-lighted on a heaven-bearing hill', bless him. Poor lamb: his state was none of his making . . . never *choose* to be gay, he answered a young questioner in his first London show. All he ever wanted was 'to be a drop of oil on the cog of the wheel of God'.

Elsewhere she described him as 'being himself but half made up, a natural freak but with an acute brain'.

But at the bottom of it all is Jessie's former boss at Cowley, the Hon. May Ammon, and Jessie's residual feelings about her (by this time dead some 14 years). Jessie must have harboured misgivings all this time, because she could not remember the exact circumstances of her departure from Cowley. Now she for the first time gets details of the drunken scene she made in 1960, for which Bertram Shuttleworth never forgave her. She writes about their 'lack of empathy' and 'the hiatus between our temperaments': she regrets hurting Miss Ammon; 'there was honour between us'. But Thelma repeatedly accuses her of 'still nourishing ill will' and a sense of 'injured merit'. Thelma calls the incident 'a crowning pity, for it spoilt a relationship beyond repair'. She was there: 'It was I who helped you off the boat, and kept us from a ducking.'

Gradually we learn more about Miss Ammon, also known as Midge and May. Thelma described her with a mixture of love and pity, and she does sound difficult, by all accounts! As late as April 1994 Thelma wrote:

Midge never *smiled* easily, poor darling. She was a more deprived child than either of us orphans and our backgrounds . . . May was born anxious, and left to anyone handy to be brought up . . . She left home to live with us – she wanted to leave home, but not to be by herself. She & I took to one another, & B & she to one another – actor, teacher boss, teacher.

A postscript to this letter adds further explanation, trying to elicit
sympathy or fellow feeling for Miss Ammon in Jessie:

> Suddenly realised I had missed out important bits. Like
> yours, when young. May had to leave the University
> (London) after her first year, following Teacher Training
> at Chichester, because her mother had cancer, so she, the
> younger daughter, able to do a day job, went straight
> into teaching. This was why, when the idea of Recreational
> Institutes were invented to catch children coming
> back from evacuee homes to heaps of rubble (Fulham,
> Kennington, Brixton; our Cowley), the Ed Inspectors &
> County Hall Council seconded such a youngster to build it
> up. The actual building in Cowley Road was a day school
> for infants and Juniors. It had to have some Women's
> Institute left-overs from a bombed boys' school in the
> neighbourhood. She got my name by chance from an
> old LCC list in 1945 when B & I were going into acting
> and teaching again. She *knew* instinctively, that just
> playing games, boxing and football were not enough.
> You had to have the educative part for which you had
> to have *real* teachers, not just instructors. See? But she
> couldn't do it by herself, so the unknown God provided me.
> See? And I stayed till my real job was ready for me, day
> school teacher at the Magdalen where I'd been off and on
> since 1921.

Jessie's draft letters to Thelma all seem to me to betray a
desperate insecurity that Thelma did not recognise. Jessie craved
her approval, for something to outweigh the past, but Thelma
was oblivious to anything but her own determined analysis of all
parties. Jessie boasted to Thelma more than to anyone else about
her achievements, and her 'punishing schedules' (although the
latter was by now a favourite topic to most correspondents). She
boasted about her son-in-law's success in Oman, about being
invited to do a reading at the South Bank, where there was
standing room only: she even boasted jokingly about 'ecclesias-

tical connections', in that her producer Marilyn Imrie had married James Runcie, son of the Archbishop of Canterbury! At the start of the renewed correspondence she brought Thelma up to date on her achievements with a whole Jiffy bag full of cuttings, doctorates and letters, such as she often included in ones and twos in ordinary correspondence. And she sent her all the books. Thelma loved them all, except for 'This Wasted Day', the last story in *Where the Apple Ripens*, where the old Tinker is admitted to Heaven where she had hoped for a bed at the Model Lodging House. Apparently this one offended Thelma's religious sensibilities.

On the whole, then, the renewal of the friendship was a success. But I suspect that there is one draft here that never went to the saintly Thelma. It includes the following:

> An even deeper regret, the end of my friendship with Bertram. Were *your* antennae working? They might have been! I had a real 'crush' on your Gude man. Partly because he was generous about the work I gave him to read. Partly because he was Individual. His only fault, he didn't allow *me* to be Individual!!!
>
> For all that, and all that, I never regretted that 'crush'. One never regrets anything that sweetened life.

For all her 'punishing schedules', which on the whole she really enjoyed, Jessie found some time to enjoy retirement. She was able to attend Philip Larkin's funeral – 'you would have enjoyed the jazz,' she told Dr Donaldson – and visit some literary sites, Gray's Stoke Poges, Lowry's grave. Her favourite pilgrimage was to Rodmell, where her beloved Virginia Woolf had lived. She was curiously obsessed with the 'Bloomsberries', and read all about them, but was put off when the house at Rodmell was taken over by the National Trust, and the guide she met knew very little of the Woolf story.

In 1982 came the last house move, a very happy one. She wrote to Dr Donaldson:

Twelve flats reconstructed within the shell of a Victorian Gothic mansion. When I arrived to view mine, electricians milling around it with others whom they euphemistically described as 'mates', were enthusiastic. 'Missis,' they informed me, 'these are the finest flats in London.' And, do you know, I think they are right.

Beautiful stonework, lovely patio, right outside my sitting room. Space, privacy – O I can't tell you the benison of *that*! I could be in the heart of a wood, yet only seven minutes walk from shopping centre.

Too late in the season for me to garden real, from seed, that is. But leaving the installation of cooker, fridge, etc to anyone who cared to undertake same, I betook myself off to the nearest Nursery, and, first things first, furnished my lovely wide patio. Abloom now with fuchsias, geraniums, French marigolds and, as an act of faith, late though it be, planted next summer seeds of forget-me-nots, lavender, night-scented stock and wallflowers.

The original mansion had belonged to a Victorian master of Black Magic. Jessie loved it, and got endless pleasure from both flat and patio.

Her health was not wonderful in the '80s. She had a lot of trouble with her teeth, and was always most loath to visit a dentist. The angina and bronchitis persisted. But she could make a great story even out of minor ailments, as in this letter to Avril and Bill Wilbourne, in which she professed to be in a deep depression, because she had priced a book at a charity sale, and the woman asked ten pence, and then leaned forward and whispered 'Five pence to you since you're an Old Lady'.

She was quite right!! I look as if I were touching 100. My psoriasis has completely covered my head so that I don't *dare* apply LOVING CARE MEDIUM ASH BROWN any more.

So
I am snow white
Truth
Furthermore
My bunion is now over the top. Agonising. I can wear
nothing but black boots two sizes larger than my normal 5s.
I look like a Witch at the top
and
Like Puss in Boots waist downwards
Truth.
I look at Dad with jaundiced eye
Couldn't find him in New Jewish Charity Shop where he
was ensconced, mouth tripping him, till I noticed his fur
Cossack hat looming between and high above the row of
'Gents' shirts 75p'. He looked, in his brown anorak and
brown fur hat, like a brown Gnome.

We walked homewards in silence. I couldn't look anyone
in the face!

Attacked Dad the moment we got inside the house,
saying
'I didn't feel like Dr Kesson, or like Scotland's top writer –
I just felt like a *Witch* going around with a Brown Gnome!!'
So
I am deeply depressed.

RECOGNITION, HONOURS, REWARDS

Fame came late to Jessie, but she was able to enjoy it. In the '80s
she was awarded an Honorary Degree at Dundee, followed by
another, particularly special for her, at Aberdeen. She was asked,
with Gaelic poet Sorley Maclean, to unveil the Neil Gunn
memorial at Heights of Brae in 1987, and most strenuously,
was celebrated in *The Scots Magazine*, for which she first wrote in
1942, when she spent three days revisiting the sites of her early
years, with magazine editor Joy Hendry and photographer Alastair Scott. She was photographed for the Scottish National
Portrait Gallery, and her portrait was painted twice. She was

given a Scottish Arts Council award for *Where the Apple Ripens.* And she was much in demand for radio and television interviews and series. She was regularly asked to perform at the Edinburgh Book Festival.

It was suggested to her in the late '80s that she write a stage adaptation of *The White Bird Passes.* She said no, claiming that she did not know enough of the techniques of the theatre. But one notes she was attempting to adapt other work for the theatre, and suspects she had had enough of writing that work. So it was adapted by Anne Downie, and directed by Andi Ross at the Theatre Workshop in Edinburgh, in March 1986, and went on to a successful tour. A little later Andi Ross went on to the Tron Theatre in Glasgow, and Downie rewrote the play with a few more characters (the Theatre Workshop production had to be pared to a tiny budget). By May 1988 they had played to 2563 people over a three-week run. Jessie went to the first nights, spoke to the Press, signed books, even faced an audience for a chat. She was supportive and appreciative, though inevitably in private a little ambivalent, voicing minor doubts about comparative effectiveness to select correspondents.

Jessie had often been to read her work in Dundee, and had become a good friend of John Norton-Smith and James Caird, Professors of English and Geography respectively. It seems it was these two who made a case for her receiving an Honorary Doctorate of Laws in July 1984. She was thrilled, but made a comic ordeal out of it, in interview:

> They were very tall men by me; I'm nae very big . . . Lovely goon. You send yer measurements right enough. But fin I gaein into my goon just the same I could have gone oot and in at the sleeve o't . . . Fin ye come in, and the Chancellor and a' the graduands are called . . . and the Lord Provost you know, marching in this long aisle and the Caird Hall packed, with everything, and they a' stand as ye process doon the narrow and up in the top the organ's playin' the Gaudeamus: and the most ridiculous thought came into my heid . . . this tall chap was behind me . . . and I thocht *Alice in*

Wonderland right enough and it wis richt, I thocht there's a
porpoise right behind me! . . . Oh, I wis awfa pleased.[3]

It was in April 1987 that Sir Kenneth Alexander was installed as
Chancellor of the University of Aberdeen. In his gift were four
Honorary Doctorates, and so it was that Jessie was at last
recognised by the university she had so longed to enter as a girl.
Sir Kenneth wrote to me:

> I have a life-long interest in Scottish literature, and particu-
> larly Northern Scottish. This began with Neil Gunn's
> *Highland River* when I was a boy, and has been fairly
> obsessive ever since. I read *The White Bird Passes* when I
> was teaching at Aberdeen in the late fifties, and was very
> impressed by it. I remember Charlie Allan singing the
> praises of Jessie's work to me some fifteen years later, and
> on reading more my admiration increased. Jessie had not
> then been given the recognition she deserved, and I was glad
> of the opportunity to have the University honour such a fine
> writer and splendid human being with such strong roots in
> our part of Scotland.

Jessie and Johnnie duly went to Aberdeen, but Johnnie's deafness
was by now so disabling that her agent, Andrew Hewson,
partnered Jessie at the celebratory buffet supper. Jessie particularly appreciated the 'scarlet goon' she had written about so long
ago, and was the first Honorary Graduate to request, through
me, a translation of her Latin diploma: this caused temporary
consternation in the Administration, but was eventually forthcoming. Sir Kenneth further demonstrated his admiration for
Jessie by presenting the portrait of her by Michael Knowles to
the newly opened Elphinstone Institute at Aberdeen University
in 1999.

That visit to Aberdeen was also marked by a very special
occasion at Skene. Jessie's old schoolmates held a reunion lunch
in her honour, which was a big thrill: this was the occasion when
she was glad she hadn't done any evil behind the bicycle sheds,

and could look her old boyfriend *and* his wife of many years, full in the face!

One of the greatest honours of all came in 1987, when Jessie was invited, along with the great Gaelic poet Sorley Maclean, to unveil the memorial to Neil Gunn, whom she had admired above all others for many years. This took place at the opening of the Memorial Viewpoint and the unveiling of the Monument at Heights of Brae, Strathpeffer, on 31st October. It was James Caird, long an admirer and critic of Gunn, who gave the main address thereafter in Dingwall.

The *Scots Magazine* story turned into a gruelling epic, although Jessie made a lot of good stories out of it. Joy Hendry, editor of *Chapman* magazine, had written to Jessie in June 1980, just after the televising of *The White Bird Passes*. She was reviewing the new edition of the book in the magazine, and asked whether Jessie had any creative work to hand for a forthcoming issue of the magazine focused on women's writing. Jessie sent her 'Morning Has Broken', later entitled 'Good Friday', which had been read on radio but never published, and was invited to send more whenever possible. So gradually more of the short stories which would be collected in *Where the Apple Ripens* were printed in *Chapman*, 'Until Such Times', 'Life Model' and 'The Bridge'. She also sent a few poems, did readings for Hendry, and even wrote a rare review, of North-East writer Sheena Blackhall's volume of poems, *The Cyard's Kist*, in summer 1985.

Friendship developed between the two, and in July 1988 Hendry asked Jessie to agree to a venture for *The Scots Magazine*, 'in which you and I would make a tour of various places which you're particularly fond of, and I would write a piece for *The Scots Magazine* out of our conversation as we were going round (with photographer).' She suggested September. In one sense, the rest is history. The resultant piece was well written and informative, with glorious colour photographs by Alastair Scott, published in *The Scots Magazine* in October 1989. But it cost too much. Financially, the magazine was parsimonious, paying Hendry and Scott but not Jessie, and only agreeing to cover Jessie's expenses from Edinburgh. The venture had to be compressed into as short a time as possible. It left Jessie physically and emotionally exhausted. Some extracts from a long letter to Avril and Bill Wilbourne describe the ordeal.

> I was fairly tired simply getting ready to go, anxious about Dad, trying to ensure everything as easy as possible for him, food stock, pills, phone numbers etc.

Her OAP privilege ticket was out of date, and getting a new one meant effectively paying full fare.

> Then started my own packing. I'd bought two nice skirts, new. But was travelling in black tracksuit. Laid skirts on sofa to pack last to save creasing. This just an hour before setting off for train. Thought I'd check ticket which Travel Agent had given me in Agency envelope: No ticket! Rang them up. They apologised profusely, had forgotten to enclose it; would I collect it on way to train! I snapped my suitcase closed and shot off . . . [no skirts]
>
> Joy met me at station. I was staying the night at her place . . . Nice supper, after climbing to top of stairs, *six flights* to Joy's flat – exhausted, desperate to get to bed . . . Set off three hours behind schedule, which we never managed to make up on. The biggest rush in my life.
>
> Anyhow, we got to Ross-shire, interviews etc., from there to Elgin to our hotel where certain friends awaited my arrival. Supposed to be 8.15 pm – nearly ten when we arrived. I had hoped to change, wash, wear my new skirts with lovely tops, in short to blind Chris, Meggie, Pat, Bella Baird and Joan Grant . . . I was too exhausted to even think of changing. You'll realise that, when Bella said, shocked, 'It's an ambulance you need, Jessie.'
>
> I know what I must have looked like. A thin scarecrow from bosom upwards, and in my tracksuit, muddy from a day spent amongst wet heather and old farmyard dirt, my tracksuit trousers baggy with drawing myself here and there.

I looked exactly like Charlie Chaplin from bust downward. I certainly felt like him.

So I didn't bother about Oil of Ulay, Tweed, Green Glass beads. My morale entirely slumped.

'Nice things' included Sir Maitland Mackie driving to meet her, hug her, give her tea, and seeing Elizabeth Adair and her lovely house:

As you know Elizabeth drinks very rarely. She took one look at me. 'You need a dram,' she said. Whisky at 10.30 in the morning isn't Elizabeth, but she was shocked by how exhausted I looked.

As to her journey home, I will quote the description she gave Alastair Scott, who was 'Cameraman' to her 'Subject' throughout the trip:

Nadir was reached with arrival of Ticket Collector . . . Finally, in lugubrious voice, 'Ye'll hae tae pay Extra.'

Self, 'What do you mean, pay extra?'

Ticket Collector, tapping ticket as if it was incendiary bomb, 'This Saver's Ticket cannot be used on Fridays. This', he informed me, as if I was an idiot – I felt like one – 'This is Friday' . . .

Repeating as if I was deaf as well as dazed, 'Five pounds ninety-five pence.'

So I brought handbag to surface, started to grope recklessly within it praying I had £5.95 in purse. I flung out cigarette ends, spent matches, two hankies, no longer Persil white, faded bits of greenery from Orphanage garden, comb with relics of hair still clinging. I could feel the eyes of nearby passengers fixed with fascinated horror on contents of Subject's handbag!

There follows an account of hearing the train was running late, which would mean a taxi from King's Cross – and taxi fares doubled at midnight:

Subject tried to unearth purse in semi-darkness under table. Bumped head in so doing, kicked lady sitting opposite by mistake in my down-bent position. And to the great delight, I am sure, of nearby passengers had to produce handbag again. Looking even more disreputable second time round.

She had the usual £5, but not the £10 she would need if they were after midnight, but got her taxi at 11.15. 'Hadn't we the gaiety, despite all the stress!'

That stress unsurprisingly caused tension between Kesson and Hendry, and Jessie raged about *The Scots Magazine* in a draft letter to Hendry. She had expected

An illustrated, photographic pilgrimage of land and people who had affected my early years, not a traumatic, stressful, rape of spirit as it was for me. Stupid question, i.e. What caused Nervous Breakdown? If I, or indeed the doctors, knew what caused it They would have had a cure without hospitalisation!

The *Impertinence*!

But having expressed her anger, Jessie put it by, and described Hendry's article as first-class. She continued to try to interest Virago in Hendry's work, while Hendry insisted that *The Scots Magazine* pay for that colourful train journey between London and Edinburgh. After Jessie's death *Chapman* published her little play, *It Was upon a Lammas Nicht*. She had sent it in April 1994. It was first produced in summer 1990 as part of 'At the Highlanders' Umbrella' at the Eden Court Theatre, Inverness. A short play, it goes right back to cottar days, and contrasts a 'fallen' farm servant who has just given birth to a son with a stereotypically prim one, like Lil Jarvis in *Glitter of Mica*.

Jessie had never had much time for literary agents: she preferred to talk or write to publishers or producers direct, as we have seen. She started working with several at different times, but found they got in the way. But from 1981 Andrew Hewson of John Johnston was her agent, not always an easy role. The fact that he had a house in the North East of Scotland, at Aboyne, where she could go for holidays was not the only reason for her choice, although Jessie and Johnnie enjoyed that very much. She confided in Hewson in 1984 that she was 'holding on to my bit of capital for a very specific purpose! A toss-up between a mobile home (caravan) in a green place and a really nice carpet!' She confided the same ambition to Carmen Callil, having lowered an earlier ambition for an unaffordable cottage:

> I'm always amused by the life and letters of Sarah Jennings, who married John, Duke of Marlborough. Her cri de coeur was for 'an hous' [sic]. The nation gave her and Duke John *Blenheim*. But it never really pleased the indomitable Sarah. Didn't she give the architect and builders *decades* of Hell! I warm always to such a Duchess.
>
> All I will have to cope with one day, some day, is with a wee man on a mobile site, three miles from Brighton. But then, my aspirations don't match up with those of Duchess Sarah.

The longing for a little time in a green place was not to be fulfilled, although Lisa St Aubin de Terán had an eye out for a little place in Banff, and during Johnnie's final illness Jessie thought about a tiny flat in Elgin. The capital would be insufficient, and so, sadly, would be the time.

THE BBC

The radio version of *Another Time, Another Place* had been produced by Marilyn Imrie in 1980. Among Jessie's effects is a draft letter to Pat Phoenix (of *Coronation Street* fame), explaining that she had taken her title from a wreath Phoenix sent to a funeral, and thanking her. Jessie had written about the Italian prisoners-of-war in *North-East Review* in 1944, mentioning them casually in 'Angie', a description of a mill-owner who swears at and wages war on 'the forkers or Italians'. The following month she produced 'Moments from Time', in which

the Italians are the focus. She describes Paulo as handsome and
homesick, and Toni, much like Luigi in the novel, 'had "gamin"
written in his face.' The picture of Toni is central: of Marianno
we learn only that he was the craftsman. They have gone, leaving
'a ring made from a half-crown. A bottle containing the portrayal
of the Crucifixion, a star worn by a soldier of the King of Italy.'
Toni has promised to send a big box of grapes from Italy, but the
piece ends:

> I appreciate the latter promise in its momentary sincerity.
> It's with gladness I realise that once Toni is reinstated
> in Italy, he'll be too engrossed, 'Too much joke for
> friends, plenty merriment,' to have time to steal the
> grapes.[4]

A letter written to entertain Peter Calvocoressi in 1957 seems full
of affectionate remembrance:

> I hope you had a good holiday in Italy. I feel I know that
> country. During the war I looked after three Italian prison-
> ers. They were such contrasts. Toni, a barrow boy from
> Naples. Paulo, a carpenter from the hills near Rome. And
> Marianno, studious and in love. We worked together in the
> fields. And how Toni hated the bleak Scottish hills. 'Noth-
> ing for look but tatties and turnips. And weend. Bloody
> weend.' Italy, now, 'plenty sun. Plenty wine. Plenty
> *divertiment.*' . . . We understood each other fine. I learned
> a lot of Italian, and they picked up Scots! . . . And I learned
> so much about their homes and way of life. And dear, how
> much 'Macaron' I consumed in these years! We cooked and
> made toffee when depression was with them! And I loved
> when they sang Italian songs. When it came to work, Toni,
> true to type, 'me no understand'. The boss, to whom all non-
> Scots – far less Italians – were suspect, used to roar, 'No!
> Dammit! But if it had *skirts* on, ye wad soon understand!'
> How Toni used to grin, for in truth all women were *bella
> ragazza* to him. I excepted, since looking after them entailed

a firm understanding from the first day: 'No posseeble!'
Toni: 'Perch? . . .'

The very different tone and outcome of both novel and film is
already clear in the radio play, where Kesson and Imrie sub-
stituted a ship in a bottle for the Crucifixion as an appropriate
final image, but of course between them Kesson and Radford
added a great deal. Says Radford, 'We had this extraordinary
capacity to respond to each other's visual ideas.' In the radio
version, as so often, Jessie made use of a voice-over commentary
by the young woman, revealing her thoughts and feelings.
In the film, of course, such things have to be done visually,
and the novel benefits from the increased visual subtleties. In
the radio version there is no Harvest Home dance, and no
complex shift in the young woman's focus from the handsome
Paolo to the city barrow boy Luigi. Radford paid tribute to her
writing:

> She really was a real writer. She really was. It's quite clear
> that she had a grasp of human psychology and a passion and
> a drive through what she did, and a capacity to bring people
> alive which was really extraordinary.

Radford, Kesson, Phyllis Logan and the whole company received
some 14 international awards, and Radford's career was greatly
forwarded, while he was able to 'rescue her from oblivion' and
'give her the kind of dignity she craved'. He summed it up: 'Our
collaboration was so important. I don't think I've made a better
film than *Another Time, Another Place*'.
    In our interview with Jessie, she discussed the necessary differ-
ences between film and novel, saying the film by its nature could
not accommodate as much as the novel could suggest, instancing
the relationship of the cottar wives, and a full account of their
relationship with Findlay:

> What you *did* get was wonderful photography and the sense
> of the faces of the countryfolk, and the parallel scene wi' the

Italians and their culture and their faces and the scenes – Mike did that brilliantly.[5]

Whatever the truth of Radford's tale of Jessie's embarrassment about discussing the sex scenes in front of Johnnie, it is clear that aesthetically film and novel diverge most over the depiction of sex. Jessie managed to treat it with extreme delicacy in the novel, while indignant Aberdeen pensioners fussed in the *Press and Journal* over Radford's treatment in the film, blaming Jessie, of course. Thus, she was particularly pleased in a later interview with Frank Delaney:

> His observation was that my descriptions of sex in *Glitter of Mica* and *Another Time* were the best he had ever read. I feel he was right about that. Unlike today's Gruntings, Groanings, Frontals – and Backwards – presentations of sex. I consider it a very private performance to be described with subtlety, so that the reader can 'feel' and thus 'feeling' can relate to what is happening.

After this there were several possible projects that took up time and energy but came to nothing. There was her dearest wish, to make a film with Mike Radford of *Glitter of Mica*, and he developed an ambition to film her life story. Her advice and help were sought on various projects: could she help with the adaptation for television of Elspeth Barker's fine novel, *O Caledonia*, and she spent a lot of time trying to produce a film version of Norman Malcolm Macdonald's radio play *The Shutter Falls*. The next work of her own to preoccupy Jessie for the BBC was *You've Never Slept in Mine*. There is a puzzle in its history. When Jessie was leaving Scotland in 1975, she asked Gordon Emslie to return scripts he did not want to use, as she thought she could place them in London. In the case of *The Matron* she was right: it went to *Woman's Hour* and was broadcast in September 1976. She hinted strongly to him that *You've Never Slept in Mine* was a different case, written for Emslie and Scotland, and unlikely to sell in London, as it was set in Glasgow and featured the subculture and language of local girls in an approved school. All the same, Emslie did return it to her in February 1976. But by 1981 Marilyn Imrie was her Scottish producer, and was interested enough to ask her, warily,

> Dear Jessie, I wonder how you are feeling about *You've Never Slept in Mine*? I very much want to do it and I think some time ago sent you a copy of the script with my thoughts about how things needed to be reworked. Can you let me know if it is going to be possible for you to work on it in the next three or four months as I would like to broadcast it in the autumn.

It is not clear why Emslie rejected it, or whether it was much changed when Imrie became interested, or whether the intervening years had brought a more relaxed attitude to the subject matter at the BBC. The subject matter is certainly unusually explicit for the BBC, but Imrie suggests it may just have been that during these intervening years Radio Scotland had acquired its own drama slots, so that producers were no longer totally dependent on London acceptance. Her radio production was particularly sensitive and intelligent. Imrie was wary of professional actresses playing the parts of these variously abused and delinquent young girls, and she and Jessie went to the Assessment Centre (the 'Sessy') at Liberton, and recorded the girls there. Imrie recalls, 'It was quite harrowing, but it made the production what it was.' She was enormously impressed by the way Jessie related to the girls, who were quite at home with her. This is the production of Jessie's work of which Imrie remains proudest.

By November the script had progressed. Imrie wrote, 'I think the script is on the right lines now, although I feel we need to do some more work on Debbie herself and Miss McCabe.' By late April 1982, the script was satisfactory. The play was scheduled for November 1982, and Imrie reported: 'I think that your script worked like a charm, and that the cast were excellent, especially Elaine Collins and Phyllis Logan.' Success is demonstrated by the fact that in September 1983 Jessie wrote to Carmen Callil, 'BBC have just commissioned me to adapt it and extend it into a 50 minute television play.' It went out in July 1985, directed by David Hayman, produced by Tom Kinninmont, and with Marilyn Imrie as script editor. Jessie, of course, acted as consultant. Hayman wrote to her, 'What a wonderfully vibrant, vivacious woman you are. You put all of us "kids" to shame.'

This story of a girl sent to an approved school, not for any crime, but because her father had been sexually abusing her, is perhaps Jessie's most controversial play. The television version is fairly explicit, and there is a fine portrait too of Debbie's friend Ginny, who finally betrays her. '*Her* problem was her Maw, who was young. Ginny was born when her mother was 14, and mother was far more physically attractive than Ginny, who had to pretend her mother was her sister. The same mother used to take over her daughter's boyfriends.' This subject was near Jessie's heart, after years of working with such disadvantaged girls, let alone her own background.

In 1983, Jessie reported to Marilyn Imrie that she had two works in the pipeline, *North of the River*, which would become *Three Score and Ten, Sir!* and 'N 13'. She produced a synopsis of the latter, which was never to be written, and seems very out of character, as it is set in a big house full of tenants, including a prostitute, a Scottish army deserter and old Miss Minter, living rent-protected, with an illicit cat. The plot involves IRA men in the basement, and climaxes in Miss Minter and Tibbles being blown up. But another letter to Imrie, who was in charge of the new radio serial *Citizens*, may shed some light on the genesis of the idea.

> We lived for a year in such a background. Westbourne Grove, near Paddington Green, Notting Hill, in a house of the Motley.
>
> All the tenants, including self, answering all rings of the bell to Policemen looking for an Army Deserter, with whom our landlady had fallen in love and was sheltering!!! Johnnie, an even greater collaborator, in Butcher's shop plucking turkeys with Deserter, to tide us over Christmas.

The immaculate pin-striped Gent, 'something in the City', with expensive briefcase, which he left lying one day on hall table. Landlady – and self – opened it out of curiosity. It contained – Bread and Dripping.

. . . And always the Vice Squad hovering around, not sure if our Rooming House was a brothel!

The project came to nothing, but this account, with comic overtones, seems much more promising than the IRA terrorising an old lady by holding a cat to ransom.

Despite the topic of incestuous sexual abuse, the radio version of *You've Never Slept in Mine* had an all-female cast, as *Dear Edith* had done. Jessie was unobtrusively focusing more and more on women characters, their situations, emotions and points of view. Her last radio play of the '80s, *Three Score and Ten, Sir!*, produced by Imrie in 1986, has one functionally necessary male character, the protagonist's son-in-law, but again it is preoccupied with women: the daughter making a home for her ageing mother, the granddaughter having to give up her room, most of all Marj herself, having to move 'North of the River', virtually out of reach of her home district and friends. The play is clear-sighted about old age, loneliness and the consciousness of the approach of death. It is occupied also with the humdrum, as the old women complain about sharing dormitories when on holiday, with others who snored about the eating habits of others at the weekly lunches, about the problems of going to live with your daughter. It is only saved from being unbearably gloomy by the unarticulated love and good will underlying the dull fabric of everyday life in the household.

Marj is initially miserable at her daughter's home, because promised lifts to the monthly 'social' at the club back 'home' do not materialise, and she feels forgotten. But when she does eventually get taken to the social, it is to find a new Secretary who does not know her; that two of her closest friends are dead, that one has been moved away compulsorily into sheltered housing, and the very street where she was born and lived has been demolished to make way for a motorway. All she can do is try to make the best of her daughter's home and family.

Jessie was particularly proud of this play because it was the first time she had ventured to write about English working-class characters, not Scots. *Dear Edith* had been set in England, but with characters in a neutral middle-class way of speaking. Now, after 35 years in London, Jessie was confident of the idiom. She was also proud that it was not inspired by her own experience:

> But now, I have a play going on quite soon which is a Cockney play in Cockney dialect in which they say the dialect's excellent. I now *know* it, and I don't think it has anything to with me, this play, at all.[6]

PUBLISHING

Jessie's publishing history in the '80s and '90s is, for once, much simpler than it looks. She herself listed *The White Bird Passes* as being issued by Paul Harris in 1980 and 1984, and also by Hogarth in 1991 and Virago in 1992. Similarly *Where the Apple Ripens and Other Stories* was issued by Chatto & Windus in 1983, by Hogarth Press in 1989 and by Virago Modern Classics in 1992. And there was an omnibus edition of all four books in one volume from Chatto & Windus in 1991. But only Paul Harris's edition is a completely separate venture, while identical in pagination.

The Paul Harris story is soon told. Harris was a young publisher in Scotland who wanted to publish new books, including his own on the trial of Sheila Garvie, and to reprint some important Scottish titles too long unavailable. He was the first to publish David Toulmin, farm worker and storyteller, who became a particularly beloved writer in North-East Scotland. Harris was advised by Trevor Royle, former Literature Director of the Scottish Arts Council, who joined the firm as Editorial Director. When a new edition of *The White Bird Passes* was mooted, to coincide with the television dramatisation, Jessie opted for the 'young Scottish publisher' over Chatto, who had apparently done nothing for the book since 1958, and where the personnel had all changed from those she formerly worked with. Harris did two printings of *The White Bird Passes*, with an Introduction by

Cuthbert Graham, and followed it up with *Glitter of Mica*, with an
Introduction by Dr William Donaldson in 1982. Harris had
youth, energy and great enthusiasm for his reprint project, which
also included titles such as Robin Jenkins's *The Cone Gatherers*, Ian
Macpherson's *Shepherds' Calendar* and *Wild Harbour*, *The Thir-
teenth Disciple* by James Leslie Mitchell (Lewis Grassic Gibbon)
and Edwin Muir's *Poor Tom*.

Unfortunately, a combination of accident, omission, inexperi-
ence and shortage of capital meant that Harris's firm was forced
into receivership in 1985. All files were removed from the office
and permanently disappeared, even including the notes for a book
Harris himself was currently writing. He wrote to me in 1997:

> I do remember that Jessie wrote me a remarkably generous
> letter following the collapse of the company. Many authors
> were, understandably, angry at losing money in the collapse
> but she wrote a most understanding letter in which, so far as
> I recall, she took the view it was only money, which, in the
> broader picture, was quite unimportant. Only two or three
> authors – out of 200 or 300 – wrote to me in those sort of
> terms and at the time, when I was feeling rather vulnerable, I
> found her sweet letter quite touching. Typically warm-
> hearted of her.

The switches of Jessie's work otherwise, from Chatto & Windus,
who were first to publish *Another Time, Another Place* in 1983 (in a
great rush, to coincide with the film), and *Where the Apple Ripens*
in 1985, to Hogarth, were largely cosmetic matters, as Chatto had
owned Hogarth for some time (although Jessie was thrilled to be
on the Hogarth list, begun by her beloved Woolfs). Similarly, by
1982, Carmen Callil was head of Chatto, Hogarth and Virago
and, when she left Chatto in 1993, she took Jessie's work with her,
so that all the books were in Virago Modern Classics by 1993.

As we would expect, Jessie soon made friends with the new
generation of staff at Chatto, and her correspondence with Callil,
Christine Carswell and others there proceeded, with the by-now-
predictable occasional bump. Jessie toyed for a long time with the

idea of an autobiography, for which Callil offered her, in her own
time, 'a large unbounceable cheque'. For a while, new life seemed
given to this project by the reunion her schoolmates had had for
her in the Red Star Inn at Skene, when she came to Aberdeen for
her Honorary Doctorate. It had been a disorienting experience.
Her 'report' to Callil and Carswell promised new inspiration:

> A most curious experience. Our roles were reversed, you see,
> and we were uncomfortable in them. Had difficulty in
> adjusting. 'Reunions' have always made good novels . . .
> The point about these novels: the protagonists all came from
> the same kind of ambience, and 20 years later remained in
> the same kind of ambience. My Reunion was a psychological
> thing. The 'Orphanage bairns', as we were described, were
> Persona Non Grata in this insular rural school playground.
> Non-rooted, unlike the local farmers' children, who were
> hereditary in their background.

She wrote to Jeremy Lewis at the firm:

> Maybe, though, Aberdeen *did* help to solve the problem. I
> had a strange psychological experience at a lunch at Skene,
> village of the Orphanage . . . It struck me at the time, maybe
> this was the method that would work. Beginning with an
> honoured Lunch given to 'recognise' an Honour . . . Then
> in Flash Back, lead up to how it was achieved. I have an
> instinct, a feeling, that this might be the way.

Her instinct was right, and she would treat the subject matter
superbly, but it would be not an autobiography, but a one-woman
television play that she would produce. *Reunion* was one of the last
acting triumphs of Anne Kristen.

The proposed title of the autobiography changed from *Mistress
of None* to *A Different Drum*:

> On reflection, I realised that in my life, the root cause of all
> my joys – and in a way, all my woes – has been that I've

'marched to the music of a different drum'. Never deliberately. Just that you can only 'keep in time' with the tune *you*
hear.

The Thoreau metaphor she picks up here highlights much the
same concept as the 'ootlin', which she underlined for us in the
interview in *Scottish Writers Talking* in 1985.[7]
Her correspondence with the publishers ranges widely, over
publishing matters and book covers, her Honorary Graduations,
her radio work, who should write the new Introductions –
Douglas Dunn for *White Bird*, Sue McGregor for *Glitter of
Mica*. But it never attained the exuberance of her letters to Peter
Calvocoressi, who was fundamentally important in her life, and
with whom she continued to enjoy the three-monthly lunches
until she herself stood him up for no reason, and they drifted out
of touch, perhaps in the mid-'80s. She never refused regular
requests to travel to publicise her work although, by 1990, it was
all becoming a bit much, with chronic angina, at least yearly
bronchitis, and horrific toothaches. As early as 1978, Bill Swainson of John Calder had written that it had been good to see her,
'even though you *were* suffering from toothache and the side
effects of your patented cure! You know, a dentist might be a wee
bit cheaper in the long run!' Increasingly, as she wrote to Dr
Donaldson:

I'm aye fine pleased to be homeward bound, curled up in my
armchair, drawing board on my knees, pen in hand; privacy
and 'sweet content'.

Coda

The last years were brief, and relatively quiet in most senses – at times horribly loud for Jessie. Johnnie progressively became completely deaf, which was a sore trial for both of them, and meant that Jessie heard much more than she wanted of extremely loud sports commentary on television. She wrote of him staring 'boss-eyed at the World Cup'. He had trouble with his legs, the after-effects of strokes, had to give up walking, a favourite occupation, and was eventually housebound. This time she was right: she *was* watching him die, and it was very hard, as he became more and more frail. She wrote to old friend Betty Wilson in February 1994:

> His health, now in his 88th year, has been failing for the past two years, another cardiac arrest + Emphysema – and Parkinson's. He's very frail. It's 'waiting in the wings' time now, a sad and anxious time, watching the deterioration, a kind of day at a time.

By April they had been married 58 years.

Jessie's own health was not improving. Her smoking had had to stop in the '60s, but later was as constant as ever, until her last two years, when her chest was very bad. The angina had forced her to cut down on alcohol. The bronchitis inevitably remained a problem. The troublesome teeth ached away. Although she would not admit to being seriously ill until the day of Johnnie's funeral, it was clear to those close to her that she had lost a lot of weight, and it is likely that the lung cancer that finally killed her had been with her some time before that.

But this does not mean that the '90s were years of retreat. She went on writing when possible, and gave a lot of her meagre free time to helping to encourage younger writers. Keith Murray, a young Scottish publisher in the North East, planned to publish *Three's Company*, stories by three local women writers, Sheena Blackhall, Rosemary Mackay and Wilma Murray. Jessie was asked to select the actual texts, which she did with care and attention, as a number of manuscript notes testify. And *The Scots Magazine* story had an aftermath. Moira Innes and Alistair Campbell of the Libraries and Museums department in her native Elgin approached her via Alastair Scott ('Cameraman'), asking if both would agree to adjudicate a local short-story competition in 1990. She agreed with alacrity, always delighted to return to Moray. The library held some very happy Elgin memories: 'One of my happiest memories of my childhood in Elgin is of my visits to the Library . . . I always made a dive for Andrew Lang's Fairy Books, in *all* their colours.' She duly spent a lot of time on the entries, presented the prizes, and gave a talk. On her return home she sent a copy of *Three's Company* for the library, and wrote:

> My one regret about Elgin visit, not quite feeling I gave either enough time or depth to help the Young Writers' Group. They could be the Inheritors, you see. I cannot think of anyone better to encourage them than the three writers in enclosed book. Also, these three girls would encourage a younger audience to Library Readings, and to the Library itself. I've always had empathy with and willingness to help the writers coming behind me.

After Moira Innes's retirement, a gentle epistolary relationship developed between Jessie and Alistair Campbell, largely concerning Elgin and her favourite haunts there, or books and writers. He asked her to judge the poetry competition held in 1993. Again she was delighted at the idea of returning to Elgin. This time the winning entries were printed as a little book, *A Poet's Quair*, for which she wrote a brief introduction, and to which she added a small group of her own poems, the only five she thought worth much, she said at the time: this certainly makes the volume a collector's item!

Not all her plans came to fruition. In 1991, Jessie exhausted herself so much at the Edinburgh Book Festival that she could not go north to celebrate the centenary of Proctor's, although she had written two fine pieces, quoted earlier, about her own time there for the *Press and Journal*. Characteristically, she wrote to send a donation – and forgot to enclose her cheque. In 1994 Banff and Buchan District Council asked her to judge a playwriting competition along with playwright Donald Campbell. Despite her own ill health, and Johnnie's frailty, she consulted with Iain Macaulay by telephone on 3rd August and did her bit. Another poignant and appropriate occasion she had to forgo because of a combination of Johnnie's illness and her own exhaustion. She was asked by George Gray (of Smeaton), now Chairman of the Hanover Housing Association, to perform the opening ceremony at West Park Court, a new development of sheltered housing just yards from Lady Lane in Elgin in December 1993. Her friend Mrs Isabel Baird stepped in at the last minute as her understudy. But earlier that year she 'ring-fenced' her plans for the poetry competition, writing to Alistair Campbell:

> Time had come for me to pace myself, for *both* our sakes. So I have cut down on commitments.
>   But
> Not *Elgin*. My daughter, and indeed Daughter In Law, both loving and caring towards their Dad, are going to stand in for me for my Elgin visit.

When she was too sick to go to Elgin to open the sheltered housing, she wrote strikingly to the Campbells:

> I couldn't bear to cancel Elgin; not even so much for my Elgin friends, but for very old friends who made the journey thinking I'd be there. That made me feel sick in the place where I *think*.

So Alistair Campbell and his wife Sheila were more or less the last new friends Jessie made, but the bond was strong. After her death he wrote to Avril, 'Jessie was an incredibly gifted writer, and an

amazing person. It was a privilege to know her.' Jessie would have
appreciated even more another sentence:

> How much we enjoyed Jessie's company: her love of poetry,
> her devotion to Neil Gunn, her feeling for Moray, and her
> empathy for humanity made her visits a delight – an
> exhausting delight!

Her heart was in Elgin, but recognition in England always moved
her. Her last plays on television reached a wide audience, of
course. But she was delighted by the implied recognition when
Maura Dooley asked her to read at the South Bank Centre in
1992: she really enjoyed the evening, and was amazed and
delighted that the theatre was full.

THE BBC

Her last two plays would be long-distilled and fine achievements.
Both survive in more than one version, indicating a freedom of
interpretation because the writer had so perfectly mastered the
situations. *Reunion*, broadcast in 1990, was a play for television. It
generally followed the pattern that Jessie had discerned as a
possible way of structuring her autobiography. This is as near
as she could approach to making an unbroken circle of her life.
She could not be reunited with her mother in Elgin, or reclaim the
White Bird, but she could survey her life from her arrival at Skene
to her return there, a Doctor of Letters, in April 1987.

The play is simplified very carefully. There is just one character,
an older woman, and just one setting, her room. The character
meditates on and responds to pictures of the class reunion recently
held, and an old one of the class that sat the 'Qualifying'
examination together. She speaks to her friend Isa by phone,
sometimes to people in the photographs – often to herself or her
mirror image. Very like Jessie herself, the character is an 'Ootlin',
completely at home in no society. She touches on many of the
themes that we have seen Jessie preoccupied by: envying of other
girls, who were ironically envious of her; singing in church,

especially the Minister's solo rendition of Blake's 'Jerusalem'; the way that all the orphans were always essentially transients, none destined to be buried in the churchyard. She remembers a fictional version of 'Missy Crooks', and the Orphanage Matron and the Dominie. She meditates on her mirror image, wrinkles 'maskin the young quine that still lives inside you', and on the first boyfriend, Band of Hope and all. At the end she puts away the photographs, shuts the drawer, and is seen contentedly alone.

One new passage here is about being an artist, about having an Ego:

> Tak ony o the Creative Arts – Music, Painting, Poetry. The folk that practise them. You could never inflict your stuff on the public, if your Ego didnae exist. Ye wadna dare think your work was worth onything if ye hadna an Ego. Mind you! I didna aye hae an Ego. It was non-existent whiles.

This perhaps supports my view that Jessie wrote herself, and effectively wrote continuity into her own personality. She went a long way towards making, and healing, herself. This last self-portrait has a quality of equanimity, however hard won.

In an early version the last play, *Cold in Coventry*, was also called *Reunion*. But that title was certainly ironic and rather misleading, as this is the final treatment of that pivotal situation, the Return to the Institution in Disgrace. This recapitulates her deepest emotional fears and anxieties. Her mother had borne her in an Institution in disgrace, and fear of this basic situation had helped to shape her psyche – and her sex life – all her life long. Again it has one main character, a female, and in a feminine quandary. It was broadcast on Radio 4 on the 9th December 1991, directed by Marilyn Imrie. Again, several versions survive, and the artist has a clear and mature grasp of her material, trying out different versions of her heroine. As always, the heroine wants to insist, virtually simultaneously, that no, she is not pregnant, but that she had no end of chances. But, in this last version, the girl thinks she may indeed be pregnant. She has had one encounter with the Boot Boy:

You'd moved too fast to notice the Boot Boy in his shed behind the garden wall and was bent down over the parsley when he pounced. Grabbing you from behind and sending you both sprawling on the ground. Give us a Kiss, he kept saying. Give us a kiss then! Hands everywhere, mouth over mine, sweating. His tongue! No! Leave me be! Leave me! Scared that Cook would come out, you struggled out of his grasp, your apron tearing in his hand, and raced into the kitchen. Capless and grubby.

Emma is extremely ignorant, naive and afraid:

He kissed me. Hot, tasting of tea and onions, hands every-where. No. No. No. All you have to do is kiss a boy. Maryann said – you start a baby kissing. No. No.

The play is suffused with the girls in the Institution singing hymns and prayers, and occasionally, more secular chants. The situation is not resolved. The play ends with Emma daydreaming about alternative scenarios, and going off to see Madam to hear her fate.

It is much more than a personal reminiscence, although Jessie *was* Returned in Disgrace, for her lack of concentration on her work. It is a final rendition of a wider universal situation, and the stark choices faced by her generation, when girls were ignorant, contraception was unknown and the glamour of romance all too often contrasted with and concealed the reality of the Workhouse: 'It's the Workhouse for us when we're pregnant.'

We all thought about the chances we might get when we went out into the world. As Madam called it. We whispered about them. Looked forward to them. We never wanted to be *pregnant*. Not until we were married. We knew what would happen to us!

The last new story she published was 'Cold in Coventry', which followed the radio play very closely, except that here Emma is less naive and ignorant, and is not afraid she may be pregnant. She contributed it to Aonghas MacNeacail's *A Writer's Ceilidh for Neil Gunn* in 1991.

Johnnie died at last in the North Middlesex Hospital on 4th August 1994. Exhausted by years of anxious nursing, Jessie had hoped for a little more time to collect herself, but it was not to be. She succumbed very quickly to the lung cancer which had been causing her unacknowledged pain for some time, and died in the Whittington Hospital on 26th September. She had famously invented her own epitaph, and told it to Joy Hendry: 'HERE, VERY MUCH AGAINST *HER* WILL, LIES JK.' But a stone did not seem appropriate: she and Johnnie had both wanted to be cremated, and their ashes scattered at Abriachan. The family went north, and Jean Lindsay, the current owner of Achbuie, and Mrs Katharine Stewart, local writer, scattered the ashes, while Avril and the family planted a rowan tree as a memorial.

> My family close, loving. Avril – daughter – was telling me that Sharon – her daughter – my eldest grandchild, mother of Sarah, my *great*-grandchild, was having a 'speakie'. Sharon was regretting that Sarah 'will never know Grandma (me). Not as *we* knew her. Dancing, kicking up her legs.' Seems such a small thing to be remembered for. But I know, I think, what was meant. Joie de vivre – maybe a good thing to be remembered for.
>
> As the poet said – William Allingham? (and poets do say things better than most):
> What a little thing to remember for years
> To remember with tears.
> I hope they never remember 'with tears' – we did have so much joy.

Notes

Jessie's own papers, freely quoted in this book, have been deposited in the National Library of Scotland, where they will in due course be catalogued. Others are in private hands. These notes will generally deal only with printed material publicly available. As well as the abbreviations for Jessie's books given in the Preface, others will be used: *SM – Scots Magazine, NER – North-East Review, P&J – Press and Journal, SWT – Scottish Writers Talking, 1996* (includes an edited version of interviews with Isobel Murray and Bob Tait) .

INTRODUCTION

1. *NER,* Oct/Nov 1941. The story is reprinted in *Somewhere Beyond: A Jessie Kesson Companion,* B&W 2000.
2. Colette Douglas-Home's interview was published in *The Scotsman,* 16/7/90.
3. Chatto & Windus, 1958. Page numbers will be given after quotations in text.
4. See Douglas Dunn's Introduction to *The White Bird Passes,* Hogarth Press, 1991.
5. See Lynn Abrams, *The Orphan Country: Children of Scotland's Broken Homes from 1845 to the Present Day,* John Donald Publishers, 1998, p 81.
6. Abrams, p 83.
7. Abrams, p 204.
8. See above, Note 2.
9. See James Ferguson, 'Talk, Talk, Talk' in George Burnett, ed., *Scotland on the Air,* Edinburgh BBC, 1938, p 72.
10. In a review of John Drakakis, ed., *British Radio Drama* in *Cencrastus* Number 6, Autumn 1981, p 37.
11. The second volume of Asa Briggs's magisterial history, *The Golden Age of Wireless,* OUP, 1965, finishes in 1939: John Gray in 'Broadcasting and Scottish Culture' in David Daiches, ed., *A New Companion to Scottish Culture,* Polygon, 1981 gives the golden age of Scottish radio as 'between 1947 and 1955' (p 40): W. H. McDowell's

The History of Broadcasting in Scotland, Edinburgh University Press, 1992, agrees with Gray, '1947 to the mid-1950s' (pp 55, 61, 86).
12. See, for example, Abrams, cited above, and John Murphy, *British Social Services: The Scottish Dimension*, Scottish Academic Press, 1992.
13. *SWT*, 1996, p 58; also 77.

CHAPTER ONE: ELGIN

1. Charles McKean, *The District of Moray: An Illustrated Architectural Guide*, Scottish Academic Press, 1987, p 7.
2. Herbert B. Mackintosh, *Elgin Past and Present*, 1914, J. D. Yeadon, p 165.
3. Jessie Kesson, 'My Scotland', *The Scottish Review: Arts and Environment* 35, August 1984, pp 39–41.
4. Mackintosh, pp 181, 147.
5. James Guthrie, 'Settlement Patterns and Communications' in Donald Omand, ed., *The Moray Book*, Paul Harris, 1976, pp 234–5.
6. *Northern Scot*, Christmas number, 1950.
7. 'Until Such Times' is the most vivid generally accessible treatment, *WAR* pp 106–17.
8. Colette Douglas-Home, *The Scotsman*, 16/7/90.
9. *SWT*, p 60.
10. *SWT*, p 56.
11. Julie Davidson, 'The Essential Jessie Kesson', *The Scotsman*, 21/4/80, p 13.
12. *The Northern Scot*, 27/5/06.
13. Douglas-Home, as above.
14. Betsy Whyte, born into a travelling family in 1919, was Jessie's near-contemporary. See *The Yellow on the Broom*, W. R. Chambers, 1979 and *Red Rowans and Wild Honey*, Corgi, 1991.
15. In a letter to Dr William Malcolm.
16. 'The Shadow', *SM*, November 1946, pp 71–4.
17. *SM*, April/September 1949, pp 21–5.
18. Joy Hendry, 'Jessie Kesson Country', *SM*, October 1989, pp 11–22.
19. She did tell radio producer Stewart Conn in the course of her correspondence with him, but not so as to suggest to him that this was a little-known fact, let alone a great secret.
20. Obituary in the *Elgin Courier*, 17/5/46.
21. Kipling's 'The Heathen', adapted.
22. See Chapter Seven: The BBC, pp 187–8.
23. *SM*, April 1942, p 14.
24. Often printed, under various titles: first in *SM*, June 1942, pp 204–5. See *Somewhere Beyond: A Jessie Kesson Companion*.

25. *SM*, August 1942, pp 387–90.
26. *SM*, January 1946, p 249.
27. *SM*, November 1949, pp 214ff.
28. *NER*, December 1943, pp 3ff.
29. Before decimalisation, threepence was 1/80 of £1.
30. *Country Living*, April 1990.

CHAPTER TWO: SKENE

1. 'Railway Journey', *NER*, October 1941, p 5. *P&J*, 12/9/91.
2. See *Third Statistical Account of Scotland*, vol. 7, 1952, 'The County of Aberdeen', pp 179–89.
3. Dorothy Haynes, *Haste Ye Back*, Jarrold, 1973.
4. *SWT*, p 58; *WBP* p 118.
5. 'My Scotland' in *The Scottish Review: Arts and Environment* 35, August 1984, p 39.
6. Maurice Hewlett's *Forest Lovers* was published in 1898, and has fairly deservedly sunk without trace. A rather arch medieval romance between Prosper le Gai and Isoult la Desirous set in the forest of Morgraunt, it is, like its hero, 'beset with white birds'. In Chapter 5 Prosper sees 'a white bird come fluttering with a dropt wing, two hen-harriers in close pursuit . . . She bled in the breast . . . her screaming, which was to him like a girl crying, moved him strangely.' As much as William Sharp's 'The Valley of White Poppies', Jessie's given source, this surely helps to produce the title of the novel, although Sharp's wording is crucial:

   A white bird floats there like a drifting leaf:

   It feeds upon faint sweet hopes and perishing dreams
   And the still breath of unremembering grief.
   And as a silent leaf the white bird passes.

   Also relevant to Jessie's experience was a belief among travelling people that a circling white dove was a forerunner of death: 'An ye will get a thing, fer Ah've seen it masel – if a buddie is gaunna die, but it's no very often an is jist a warnin – thir a thing like a white pigeon comes an hit traivels in fron o ye. Ye cannae get it oot o yer een an ye ken somebuddie is gaunna go' (Roger Leitch, ed., *The Book of Sandy Stewart*, Scottish Academic Press, 1988).
7. These sayings are not, of course, all from the Bible. Sources; Proverbs 22:6; Ecclesiastes 9:10; an English proverb from the Latin; *Othello*. *P&J*, 12/9/91.

8. *P&J*, 12/9/91.
9. *NER*, April 1946, p 5.
10. *NER*, September 1946, pp 5–8.
11. *Country Living*, April 1990.
12. 'Pilgrimage', *SM*, June 1946, pp 167–70.
13. 'The Years Between', *SM*, April 1942, pp 14–18.
14. *NER*, September 1946, pp 5–8.
15. *SM*, January 1946, pp 249–53.
16. Chrissie Gibson, *Memories of Finzean: Schooldays 1925–1933*, Braw Promotions, 1997, pp 82–83.
17. 'The silver birch is a dainty Lady' – first line of E. Nesbit's poem, 'Child's Song in Spring'.
18. 'L'Envoi': in fact, his 'The Long Trail'.
19. H. M. Paterson, 'Incubus and Ideology: The Development of Secondary Schooling in Scotland, 1900–1939' in *Scottish Culture and Scottish Education 1800–1980*, eds. Walter M. Humes and Hamish M. Paterson, John Donald, 1983, pp 204–5.
20. G. S. Osborne, *Scottish and English Schools: A Comparative Study of the Last Fifty Years*, Longman, 1966, p 169.
21. See Jayne D. Stephenson and Callum G Brown, 'The View from the Workplace: Women's Memories of Work in Stirling c 1910 – c 1950', in Eleanor Gordon and Esther Breitenbach, eds, *The World is Ill Divided: Women's Work in Scotland in the Nineteenth and Early Twentieth Centuries*, Edinburgh University Press 1990, pp 11–15. Cf. Lynn Jamieson, ' "We all left at 14": girls' and boys' schooling 1900–1930' in Judith Fewell and Fiona Paterson, eds, *Girls in their Prime: Scottish Education Revisited*, Scottish Academic Press, 1990, pp 16–37.
22. 'no continuing city': see Hebrews 13:14.
23. Chrissie Gibson, pp 59–60.

CHAPTER THREE: `CHRONICLE OF FAILURE´

1. Julie Davidson, *The Scotsman*, 21/4/80.
2. See, eg, *SWT*, pp 68–70.
3. 'The Years Between', *SM*, April 1942, pp 14–18.
4. 'Ferm Deem', *SM*, February 1946, pp 339–44, p 132.
5. Quoted in T. C. Smout and Sydney Wood, *Scottish Voices 1745–1960*, Collins, 1990, p 132.
6. Members' Handbook 1945–46, which retrospectively covers the war years: courtesy of Grace Law.
7. 'I'll Walk Beside You', *NER*, May 1942, p 9.

CHAPTER FOUR: MENTAL HOSPITAL

1. Colette Douglas-Home, Interview with Jessie Kesson, *The Scotsman*, 16/7/90.
2. Elaine Showalter, *The Female Malady: Women, Madness and English Culture 1830–1980*, Virago, 1987, p 121.
3. Showalter, p 134.
4. Showalter, p 137.

CHAPTER FIVE: NEW LIFE

1. See Murphy, p 97.
2. Abrams, p 37.
3. Abrams, p 41.
4. Abrams, p 42.
5. Cited in Abrams, p 45.
6. Abrams, p 29.
7. Cited in Abrams, pp 51–2.
8. Abrams, p 66.
9. Reissued by House of Lochar, 1998.
10. Abrams, p 69.
11. See above Introduction, p 4.
12. When she was asked by J. B. Salmond, the editor, to take over Neil Gunn's 'Country Dweller's Year' series, she followed his example of using an alternative name, in this case her early childhood name, Ness Macdonald.
13. *SM*, April 1946, pp 17–19.
14. *SM*, July 1946, p 268.
15. *SM*, September 1946, pp 415–18. For a fuller account of many aspects of Abriachan, see the books of Katharine Stewart, especially *A Croft in the Hills*, Oliver & Boyd, 1960.
16. Isaiah 35:4.
17. *SWT*, p 57.
18. *NER*, October 1946, pp 7–10.
19. It was produced by Elizabeth Adair on 24th March 1946.
20. Colette Douglas-Home, *The Scotsman*, 16/7/90.

CHAPTER SIX: COTTAR WIFE AND WRITER

1. David Kerr Cameron, *The Ballad and the Plough*, Gollancz, 1978, p 65. John R. Allan, *Farmer's Boy*, repr. Serif Books, 1935, repr. 1948, p 47.

2. *SWT*, p 65.

3. Kerr Cameron, p 70.

4. Kerr Cameron, *The Cornkister Days*, Gollancz, 1984, p 18; *The Ballad and the Plough*, p 75.

5. *SWT*, pp 172–3. David Toulmin wrote many documentary articles and short stories about cottar life in the North East, which shed light on the working conditions the Kessons experienced. See especially *Hard Shining Corn*, Impulse Publications, 1972, *Harvest Home*, Paul Harris Publishing 1978, *Straw into Gold*, Impulse Publications, 1981, *A Chiel Among Them*, Gourdas House, 1982.

6. *NER*, December 1943, p 9. Psalm 45 is a love song, and verse 8 reads: 'All thy garments smell of myrrh, and aloes, and cassia, out of the ivory palaces, whereby they have made thee glad.'

7. 'Nan Shepherd in Recollection', *Aberdeen University Review*, Spring 1990, pp 187–91.

8. Nan Shepherd's review of *WBP* was in *Aberdeen University Review*, Vol. XXXVII, No. 119, Autumn 1958, p 389.

9. Silvie Taylor, 'Remembering J.B.', *SM*, December 1991, pp 267–78.

CHAPTER SEVEN: THE BBC

1. John Gray, 'Broadcasting and Scottish Culture' in David Daiches, ed., *The New Companion to Scottish Culture*, pp 27–32.

2. 'Some memories of my 21 years of radio in the BBC Aberdeen' in *The Book of the Braemar Gathering and Scottish Annual*, Braemar, 1989, p 61.

3. Ibid., p 65.

4. *SWT*, p 58.

5. 'Nan Shepherd in Recollection' in *Aberdeen University Review*, Spring 1990, pp 187–91.

6. '& a Portrait of Jessie Kesson' by Elizabeth Adair, *Leopard Magazine*, June 1980, p 23.

7. Abrams, p 69.

8. 'Report of the Boarding-Out Committee of the Scottish Advisory Council on Child Care', HMSO, Edinburgh, 1950.

CHAPTER EIGHT: LONDON: THE FIFTIES

1. *SWT*, p 73.

2. 'Writers in Exile – Jessie Kesson', *Leopard Magazine*, December 1992, p 5.

CHAPTER NINE: THE SIXTIES

1. *SWT*, p 74.
2. Jessie often quotes this sentence from Neil Gunn.
3. See Hugh Macpherson, 'Jessie Kesson', *The Scottish Book Collector*, December/January 1990/91, pp 22–5.
4. *SWT*, pp 68–69.
5. Kenneth Roy, *The Closing Headlines: Inside Scottish Broadcasting*, Carrick Media, 1993, p 72.
6. See David Cleghorn Thomson, ed., *Scotland in Quest of Her Youth*, Oliver & Boyd, 1932, pp 69–86.
7. 'A Far Cry from the Kailyard: Jessie Kesson's *Glitter of Mica*', in Aileen Christianson and Carol Anderson, eds, *Scottish Women's Fiction, 1920s to 1960s: Journeys into Being*, Tuckwell Press, 2000.
8. *SWT*, p. 65.
9. *SWT*, p 58.

CHAPTER TEN: THE SEVENTIES

1. Hugh Macpherson, 'Jessie Kesson', *The Scottish Book Collector*, December/January 1990/91, pp 22–5.
2. *SWT*, p 71.
3. *SWT*, p 68.
4. *WAR*, pp 126–9.
5. John Gray, 'Broadcasting and Scottish Culture' in David Daiches, ed., *The New Companion to Scottish Culture*, pp 29–30.
6. *SWT*, p 82.
7. *SWT*, p 81.

CHAPTER ELEVEN: THE EIGHTIES

1. *SWT*, pp 59–60.
2. *SWT*, p 63.
3. *SWT*, p 76.
4. *NER*, July 1944, p 11.
5. *SWT*, pp 62–3.
6. *SWT*, p 59.
7. *SWT*, p 58.

Index

NOTES
JK's family name is spelt in different ways, even in official documents: in the index it is regularised to McDonald. Where family members (such as 'the grandfather') and other characters are clearly taken from life, and where institutions such as the orphanage or the mental hospital as clearly reflect reality, these are indexed under the real names. Shorter works of JK currently in print are followed by *WAR – Where the Apple Ripens* or *SB:AJKC – Somewhere Beyond: A Jessie Kesson Companion.*